Introduction

Here is what Isaiah spoke/w chapter 30 verses 25 and 26

25 And upon every high mountain and upon every elevated hill there must come to be streams, water ditches, in the day of the big slaughter when the towers fall.
26 And the light of the full moon must become as the light of the glowing [sun]; and the very light of the glowing [sun] will be [for] 7 times, like the light of 7 days, in the day that Jehovah binds up the breakdown of his people and heals even the severe wound resulting from the stroke by him (Isaiah 30 - New World Translation adapted from the Hebrew)

Now at first sight this looks like it could refer to the twin towers falling, since there certainly was a great slaughter of, well of what is now said to be 2,800 souls on that very day of September 11th 2001 when the twin towers fell. Many Christian commentators before us, have indicated that they believe that it might relate to the fall of the twin towers, but that they are not absolutely sure.

It is the purpose of this book to prove beyond any doubt that this scripture does refer to the fall of the Twin Towers.

In order to prove this we need first to prove the following:

[1]   The above is an accurate translation of the true words of Isaiah who lived over 700 years before Christ.

[2]   Every scripture has a second fulfilment, a second meaning.

[3]   The bible is written in a code which defines rules for interpreting the first meaning which is the literal meaning in the case of a historical account and is a straight symbolic meaning in the case of a prophecy a dream a vision or a parable. This code also defines the rules for interpreting the second meaning which we call the word symbolism because it is a symbolic interpretation not of the events that a bible account describes, but of the words of the bible account themselves.

[4]   Dates and times in the bible are stated in terms of the Biblical Lunar Calendar, which is a lunar calendar and was the first calendar used by Mankind in the period before 1000 BC. It has 12 months of 30 days making a total of 360 days in a year. This calendar is the reason that there are 360 degrees in a circle.

[5]   The bible prophesies that the battle of Armageddon starts on 2008Nisan16 (March 23rd 2008) and ends 150 days later on 2008Elul15 (August 20th 2008).

[6]   The phrase '7 times' means '7 years' of the biblical lunar calendar in the bible.

[7]   The 'day' of the big slaughter of Isaiah 30:25 is a 'day' starting with the slaughter of the Twin Towers and ending with the end of the slaughter of Armageddon. The word 'day' is meant in the sense of 'in Queen Victoria's day', it is merely a period of time. During this 'day', streams of people respond to the true light of God, the light of the sun, the light of the world, Jesus Christ. This 'day' of true light, last for 7 times which is 7 years. So the 'day' of big slaughter, which is the day of great light and of the streaming response to that light also lasts for 7 years, which run from 2001Elul19 (2001 September 11th), the fall of the Twin Towers, until 2008Elul15 (August 20th), the last day of Armageddon. This is 7 biblical lunar years precisely.

It would be great if mankind or if the majority of Christian churches were up to speed with any of the points above, but sadly they are not. So we have to start from nowhere and build all 7 points one by one. For we are a race that can write millions of lines of complicated computer code, but cannot understand fully even one line of the true bible code. We can invent elaborate flawed deceptions, which we readily accept, to explain our existence in the absence of God, and yet we fail to unravel even the simplest of puzzles in the holy book which explains not only our existence but actually our entire future, our birthright and our heritage, to be not only perfect humans for 1,000 years from 2008 onwards, but to be also angels after that and Gods after that. Yes, even the lowliest Muslim slave girl hiding her face in her Burka will one day rule an entire galaxy as a God with a face too glorious for her subjects even to look upon. For she is not now and has never been a product of random chance, no, rather, she is a product of the generosity of Jehovah, who having elevated his angelic son Jesus Christ to the status of God, will not fail to show the same love for and confidence in many others of his sons and daughters. We are children of God, our future is to be God's just like our father. That is the race that we come from, that is the family we are talking about, and there is the jealousy of Satan.

Contents

Isaiah and the Twin Towers Prophecy

0 The Big Picture
1 The accurate translation of the true words of Isaiah 30, spoken or written over 2700 years ago.
2 The Prophetic Principle: Every scripture has a 2nd fulfilment, a 2nd meaning
3 The Bible is written in a code
4 Dates in the bible are stated in terms of the Biblical Lunar Calendar
5 The bible prophesies that the battle of Armageddon starts on 2008Nisan16 (March 23rd 2008) and ends 150 days later on 2008Elul15 (August 20th 2008).
6 The phrase '7 times' means '7 years' of the biblical lunar calendar in the bible
7 Conclusion

Basic Bible Understandings (numbering as in www.truebiblecode.com)

1 Millions of years of human fossils reconciled with Genesis
3 The Bible and its Translations
4 The Biblical Lunar Calendar (BLC)
5 How Ages & Reigns are counted
5a There is a God
6 What is a Soul
7 The Ransom of Jesus for Adam
8 The Kingdom of God and the Great Crowd
16 The Date of Armageddon without using the Code
16a The Dates of Jesus' birth and death
17 Logical Pathways and One Step Thinking

The True Bible Code

18 The Bible Code

Glossary of abbreviations

[0] The Big Picture

Before we start proving anything, since your time is limited (more limited than you had imagined), here is the whole deal. Firstly we present the first meaning, the event symbolism of Isaiah 30, which related to the saving of Jerusalem from the army of the Assyrian king Sennacherib by God in 715 BC and then destruction of Jerusalem in 586 BC by the Babylonian King, Nebuchadnezzar. We then present the current fulfilment of the account symbolism of Isaiah 30, which relates to the Twin Towers. You are not expected fully to understand or accept these interpretations at this point. But the writer thought you might want to know the bottom line before you invest your valuable (and rapidly expiring) time into reading this book.

We ask you to take the following 5 assertions on trust. We do not prove these points in this section. If you want to know more about them please visit www.truebiblecode.com. These assertions are not necessary to prove that Isaiah foretold the fall of the Twin Towers in the last 7 years but they are necessary to understand the full account symbolic meaning of the whole of Isaiah chapter 30. And we need to decode the whole of the chapter to prove that it really does refer to the Twin Towers. Some of these assertions may sound pretty fantastic and unbelievable. But, firstly they are not necessary to logically prove that Isaiah 30 refers to the twin towers, secondly any serious bible student must give Satan some credit for misleading mankind - which includes YOU:

9 So down the great dragon was hurled, the original serpent, the one called Devil and Satan, who is misleading the entire inhabited earth; he was hurled down to the earth, and his angels were hurled down with him (Revelation 12).

and thirdly, they are less fantastic than what we are trying to prove!

[1]   The 3rd true Christian church, FDS3, (the 3rd Faithful and Discreet Slave of the Master Jesus according to the parable of Matthew 24: 45-51) was the Jehovah's Witnesses, the JWs, whose administration is called the Watchtower. And all of the remaining (2000 odd) new covenant saints today (May 2002) are members of that religion, which has now fallen and become a false religion. New covenant saints are those of mankind who truly are in the new covenant that Jesus made at the last supper.

[2]   The JWs were rejected by God in 1994, and their leaders are now referred to in scripture as the Wicked and Sluggish Slave of Matthew 25 (the WSS) and as those of their leaders who are new covenant saints are referred to as the Evil Slave of Matthew 24.

[3] The 4th and last true Christian church, FDS4, is the Lord's Witnesses, who publish this book.

[4] In case you are wondering, the first true Christian church (FDS1) was started by Jesus in Jerusalem, and the second (FDS2) was started by St. Paul in Rome. The second true Christian church was finally rejected by God in 455 AD. There was no true Christian church, by which we mean a Christian church whose baptism actually resulted in a forgiveness of sins by God, between 455 AD and 1884 AD

[5] Jesus' first presence ended in 119 AD (120 years after his birth) and his second presence started in 1884 AD (and lasts until 2004, a total of 120 years). He is absent when no true new covenant saints (those who truly are authorised to take the bread and wine of communion) are alive on earth. This is because the new covenant saints are his wife to be, and the Law of Moses equated a fiancee with a wife (not allowing for the possibility that someone might break their word), and God's law regards the flesh of a wife as being the flesh of a husband. So new covenant saints are Jesus' flesh, and so their presence or absence is his presence or absence.

Isaiah 30 (New World Translation adapted from Hebrew)

1 Woe to the stubborn sons, is the utterance of Jehovah, [those disposed] to carry out a plan, but not from me; and to weave a covering web (GLT), but not with my spirit, in order to add sin to sin;
2 those who are setting out to go down to Egypt and who have not inquired of my own mouth, to take shelter in the stronghold of Pharaoh and to take refuge in the shadow of Egypt!
3 And the stronghold of Pharaoh must become even for you men a reason for shame, and the refuge in the shadow of Egypt a cause for humiliation.
4 For his princes have come to be in Zoan itself, and his own envoys reach even Hanes.
5 Every one will certainly become ashamed of a people that bring no benefit to one, that are of no help and bring no benefit, but are a reason for shame and also a cause for reproach.
6 The pronouncement against the beasts of the Negeb (semi-desert): Through the land of distress and hard conditions, of the lion and the leopard growling, of the viper and the flying fiery snake, on the shoulders of full-grown asses they carry their riches, and on the humps of camels their treasures. In behalf of the people they will prove of no benefit.
7 And the Egyptians are mere vanity, and they will help simply for nothing. Therefore I have called this one: Rahab -- they are for sitting still.
8 Now come, write it upon a tablet with them, and inscribe it even in a book, that it may serve for a future day, for a witness to time indefinite.

9 For it is a rebellious people, untruthful sons, sons who have been unwilling to hear the law of Jehovah;
10 who have said to the ones seeing, 'You must not see,' and to the ones having visions, 'You must not envision for us any straightforward things. Speak to us smooth things; envision deceptive things.
11 Turn aside from the way; deviate from the path. Cause the Holy One of Israel to cease just on account of us.'
12 Therefore this is what the Holy One of Israel has said: In view of your rejecting of this word, and [since] you men trust in defrauding and in what is devious and you support yourselves on it,
13 therefore for you this error will become like a broken section about to fall down, a swelling out (a bulge) in a highly raised wall, the breakdown of which may come suddenly, in an instant.
14 And one will certainly break it as in the breaking of a large jar of the potters, crushed to pieces without one's sparing [it], so that there cannot be found among its crushed pieces a fragment of earthenware with which to rake the fire from the fireplace or to skim water from a marshy place.
15 For this is what the Sovereign Lord Jehovah, the Holy One of Israel, has said: By coming back and resting you people will be saved. Your mightiness will prove to be simply in keeping undisturbed and in trustfulness. But you were not willing.
16 And you proceeded to say: No, but on horses we shall flee! That is why you will flee. And on swift [horses] we shall ride! That is why those pursuing you will show themselves swift.
17 1,000 will tremble on account of the rebuke of one; on account of the rebuke of 5 you will flee until you will have remained over like a mast on the top of a mountain and like a signal (sign) on a hill.
18 And therefore Jehovah will keep in expectation of showing you favor, and therefore he will rise up to show you mercy. For Jehovah is a God of judgment. Happy are all those keeping in expectation of him.
19 When the very people in Zion will dwell in Jerusalem, you will by no means weep. He will without fail show you favor at the sound of your outcry; as soon as he hears it he will actually answer you.
20 And Jehovah will certainly give you people bread in the form of distress and water in the form of oppression; yet your Grand Instructor will no longer hide himself, and your eyes must become [eyes] seeing your Grand Instructor.
21 And your own ears will hear a word behind you saying: This is the way. Walk in it, you people, in case you people should go to the right or in case you should go to the left.
22 And you people must defile the overlaying of your graven images of silver and the close-fitting covering of your molten statue of gold. You will scatter them. Like a menstruating woman, you will say to it: Mere dirt!
23 And he will certainly give the rain for your seed with which you sow the ground, and as the produce of the ground bread, which must become fat and oily. Your livestock will graze in that day in a spacious pasture.

24 And the cattle and the full-grown asses cultivating the ground will eat fodder seasoned with sorrel, which was winnowed with the shovel and with the fork.
25 And upon every high mountain and upon every elevated hill there must come to be streams, water ditches, in the day of the big slaughter when the towers fall.
26 And the light of the full moon must become as the light of the glowing [sun]; and the very light of the glowing [sun] will be [for] 7 times, like the light of 7 days, in the day that Jehovah binds up the breakdown of his people and heals even the severe wound resulting from the stroke by him.
27 Look! The name of Jehovah is coming from far away, burning with his anger and with heavy clouds. As for his lips, they have become full of denunciation, and his tongue is like a devouring fire.
28 And his spirit is like a flooding torrent that reaches clear to the neck, to swing the nations to and fro with a sieve of worthlessness/destruction; and a bridle that causes one to wander about/astray will be in the jaws of the peoples.
29 you people will come to have a song like that in the night that one sanctifies oneself for a festival, and rejoicing of heart like that of one walking with a flute to enter into the mountain of Jehovah, to the Rock of Israel.
30 And Jehovah will certainly make the dignity of his voice to be heard and will make the descending of his arm to be seen, in the raging of anger and the flame of a devouring fire [and] cloudburst and rainstorm and hailstones.
31 For because of the voice of Jehovah Assyria will be struck with terror; he will strike [it] even with a staff.
32 And every swing of his rod of chastisement that Jehovah will cause to settle down upon [Assyria] will certainly prove to be with tambourines and with harps; and with battles of brandishing he will actually fight against them.
33 For his Topheth is set in order from recent times; it is also prepared for the king himself. He has made its pile deep. Fire and wood are in abundance. The breath of Jehovah, like a torrent of sulphur, is burning against it.

Isaiah 30: Green's Literal Version (LITV)

1 Woe *to* rebellious sons, declares Jehovah, to make counsel, but not from Me; and to weave a covering web, but not of My Spirit, in order to add sin on sin;
2 who are walking to go down *to* Egypt, but have not asked at My mouth, to take refuge in the stronghold of Pharaoh, and to trust in the shadow of Egypt.
3 And the stronghold of Pharaoh shall become a shame to you; and relying on the shadow of Egypt shall be a disgrace.
4 For his rulers were in Zoan, and his ambassadors reached *to* Hanes.
5 Every one is ashamed over a people who do not profit them; *they are* not for a help, and not for profiting, but for a shame; yea, also for a reproach.
6 The burden of the beasts of the south: Into the land of trouble and constraint. The lioness and the lion *are* from them; the viper and fiery flying

serpent. They carry their riches on the shoulders of young asses, and their treasures on the humps of camels, to a people who cannot profit *them*.
7 And Egypt; vainly and emptily they help. So I have called to this: Their strength *is* to sit still.
8 Now come, write it before them on a tablet, and note it on a book, so that it may be for the latter day, until forever;
9 that this *is* a rebellious people, lying sons; sons who are not willing to hear the Law of Jehovah;
10 who say to the seers, Do not see; and to visioners, Do not have a vision for right things *to* us; speak smooth things to us; have a vision of trifles.
11 Turn aside from the way; stretch from the path; cause the Holy One of Israel to cease from before us.
12 For this reason, so says the Holy One of Israel, Because of your rejection of this Word, and your trust in oppression and perversity, even resting on it;
13 So this iniquity shall be to you as a broken *section* falling, like the bulging out of a high wall, the breaking of which comes suddenly, in an instant.
14 And its smashing *is* as the smashing of a potter's vessel; *when* broken in pieces, he has no pity; for in its breaking there is not found a shard to carry fire from the hearth, nor to skim water from a well.
15 For so says the Lord Jehovah, the Holy One of Israel, In returning and rest you shall be saved; and in quietness and hope shall be your strength. But you were not willing.
16 For you said, No! For we will flee on horseback. On account of this you shall flee. Also, *you say*, We will ride on swift ones. On account of this, those who pursue you shall be swift.
17 One thousand *shall flee* at the rebuke of one. You shall flee from the rebuke of five, until you are left like a pole on the top of the mountain, and like a sign on a hill.
18 And so Jehovah waits to be gracious to you. And for this He is exalted to have mercy on you; for Jehovah *is* a God of justice. Blessed *are* all who wait for Him.
19 For the people shall live in Zion, at Jerusalem; you shall surely cry no more. He surely will be gracious to you at the sound of your cry. When He hears, He will answer you.
20 And the Lord gives you the bread of adversity, and the water of affliction; but your teachers shall not be hidden any more; but your eyes shall be *able* to see your teachers.
21 And your ears shall hear a word behind you, saying, This is the way, walk in it, when you go right, or when you go left.
22 And you shall defile the covering of your carved images of silver; and the covering of your molten images of gold. You shall strew them as a menstruous cloth; you shall say to it, Go out!
23 Then He shall give rain *for* your seed, with which you sow the ground. And the bread of the produce of the earth also shall be fat and plentiful. In that day your livestock shall feed in a pasture made wide.
24 Also, the oxen and the young asses that till the ground shall eat seasoned

fodder which one winnows with the shovel and with the fork.
25 And on every high mountain, and on every high hill, shall be rivulets lifted up, streams of water, in a day of great slaying, when towers fall.
26 And the moonlight shall be like the light of the sun. And the sun's light shall be sevenfold, as the light of seven days, in the day of binding up, Jehovah *binding* the break of His people, and healing the wound of His blow.
27 Behold, the name of Jehovah comes from afar; His anger burns; and *is* heavy *as* the uplifting *of smoke*; His lips are full of fury, and His tongue like a devouring fire.
28 And like an overflowing torrent, His breath shall divide to the neck, to sift the nations with the sieve of vanity, and a misleading bridle on the jaws of the peoples.
29 The song shall be to you, as the night when the feast is sanctified, and gladness of heart, as one going with the flute, to come into the mount of Jehovah, to the Rock of Israel.
30 And Jehovah shall make the majesty of His voice heard; and He causes His arm to be seen coming down with raging anger and flame of consuming fire, cloudburst and storm, and hailstones.
31 For through the voice of Jehovah, Assyria shall be crushed, the rod with which He strikes.
32 And every passage of the appointed staff that Jehovah causes to rest on him will be with timbrels and with harps. And in brandishing battles He fights with her.
33 For Topheth is ordained from yesterday. Also, it is prepared for the king; He deepened; He widened its pyre; *He* makes great *with* fire and wood. The breath of Jehovah burns in it like a torrent of brimstone (Isaiah 30 Green's LITV).

1 Woe to those who go down to Egypt for help, and lean on horses, and trust on chariotry, because *it is* great; and in horsemen because they are very strong! But they do not look to the Holy One of Israel, nor seek Jehovah.
2 And He also *is* wise, and brings evil, and will not turn aside His Words, but will rise against the house of evildoers, and against the help of those who work iniquity.
3 And Egypt *is* a man, and not God. And their horses are flesh, and not spirit. And Jehovah stretches out His hand, and both he who helps shall fall, and he who is helped shall fall; and they shall all cease together.
4 For so Jehovah has said to me: As the lion roars, even the young lion on his prey when the multitude of shepherds are gathered against him, *he* will not fear their voice, nor fret himself because of their noise. So Jehovah of Hosts shall go down to fight on Mount Zion, and on its hill.
5 As birds that fly, so Jehovah of Hosts will shield over Jerusalem; shielding and delivering, and passing over, He will save *it.*
6 Turn back to *Him against* whom you have made a deep revolt, sons of Israel.

7 For in that day each shall despise his silver idols and his golden idols, which your hands have made for you; a sin.
8 Then Assyria shall fall by a sword, not *of* man; yea, a sword, not of man, shall devour him. For he shall flee from the sword, and his young men shall become forced labor.
9 And his rock will pass away from fear; and his commanders shall tremble at the banner, declares Jehovah, whose fire *is* in Zion, and His furnace in Jerusalem (Isaiah 31 Green's LITV)

Time of prophecy: After the death of King Ahaz (Isaiah 14:28) and before the 14th year of King Hezekiah (Isaiah 36:1). So the prophecy was made after 728 BC, the 16th and last regnal year of King Ahaz, which was the first regnal year of King Hezekiah, his son - see [91]. And it was made before 716 BC, the 14th regnal year of Hezekiah. So Isaiah said these things over 2700 years ago!

Translation points: Negeb (נגב) can mean South, since the Negeb desert was the land South of Judah, but Exodus and Numbers use Negeb (נגב) to mean the Negeb desert and (תימנה) to mean South. So we translate 'Negeb' as Negeb here.

The Event Symbolism

Stubborn sons	Stubborn sons of Israel (Jacob) in Isaiah's day
Weave a web	Prepare a system of lies as a cover up
Zoan	Defence Department of Egypt
Hanes	State Department of Egypt (Foreign Office)
Beasts of the Negeb	Pagan ruling groups in the Negeb Desert South of Judah
Flying fiery snake	Satan
Called this one Rahab	The Egyptians as a group are called 'Rahab', the faithful prostitute of Jericho. They make meaningless alliances with everybody (as does a prostitute)!
They are for sitting still	When the Assyrians attacked under Sennacherib, the Egyptians did nothing, it was God who saved Jerusalem.
Land of distress and hard conditions	Route to Egypt from Judah
Future day	The fall of Jerusalem to Nebuchadnezzar in 586Ab BC and the subsequent release of the people from Babylon in 539Tishri BC
Cause the holy one of Israel to cease just on account of us	We (your temporary administrators) are more important than God your permanent father.
Broken section, bulge in a wall	They know the house of Judah will fall (from ruling over God's people - the sons of Israel), but it hasn't fallen yet
Jar broken, not a fragment remaining	All administrative groups of Judah will be destroyed when/after the house falls. It fell in 608Chislev10 to Pharaoh Necho. Then Nebuchadnezzar burnt Jerusalem and the temple and scattered all the Jews on 586Ab10
Remain like a mast on a hill	People left over will be in tiny exposed groups.

He will rise up to show you mercy	He will then rescue you and forgive you after you have been captured
He will give you bread in the form of distress and water in the form of oppression	He will discipline you for your benefit. He will teach you and feed you spiritually by punishing you physically.
You eyes must see your grand instructor	His actions will be obvious to the Jews.
Hear a word behind you saying this is the way, walk in it	They will eventually re adopt the law of Moses written before (behind them), after they have learned their lesson
Like a menstruating woman, you will say: Mere dirt	Their idols they will regard as the unclean product of a woman's menstruation - euch.
Streams	Moving streams of fleeing people
Water ditches	Stationary groups of hiding people
Day of the big slaughter when the towers fall	The destruction of Jerusalem by Nebuchadnezzar. The wall of Jerusalem was punctuated with Towers.
Light of the moon	Understandings of false religion
Light of the sun	Understandings of true religion

7 So he said to Judah: Let us build these cities and make walls around and towers, double doors and bars. For us the land is yet available, because we have searched for Jehovah our God. We have searched, and he gives us rest all around. And they went building and proving successful (2 Chronicles 14).

9 Moreover, Uzziah built towers in Jerusalem by the Corner Gate and by the Valley Gate and by the Buttress, and made them strong (2 Chronicles 26).

17 So he brought up against them the king of the Chaldeans, who proceeded to kill their young men with the sword in the house of their sanctuary, neither did he feel compassion for young man or virgin, old or decrepit. Everything he gave into his hand.
18 And all the utensils, great and small, of the house of the [true] God and the treasures of the house of Jehovah and the
treasures of the king and of his princes, everything he brought to Babylon.
19 And he proceeded to burn the house of the [true] God and pull down the wall of Jerusalem; and all its dwelling towers they burned with fire and also all its desirable articles, so as to cause ruin (2 Chronicles 36).

The 7 times of verse 26 cannot be 7 prophetic times in the event symbolism, because no time substitution is permitted in the this symbolism by the code.

So 7 times God heals the breakdown resulting from the stroke by him through a period of intense enlightenment wherein the good light eclipses the bad. These 7 must be as follows:

Healing	Stroke	True light eclipses false light
Jacob enters Egypt in 1728Nisan BC, fleeing the famine	Regional Famine	Joseph explains Pharaoh's dreams, no other magic practicing priests can.
Moses takes sons of Israel out of Egypt	Permitting slavery to the Egyptians	Moses and Aaron prove superior to Egyptian magicians
Jews leave Babylon after 539Tishri and go back under law in 455Tishri	Fall of Samaria to Shalmanezer in 723 and of Jerusalem to Nebuchadnezzar in 586	Cyrus (the Mede) proves Jehovah superior to all the God's of Babylon. He gives the temple equipment back to Sheshbazzar or Zerubbabel to take back to Judah.
FDS1	End of the Law of Moses	Jesus eclipses the Pharisees
FDS2	Disfellowshipping of FDS1	Paul eclipses the followers of FDS1
FDS3	Disfellowshipping of FDS2	Russell eclipses Babylon the great (the false churches of Christendom)
FDS4	Disfellowshipping of FDS3	Gordon eclipses FDS3

The 4 true Christian churches all contain God's chosen people, who are Abraham's children through the 1AC (the first Abrahamic Covenant of Genesis 12, the true seed - see [9]). They are children of faith through baptism in water, sons of the first Abrahamic covenant.

Lips full of denunciation, tongue like a devouring fire	Each previous system is denounced by the prophets of the next system
A bridle that causes one to wander about/astray will be in the jaws of the peoples	The prevailing tendency on everyone will be to go astray, but God's people will be saved from this.
The descending of his arm to be seen	His fighting arm.
God will strike Assyria with a staff	His angel killed 185,000 Assyrians in one night in the 14th year of Hezekiah - 715 BC (Isaiah 37:6)
Topheth was where the Jews burnt their sons and daughters in the fire in a misguided offering to God or in a misguided offering to Molech. God's Topheth is everlasting death, Gehenna. (Topheth was in Gehenna, the valley of Hinnom outside the wall of Jerusalem)	God has his everlasting destruction means ready. It is prepared for the King of Assyria himself - Sennacherib. He taunted Jerusalem saying: Do not let Hezekiah cause you to trust in Jehovah saying: Without fail Jehovah will deliver us (Isaiah 36:15)

Isaiah 30 Decoded (Literal Meaning/Event Symbolism) Interlinearized

Black text = Scriptures (New World Translation)
Green text = Literal Meaning/Event Symbolism

1 Woe to the stubborn sons, is the utterance of Jehovah, [those disposed] to carry out a plan, but not from me; and to weave a covering web (GLT), but not with my spirit, in order to add sin to sin;
1 Woe to the stubborn sons of Israel, is the utterance of Jehovah, [those disposed]

to act on advice, but not advice that came from me; and to manufacture a cover up, but not with my spirit, in order to add sin to sin;

2 those who are setting out to go down to Egypt and who have not inquired of my own mouth, to take shelter in the stronghold of Pharaoh and to take refuge in the shadow of Egypt!
2 those who are setting out to go down to Egypt and who have not consulted with my prophets first, to take shelter in the stronghold of Pharaoh and to take refuge in the shadow of Egypt!

3 And the stronghold of Pharaoh must become even for you men a reason for shame, and the refuge in the shadow of Egypt a cause for humiliation.
3 And the stronghold of Pharaoh must become even for you men a reason for shame, and the refuge in the shadow of Egypt a cause for humiliation.

4 For his princes have come to be in Zoan itself, and his own envoys reach even Hanes.
4 For his princes have come to be in the Egyptian Defence department itself, and his own envoys reach even the State department.

5 Every one will certainly become ashamed of a people that bring no benefit to one, that are of no help and bring no benefit, but are a reason for shame and also a cause for reproach.
5 Every one will certainly become ashamed of a people that bring no benefit to one, that are of no help and bring no benefit, but are a reason for shame and also a cause for reproach (when the Assyrians come to attack Judah and the Egyptians fail to help at all).

6 The pronouncement against the beasts of the Negeb (semi-desert): Through the land of distress and hard conditions, of the lion and the leopard growling, of the viper and the flying fiery snake, on the shoulders of full-grown asses they carry their riches, and on the humps of camels their treasures. In behalf of the people they will prove of no benefit.
6 The pronouncement against the pagan ruling groups of the Negeb Desert: Through the land of distress and hard conditions, of the lion and the leopard growling, and of the viper, the Negeb Desert and the Sinai peninsular, and through to the land of Satan himself (Egypt - the dominant World Power) on the shoulders of full-grown asses they carry their resources/riches, and on the humps of camels their supplies/treasures. In behalf of the people they will prove of no benefit.

7 And the Egyptians are mere vanity, and they will help simply for nothing. Therefore I have called this one: Rahab -- they are for sitting still.
7 And the Egyptians are mere vanity, and they will help simply for nothing. Therefore I have called this one: Rahab the prostitute of Jericho, since they will make meaningless alliances with anyone. The Egyptians will sit still when Judah is in trouble.

8 Now come, write it upon a tablet with them, and inscribe it even in a book, that it may serve for a future day, for a witness to time indefinite.
8 Now come, write it upon a tablet with them, and inscribe it even in a book, that it may serve for a future day (in 715 when Assyria attacks Jerusalem and in 586 when

Nebuchadnezzar attacks and destroys Solomon's temple and in 515 when Zerubbabel rebuilds the temple and in 455 when the Law of Moses is finally restored in Jerusalem), for a witness to time indefinite.

9 For it is a rebellious people, untruthful sons, sons who have been unwilling to hear the law of Jehovah;
9 For it is a rebellious people, untruthful sons, sons who have been unwilling to hear the law of Jehovah;

10 who have said to the ones seeing, 'You must not see,' and to the ones having visions, 'You must not envision for us any straightforward things. Speak to us smooth things; envision deceptive things.
10 who have said to the ones understanding God's word, God's prophets, 'You must not literally interpret', and to the ones decoding accounts, 'You must not decode anything concrete for us. Speak to us diplomatically, decode deceptively.

11 Turn aside from the way; deviate from the path. Cause the Holy One of Israel to cease just on account of us.'
11 Turn aside from the way; deviate from the path. Pay attention to us (who are deranged toddlers) rather than to the Holy One of Israel who created the whole universe and wrote the laws of our country and caused this whole nation to exist and gave it this land where we live etc etc.

12 Therefore this is what the Holy One of Israel has said: In view of your rejecting of this word, and [since] you men trust in defrauding and in what is devious and you support yourselves on it,
12 Therefore this is what the Holy One of Israel has said: In view of your rejecting of this word, and [since] you men trust in defrauding and in what is devious and you support yourselves on it,

13 therefore for you this error will become like a broken section about to fall down, a swelling out (a bulge) in a highly raised wall, the breakdown of which may come suddenly, in an instant.
13 therefore for you this error will become like a broken girder about to fall down, like bulge in a highly raised wall, the breakdown of which may come suddenly, in an instant. You know the house of Judah is going to fall, it is just a matter of time.

14 And one will certainly break it as in the breaking of a large jar of the potters, crushed to pieces without one's sparing [it], so that there cannot be found among its crushed pieces a fragment of earthenware with which to rake the fire from the fireplace or to skim water from a marshy place.
14 And one will certainly break it as in the breaking of a large jar of the potters, crushed to pieces without one's sparing [it], so that there cannot be found among its crushed pieces a fragment of earthenware with which to rake the fire from the fireplace or to skim water from a marshy place. When Judah falls, there will be no part of the administration left at all, there will not even be left a few people huddling together trying to organise a discussion group.

15 For this is what the Sovereign Lord Jehovah, the Holy One of Israel, has said: By coming back and resting you people will be saved. Your mightiness will prove to be simply in keeping undisturbed and in trustfulness. But you

were not willing.
15 For this is what the Sovereign Lord Jehovah, the Holy One of Israel, has said as regards your future salvation from his punishment: By coming back (to Jerusalem from Babylon) and resting you people will be saved. Your mightiness will prove to be simply in keeping undisturbed and in trustfulness. But you were not willing.

16 And you proceeded to say: No, but on horses we shall flee! That is why you will flee. And on swift [horses] we shall ride! That is why those pursuing you will show themselves swift.
16 And you proceeded to say: No, but on horses we shall flee! That is why you will flee. And on swift [horses] we shall ride! That is why those pursuing you will show themselves swift.

17 1,000 will tremble on account of the rebuke of one; on account of the rebuke of 5 you will flee until you will have remained over like a mast on the top of a mountain and like a signal (sign) on a hill.
17 1,000 will tremble on account of the rebuke of one; on account of the rebuke of 5 you will flee until those who remain will be in tiny isolated groups on the tops of mountains and hills.

18 And therefore Jehovah will keep in expectation of showing you favor, and therefore he will rise up to show you mercy. For Jehovah is a God of judgment. Happy are all those keeping in expectation of him.
18 And therefore Jehovah will keep in expectation of showing you favor, and therefore he will rise up to show you mercy after you have learned from your punishment. For Jehovah is a God of judgment. Happy are all those keeping in expectation of him.

19 When the very people in Zion will dwell in Jerusalem, you will by no means weep. He will without fail show you favor at the sound of your outcry; as soon as he hears it he will actually answer you.
19 When the very people in Zion, whom God has chosen to rule, you will dwell in Jerusalem, you will by no means weep. He will without fail show you favor at the sound of your outcry; as soon as he hears it he will actually answer you.

20 And Jehovah will certainly give you people bread in the form of distress and water in the form of oppression; yet your Grand Instructor will no longer hide himself, and your eyes must become [eyes] seeing your Grand Instructor.
20 And Jehovah will certainly before that time give you people bread in the form of distress and water in the form of oppression; yes, he will teach you humility and loyalty and quite simply obedience, through calamity, he will give you pain and you will gain, yet your Grand Instructor will no longer hide himself, and your eyes must become [eyes] seeing your Grand Instructor.

21 And your own ears will hear a word behind you saying: This is the way. Walk in it, you people, in case you people should go to the right or in case you should go to the left.
21 And your own ears will hear a word behind you, which is the Law of Moses, saying: This is the way. Walk in it, you people, in case you people should go to the

right or in case you should go to the left.

22 And you people must defile the overlaying of your graven images of silver and the close-fitting covering of your molten statue of gold. You will scatter them. Like a menstruating woman, you will say to it: Mere dirt!

22 And you people must defile the overlaying of your graven images of silver and the close-fitting covering of your molten statue of gold. You will scatter them. Like a menstruating woman, you will say to it: Mere dirt! You will regard idolatry and disobedience to God as being as disgusting and the produce of a menstruating woman.

23 And he will certainly give the rain for your seed with which you sow the ground, and as the produce of the ground bread, which must become fat and oily. Your livestock will graze in that day in a spacious pasture.

23 And he will certainly give the rain for your seed with which you sow the ground, and as the produce of the ground bread, which must become fat and oily. Your livestock will graze in that day in a spacious pasture.

24 And the cattle and the full-grown asses cultivating the ground will eat fodder seasoned with sorrel, which was winnowed with the shovel and with the fork.

24 And the cattle and the full-grown asses cultivating the ground will eat fodder seasoned with sorrel, which was winnowed with the shovel and with the fork.

25 And upon every high mountain and upon every elevated hill there must come to be streams, water ditches, in the day of the big slaughter when the towers fall.

25 And upon every high mountain and upon every elevated hill there must come to be streams of moving people, and groups of stationary hiding people, in the day of the big slaughter when the towers of Jerusalem fall (to Nebuchadnezzar in 586BC).

26 And the light of the full moon must become as the light of the glowing [sun]; and the very light of the glowing [sun] will be [for] 7 times, like the light of 7 days, in the day that Jehovah binds up the breakdown of his people and heals even the severe wound resulting from the stroke by him.

26 But the understandings of false religion must become as the understandings of the true religion; and the very light of the true religion will eclipse the light of false religion 7 times, like the light of 7 days, in the 'day' (of which there are 7 instances) that Jehovah binds up the breakdown of his people and heals even the severe wound resulting from the stroke by him. And when you are rescued from Babylon one of these 'days' of increased bible understanding and acceptance by both your leaders and your people will occur.

27 Look! The name of Jehovah is coming from far away, burning with his anger and with heavy clouds. As for his lips, they have become full of denunciation, and his tongue is like a devouring fire.

27 Look! The reputation, authority and status of Jehovah arises from a place a long way away (heaven), his heart is burning with his anger and with heavy clouds. As for his lips, they have become full of denunciation, and his tongue is like a devouring fire.

28 And like an overflowing torrent, His breath shall divide to the neck, to sift the nations with the sieve of vanity, and a misleading bridle on the jaws of the peoples.
28 And his spirit is like a flooding torrent that reaches clear to the neck, to swing the nations to and fro with a separating judgmental sieve of worthlessness/destruction for those who fall through it; and a bridle that causes one to wander about/astray will be in the jaws of the peoples who are not his own.

29 you people will come to have a song like that in the night that one sanctifies oneself for a festival, and rejoicing of heart like that of one walking with a flute to enter into the mountain of Jehovah, to the Rock of Israel.
29 you people, the loyal ones of Israel, will come to have a song like that in the night that one sanctifies oneself for a festival, and rejoicing of heart like that of one walking with a flute to enter into the new administration/mountain of Jehovah in Jerusalem after the exile in Babylon, to the Rock of Israel.

30 And Jehovah will certainly make the dignity of his voice to be heard and will make the descending of his arm to be seen, in the raging of anger and the flame of a devouring fire [and] cloudburst and rainstorm and hailstones.
30 And Jehovah will certainly make the dignity of his voice to be heard and will make the descending of his fighting arm to be seen, in the raging of anger and the flame of a devouring fire [and] cloudburst and rainstorm and hailstones.

31 For because of the voice of Jehovah Assyria will be struck with terror; he will strike [it] even with a staff.
31 For because of the voice of Jehovah Assyria will be struck with terror; he will strike [it] even with a staff. He will in fact kill 185,000 Assyrians who are attacking Jerusalem in one night in 715 BC - see Isaiah 36:7.

32 And every swing of his rod of chastisement that Jehovah will cause to settle down upon [Assyria] will certainly prove to be with tambourines and with harps; and with battles of brandishing he will actually fight against them.
32 And every swing of his rod of chastisement that Jehovah will cause to settle down upon [Assyria] will certainly prove to be with tambourines and with harps; and with battles of brandishing he will actually fight against them.

33 For his Topheth is set in order from recent times; it is also prepared for the king himself. He has made its pile deep. Fire and wood are in abundance. The breath of Jehovah, like a torrent of sulphur, is burning against it.
33 For God's destructive incinerator is set in order from recent times; it is also prepared for the king of Assyria himself. He has made its pile deep. Fire and wood are in abundance. The breath of Jehovah, like a torrent of sulphur, is burning against it.

Isaiah 30 Decoded (Event Symbolism)

1 Woe to the stubborn sons of Israel, is the utterance of Jehovah, [those disposed] to act on advice, but not advice that came from me; and to

manufacture a cover up, but not with my spirit, in order to add sin to sin;
2 those who are setting out to go down to Egypt and who have not consulted with my prophets first, to take shelter in the stronghold of Pharaoh and to take refuge in the shadow of Egypt!
3 And the stronghold of Pharaoh must become even for you men a reason for shame, and the refuge in the shadow of Egypt a cause for humiliation.
4 For his princes have come to be in the Egyptian Defence department itself, and his own envoys reach even the State department.
5 Every one will certainly become ashamed of a people that bring no benefit to one, that are of no help and bring no benefit, but are a reason for shame and also a cause for reproach (when the Assyrians come to attack Judah and the Egyptians fail to help at all).
6 The pronouncement against the pagan ruling groups of the Negeb Desert: Through the land of distress and hard conditions, of the lion and the leopard growling, and of the viper, the Negeb Desert and the Sinai peninsular, and through to the land of Satan himself (Egypt - the dominant World Power) on the shoulders of full-grown asses they carry their resources/riches, and on the humps of camels their supplies/treasures. On behalf of the people they will prove of no benefit.
7 And the Egyptians are mere vanity, and they will help simply for nothing. Therefore I have called this one: Rahab the prostitute of Jericho, since they will make meaningless alliances with anyone. The Egyptians will sit still when Judah is in trouble.
8 Now come, write it upon a tablet with them, and inscribe it even in a book, that it may serve for a future day (in 715 when Assyria attacks Jerusalem and in 586 when Nebuchadnezzar attacks and destroys Solomon's temple and in 515 when Zerubbabel rebuilds the temple and in 455 when the Law of Moses is finally restored in Jerusalem), for a witness to time indefinite.
9 For it is a rebellious people, untruthful sons, sons who have been unwilling to hear the law of Jehovah;
10 who have said to the ones understanding God's word, God's prophets, 'You must not literally interpret', and to the ones decoding accounts, 'You must not decode anything concrete for us. Speak to us diplomatically, decode deceptively.
11 Turn aside from the way; deviate from the path. Pay attention to us (who are deranged toddlers) rather than to the Holy One of Israel who created the whole universe and wrote the laws of our country and caused this whole nation to exist and gave it this land where we live etc etc.
12 Therefore this is what the Holy One of Israel has said: In view of your rejecting of this word, and [since] you men trust in defrauding and in what is devious and you support yourselves on it,
13 therefore for you this error will become like a broken girder about to fall down, like bulge in a highly raised wall, the breakdown of which may come suddenly, in an instant. You know the house of Judah is going to fall, it is just

a matter of time.

14 And one will certainly break it as in the breaking of a large jar of the potters, crushed to pieces without one's sparing [it], so that there cannot be found among its crushed pieces a fragment of earthenware with which to rake the fire from the fireplace or to skim water from a marshy place. When Judah falls, there will be no part of the administration left at all, there will not even be left a few people huddling together trying to organise a discussion group.

15 For this is what the Sovereign Lord Jehovah, the Holy One of Israel, has said as regards your future salvation from his punishment: By coming back (to Jerusalem from Babylon) and resting you people will be saved. Your mightiness will prove to be simply in keeping undisturbed and in trustfulness. But you were not willing.

16 And you proceeded to say: No, but on horses we shall flee! That is why you will flee. And on swift [horses] we shall ride! That is why those pursuing you will show themselves swift.

17 1,000 will tremble on account of the rebuke of one; on account of the rebuke of 5 you will flee until those who remain will be in tiny isolated groups on the tops of mountains and hills.

18 And therefore Jehovah will keep in expectation of showing you favor, and therefore he will rise up to show you mercy after you have learned from your punishment. For Jehovah is a God of judgment. Happy are all those keeping in expectation of him.

19 When the very people in Zion, the people who God has chosen to rule you, will dwell in Jerusalem, you will by no means weep. He will without fail show you favor at the sound of your outcry; as soon as he hears it he will actually answer you.

20 And Jehovah will certainly before that time give you people bread in the form of distress and water in the form of oppression; yes, he will teach you humility and loyalty and quite simply obedience, through calamity, he will give you pain and you will gain, yet your Grand Instructor will no longer hide himself, and your eyes must become [eyes] seeing your Grand Instructor.

21 And your own ears will hear a word behind you, which is the Law of Moses, saying: This is the way. Walk in it, you people, in case you people should go to the right or in case you should go to the left.

22 And you people must defile the overlaying of your graven images of silver and the close-fitting covering of your molten statue of gold. You will scatter them. Like a menstruating woman, you will say to it: Mere dirt! You will regard idolatry and disobedience to God as being as disgusting and the produce of a menstruating woman.

23 And he will certainly give the rain for your seed with which you sow the ground, and as the produce of the ground bread, which must become fat and oily. Your livestock will graze in that day in a spacious pasture.

24 And the cattle and the full-grown asses cultivating the ground will eat

fodder seasoned with sorrel, which was winnowed with the shovel and with the fork.

25 And upon every high mountain and upon every elevated hill there must come to be streams of moving people, and groups of stationary hiding people, in the day of the big slaughter when the towers of Jerusalem fall (to Nebuchadnezzar in 586BC).

26 But the understandings of false religion must become as the understandings of the true religion; and the very light of the true religion will eclipse the light of false religion 7 times, like the light of 7 days, in the 'day' (of which there are 7 instances) that Jehovah binds up the breakdown of his people and heals even the severe wound resulting from the stroke by him. And when you are rescued from Babylon one of these 'days' of increased bible understanding and acceptance by both your leaders and your people will occur.

27 Look! The reputation, authority and status of Jehovah arises from a place a long way away (heaven), his heart is burning with his anger and with heavy clouds. As for his lips, they have become full of denunciation, and his tongue is like a devouring fire.

28 And his spirit is like a flooding torrent that reaches clear to the neck, to swing the nations to and fro with a separating judgmental sieve of worthlessness/destruction for those who fall through it; and a bridle that causes one to wander about/astray will be in the jaws of the peoples who are not his own.

29 you people, the loyal ones of Israel, will come to have a song like that in the night that one sanctifies oneself for a festival, and rejoicing of heart like that of one walking with a flute to enter into the new administration/mountain of Jehovah in Jerusalem after the exile in Babylon, to the Rock of Israel.

30 And Jehovah will certainly make the dignity of his voice to be heard and will make the descending of his fighting arm to be seen, in the raging of anger and the flame of a devouring fire [and] cloudburst and rainstorm and hailstones.

31 For because of the voice of Jehovah Assyria will be struck with terror; he will strike [it] even with a staff. He will in fact kill 185,000 Assyrians who are attacking Jerusalem in one night in 715 BC - see Isaiah 36:7.

32 And every swing of his rod of chastisement that Jehovah will cause to settle down upon [Assyria] will certainly prove to be with tambourines and with harps; and with battles of brandishing he will actually fight against them.

33 For God's destructive incinerator is set in order from recent times; it is also prepared for the king of Assyria himself. He has made its pile deep. Fire and wood are in abundance. The breath of Jehovah, like a torrent of sulphur, is burning against it.

Isaiah 30 Decoded Second Presence Account Symbolism

The Event symbolism of an account is the symbolic interpretation of the events which the account describes. The Account symbolism of an account is the symbolic interpretation of the description of the events. It is the interpretation of the words of the account themselves rather than the interpretation of what happened.

The Repetition Principle of the code tells us that repeated words or phrases (such as Pharaoh) take a different meaning in the account symbolism to the meaning that they take in the event symbolism, but non repeated words or phrases such as:

'In the day of the big slaughter when the towers fall'

take the same meaning in both symbolisms. In the case of Pharaoh, he stands for the King of ancient Egypt in the event symbolism and he stands for the King of the UN in the account symbolism (which is presently the 7th biblical king, the UK/US world power). In the case of towers falling, we know that physical towers must fall in the account symbolism as they did in the event symbolism. This really leaves us with the Twin Towers. Since account symbolism is always an end times prophecy (either the end of the Jewish system of things or the end of the first presence or the end of FDS2 or the end of the second presence or the end of this system of things) and no other significant towers have fallen in Jesus' second presence which is all but over. Also the Twin Towers fell exactly 7 years before the end of Armageddon, as witnessed in verse 26, which completely nails this account as referring to the Twin Towers. We have had the end date of Armageddon as being 2008Elul since 1992. We also prophesied in the Second Edition of the True Bible Code in January 2001 in section [158] on page 535 that:

'War (possibly unofficial war i.e. terrorism) will be the trigger for the UN to take over the world'

The Twin Towers fell on 2001Elul19 (September 11), which was precisely 7 years to the Hebrew month before the end of Armageddon on 2008Elul15 (August 20). Now it is true that the Twin Towers were not in the antetypical Jerusalem (which is the Watchtower, the fallen FDS3, in this account). But this is an account symbolism, we are interpreting words not events. They are not stated to be in Jerusalem in the account, so in the account symbolism we are free to take them as being elsewhere. In fact we are lead to take them as being elsewhere by the Omission Principle of the code (it is not as if God forgot to mention where they were). The account symbolism cannot refer to a metaphorical fall, as in a fall from favour with God of a metaphorical tower, such as a stronghold of a religion, since their fall is only recited once and therefore must take the same meaning in the account symbolism as it did in the literal prophecy. This meaning is a literal fall of literal towers.

The Successive Descriptions Principle applied to verse 8 below, shows us that the account symbolism has two fulfilments (which occur one in each presence of the Christ).

8 Now come, write it upon a tablet with them, and inscribe it even in a book, that it may serve for a future day, for a witness to time indefinite.

We are only going to look at the one in the current presence of the Christ, through his wife, the new covenant saints (1884 to 2004).

Stubborn sons	Stubborn sons of Jesus, the eternal father today (the New covenant saints in the Watchtower)
Weave a web	Prepare a system of lies as a cover up
Egypt	UN
Shadow of Egypt	UN protection for associated NGO's
Pharaoh	7th biblical king of the world the UK/US world power (at the time the Watchtower was riding the beast), it rules over the UN until the 10 kings give their authority.
Stronghold of Pharaoh	UN security council
Zoan	UN General assembly
Hanes	UN NGO conferences
Beasts of the Negeb	Apostate ruling groups in the WSS
Land of distress and hard conditions	Administration of the WSS (Wicked and Sluggish Slave of Matthew 25).
Flying fiery snake	Satan
Called this one Rahab	The UN has formed meaningless NGO alliances with every major religion. The beast itself behaves like a prostitute.
They are for sitting still	The UN will do nothing to protect religion and will eventually destroy it!
Full grown asses	Mature congregations
For a future day, for a witness to time indefinite (which is a future day)	This is an immediate repetition, so there are two greater future days that this prophecy serves in the account symbolism in addition to the day of the error and the destruction of Physical Jerusalem in the event symbolism. We will not cover the first century account symbolism fulfillment here - it relates to the transgression which causes desolation of FDS1 on 60Sivan12, their idolatry with Rome - see [157]. The current future 'day' is the day of the transgression that causes desolation to FDS3, the joining up with the UN on 1992January28 and thereafter. Incidentally the future day of the account symbolism does not have to be the same time period as the future day of the event symbolism, they are both 'future days'. Likewise the Twin Towers are not Towers on the wall of Jerusalem, they are just Towers that physically fall down as the account says.
Cause the holy one of Israel to cease just on account of us	We (your temporary spiritual administrators of the Watchtower) are more important than God your permanent father.

Broken section, bulge in a wall	They know the house of FDS3 will fall down (from ruling over God's people - the sons of Abraham through the 1AC), but it hasn't fallen down physically yet.
Jar broken, not a fragment remaining	All administrative groups of FDS3 will be destroyed when/after the house falls.
1,000 will tremble on account of the rebuke of one	1,000 new covenant saints will join the LWs due to the rebuke of Gordon. (We do not get 2,000 of them).
on account of the rebuke of 5 you will flee until you will have remained over like a mast on the top of a mountain and like a signal (sign) on a hill.	5 years of rebuke from 1999Elul when the first horseman of the Apocalypse (Gordon) started to ride until 2004Elul when the last remnant brother dies and goes to the top of mount Zion.
He will rise up to show you mercy	He will then rescue you and forgive you after you have been captured
He will give you bread in the form of distress and water in the form of oppression	He will discipline you for your benefit. He will teach you and feed you spiritually by punishing you physically.
Your eyes must see your grand instructor	His actions will be obvious to the true and faithful New covenant saints
Hear a word behind you saying this is the way, walk in it	They will eventually re read the scriptures, the law of God, and accept the new decoded meanings, the new wine, after they have learned their lesson.
Like a menstruating woman, you will say: Mere dirt	Their idols (the Governing body, the Writing committee, the Bethelites, the Elders etc.) they will regard as the unclean product of a woman's menstruation - euch.
And he will certainly give the rain for your seed with which you sow the ground	The LW baptism will be accepted by God (this was spoken 2700 years ago)
Your livestock will graze in that day in a spacious pasture.	The new flock of the LWs will have a non oppressive and loving administration
And the cattle and the full-grown asses cultivating the ground will eat fodder seasoned with sorrel, which was winnowed with the shovel and with the fork.	The new flock of the LWs will eat fantastically prepared spiritual food - like this?
Mountain	(False) religion
Elevated Hill	Worldly organisation
Streams	Moving streams of people leaving to join the LWs
Water ditches	Stationary groups of LW believers hiding in the hills and mountains
Day of the big slaughter when the towers fall	7 year 'day' of the big slaughter of mankind from 2001Elul when the Twin Towers fell to the end of Armageddon in 2008Elul when the slaughter stops.
Light of the moon	Understandings of false religion
Light of the sun	Understandings of true religion
Light will be 7 times, like the light of 7 days (which takes 7 days to arrive)	True understandings are not 7 times brighter than false ones, in some luminosity contest, they eclipse them completely. So the 7 times means 7 years not sevenfold. Isaiah just says that the Twin Towers fall within the last 7 years (7 times). We know from our Chronology that they fall in the first month of the last 7 years, 2001Elul19, 2001 September 11.

Light of the moon must become as the light of the sun	The understandings of false religion are eclipsed by and are abandoned for the understandings of true religion.
Jehovah heals the breakdown of his people	By baptism into FDS4 the LWs. He heals his people, not their fallen administration.
Stroke by him	Disfellowshipping of FDS3 and all the JWs. Strike the shepherd and let the flock be scattered (Zechariah 13:7, Matthew 26:31, Mark 14:27)
Assyria	The new covenant saints in the Watchtower - beaten with many strokes (Luke 12:47). Many will repent and join the LWs - over 1,000 will repent.
Staff	Authority and rulership of FDS4 the LWs
Topheth	Gehenna, everlasting death
The King	Not Milton Henschel, or Don Adams (neither of whom are new covenant saints), but all the ruling ones, the men, the rotten new covenant saints with authority who remain in the Watchtower until they die (Gordon thinks). The evil members of the evil slave of Matthew 24. Serpents! Offspring of vipers! How will you flee the judgement of Gehenna?

Assyria is only mentioned once in Isaiah 30, but biblical chapters are not canonical and the account continues until the end of Isaiah 31 where we read:

8 And Assyria (NIVHEOT) must fall by the sword, not [that of] a man; and a sword, not [that of] earthling man, will devour him. And he must flee because of the sword, and his own young men will come to be for forced labor itself. 9 And his own crag will pass away out of sheer fright, and because of the sign his princes must be terrified, is the utterance of Jehovah, whose light is in Zion and whose furnace is in Jerusalem (Isaiah 31).

If the word 'Assyria' only appeared once in the whole account then the account symbolic meaning would have to be 'Assyria'. But it appears twice, so we are free to give it a greater meaning as some great enemy of God's true people. Assyria of course did fall by the sword of God when 185,000 of her soldiers were killed by God's angel as recorded in Isaiah 36:7. But in the greater meaning those sanctified ones who remain in the Watchtower are judged by God and suffer the 2nd death it would appear. For the light of Jehovah is in his true administration, Zion, now the LWs. And his smelting furnace for sanctified Christians is in Jerusalem, the true congregation, neither his light nor his smelting furnace are any longer in FDS3 which has become Assyria.

Isaiah 30 Decoded Second Presence Account Symbolism Interlinearized

Black text = Scripture (New World Translation)
Red text = Account symbolism

1 Woe to the stubborn sons, is the utterance of Jehovah, [those disposed] to carry out a plan, but not from me; and to weave a covering web (GLT), but not with my spirit, in order to add sin to sin;
1 Woe to the stubborn sons of the new covenant in the JWs, is the utterance of Jehovah, [those disposed] to act on advice, but not advice that came from me; and to manufacture a cover up, but not with my spirit, in order to add sin to sin;

2 those who are setting out to go down to Egypt and who have not inquired of my own mouth, to take shelter in the stronghold of Pharaoh and to take refuge in the shadow of Egypt!
2 those who are setting out to go down to the UN having deliberately ignored the word of God with which they are fully familiar, to take shelter in the UN security council and to take refuge in the protection of the UN!

3 And the stronghold of Pharaoh must become even for you men a reason for shame, and the refuge in the shadow of Egypt a cause for humiliation.
3 And the UN security council must become even for you men a reason for shame, and the refuge in the protection of the UN a cause for humiliation.

4 For his princes have come to be in Zoan itself, and his own envoys reach even Hanes.
4 For Jesus' princes have come to be in the UN General Assembly itself, and his own envoys participate in UN NGO conferences.

5 Every one will certainly become ashamed of a people that bring no benefit to one, that are of no help and bring no benefit, but are a reason for shame and also a cause for reproach.
5 Every one will certainly become ashamed of a people that bring no benefit to one, that are of no help and bring no benefit, but are a reason for shame and also a cause for reproach.

6 The pronouncement against the beasts of the Negeb (semi-desert): Through the land of distress and hard conditions, of the lion and the leopard growling, of the viper and the flying fiery snake, on the shoulders of full-grown asses they carry their riches, and on the humps of camels their treasures. In behalf of the people they will prove of no benefit.
6 The pronouncement against the apostate ruling groups of the WSS (the Negeb desert with no food and no accepted water baptism): Through the administration of the Wicked and Sluggish Slave of Matthew 25, an administration of distress and hard conditions, of the lion and the leopard growling, of the viper and of Satan himself, on the shoulders of mature congregations they carry their understandings, and on the backs of those trying to maintain a discredited water baptism they carry their food. In behalf of JWs loyal to God they will prove of no benefit.

7 And the Egyptians are mere vanity, and they will help simply for nothing.

Therefore I have called this one: Rahab -- they are for sitting still.
7 And the UN are mere vanity, and they will help simply for nothing. Therefore I have called this one: Rahab (the prostitute of Jericho, because the UN is quick to form meaningless unions) but they will do nothing whatsoever to help the Watchtower (in fact they will sit still when the Watchtower is attacked - and they will eventually attack it themselves just as the Egyptians under Pharaoh Necho attacked Josiah in 608 BC).

8 Now come, write it upon a tablet with them, and inscribe it even in a book, that it may serve for a future day, for a witness to time indefinite.
8 Now come, write the first presence fulfilment of the account symbolism upon a tablet with them, and inscribe a further second presence fulfilment of the account symbolism even in a book using the same set of words, that it may serve for a future day in the first presence of the Christ, for a witness to time indefinite in the second presence of the Christ.

9 For it is a rebellious people, untruthful sons, sons who have been unwilling to hear the law of Jehovah;
9 For it is a rebellious people the JWs, untruthful sons, the new covenant saints, sons who have been unwilling to hear the law of Jehovah;

10 who have said to the ones seeing, 'You must not see,' and to the ones having visions, 'You must not envision for us any straightforward things. Speak to us smooth things; envision deceptive things.
10 who have said to the ones seeing the true bible code in the JWs, 'You must not literally interpret', and to the ones decoding accounts, 'You must not decode anything concrete for us. Speak to us diplomatically, decode deceptively. Say things like: 'The end of the world is very soon' and 'we are in the time of the end of the time of the end', but do not tell them that Armageddon is in 2008 and starts on March 23rd.

11 Turn aside from the way; deviate from the path. Cause the Holy One of Israel to cease just on account of us.'
11 Turn aside from the way; deviate from the path. Pay attention to us (who are deranged spiritual toddlers) rather than to the Holy One of Israel who created the whole universe and wrote the bible and created love etc. etc.

12 Therefore this is what the Holy One of Israel has said: In view of your rejecting of this word, and [since] you men trust in defrauding and in what is devious and you support yourselves on it,
12 Therefore this is what the Holy One of Israel has said: In view of your rejecting of this word, and [since] you men trust in defrauding and in what is devious and you support yourselves on it,

13 therefore for you this error will become like a broken section about to fall down, a swelling out (a bulge) in a highly raised wall, the breakdown of which may come suddenly, in an instant.
13 therefore for you this error will become like a broken girder about to fall down, like bulge in a highly raised wall, the breakdown of which may come suddenly, in an instant. You know the house of the fallen FDS3 is going to be destroyed, it is just a matter of time.

14 And one will certainly break it as in the breaking of a large jar of the potters, crushed to pieces without one's sparing [it], so that there cannot be found among its crushed pieces a fragment of earthenware with which to rake the fire from the fireplace or to skim water from a marshy place.
14 And one will certainly break it as in the breaking of a large jar of the potters, crushed to pieces without one's sparing [it], so that there cannot be found among its crushed pieces a fragment of earthenware with which to rake the fire from the fireplace or to skim water from a marshy place. When FDS3 goes, there will be no part of the administration left at all, there will not even be left two people having a coffee break. (Let his lodging place become desolate - Acts 1:20)

15 For this is what the Sovereign Lord Jehovah, the Holy One of Israel, has said: By coming back and resting you people will be saved. Your mightiness will prove to be simply in keeping undisturbed and in trustfulness. But you were not willing.
15 For this is what the Sovereign Lord Jehovah, the Holy One of Israel, has said as regards your future salvation from his punishment: By coming back (from the Watchtower to God in FDS4) and resting from the physical works required by FDS3 (which is now the WSS), which are not required by God, you people will be saved. Your mightiness will prove to be simply in keeping undisturbed and in trustfulness. Not in door to door ministry service or frequent meeting attendance. But you were not willing.

16 And you proceeded to say: No, but on horses we shall flee! That is why you will flee. And on swift [horses] we shall ride! That is why those pursuing you will show themselves swift.
16 And you proceeded to say: No, but on the great understandings of the Watchtower we shall flee Armageddon! That is why you will flee not Armageddon, but the Watchtower. And on swift [horses] we shall ride! That is why those pursuing you in FDS4 will show themselves to have greater understandings than you.

17 1,000 will tremble on account of the rebuke of one; on account of the rebuke of 5 you will flee until you will have remained over like a mast on the top of a mountain and like a signal (sign) on a hill.
17 1,000 new covenant saints will repent on account of the rebuke of one, Gordon; on account of the rebuke lasting for the final 5 years of the second presence from 1999Elul to 2004Elul you will flee from FDS3 until only one new covenant saint is left, like a mast on the top of a mountain and like a sign on a hill.

18 And therefore Jehovah will keep in expectation of showing you favor, and therefore he will rise up to show you mercy. For Jehovah is a God of judgment. Happy are all those keeping in expectation of him.
18 And therefore Jehovah will keep in expectation of showing you favor, and therefore he will rise up to show you mercy, once you have fled. For Jehovah is a God of judgment. Happy are all those keeping in expectation of him.

19 When the very people in Zion will dwell in Jerusalem, you will by no means weep. He will without fail show you favor at the sound of your outcry; as soon

as he hears it he will actually answer you.
19 When the very people approved by God will rule over you, you will by no means weep. He will without fail show you favor at the sound of your outcry; as soon as he hears it he will actually answer you.

20 And Jehovah will certainly give you people bread in the form of distress and water in the form of oppression; yet your Grand Instructor will no longer hide himself, and your eyes must become [eyes] seeing your Grand Instructor.
20 And Jehovah will certainly teach you people with distress and feed you with oppression; yet your Grand Instructor will no longer hide himself, and your eyes must become [eyes] seeing your Grand Instructor through the true bible code.

21 And your own ears will hear a word behind you saying: This is the way. Walk in it, you people, in case you people should go to the right or in case you should go to the left.
21 And your own ears will understand the current meanings of the scriptures written millennia ago saying: This is the way. Walk in it, you people, in case you people should go to the right or in case you should go to the left.

22 And you people must defile the overlaying of your graven images of silver and the close-fitting covering of your molten statue of gold. You will scatter them. Like a menstruating woman, you will say to it: Mere dirt!
22 And you people must defile the respectability of your Governing body, your Bethelites (head office guys), your Elders. You will scatter them. Like a menstruating woman, you will say to them: Mere dirt!

23 And he will certainly give the rain for your seed with which you sow the ground, and as the produce of the ground bread, which must become fat and oily. Your livestock will graze in that day in a spacious pasture.
23 And God will certainly accept the baptism you then give to new disciples, and the spiritual food, the bible understandings, will be very up-building. Your flock will be taught in a non oppressive atmosphere.

24 And the cattle and the full-grown asses cultivating the ground will eat fodder seasoned with sorrel, which was winnowed with the shovel and with the fork.
24 And your evangelisers will be given top class bible understandings, worked on and refined by unpretentious honest and industrious lovers of God (who do not regard themselves as being anything special or as having any sort of exclusivity on the holy spirit or on correct bible interpretation).

25 And upon every high mountain and upon every elevated hill there must come to be streams, water ditches, in the day of the big slaughter when the towers fall.
25 And in every false religion and in every secular oganisation there must come to be streams of courageous decisive enlightened people heading for the LWs, and groups of less motivated believers hiding within these religions and secular organisations, in the 7 year long last 'day' of the big slaughter of mankind within which the TWIN TOWERS fall.

26 And the light of the full moon must become as the light of the glowing [sun]; and the very light of the glowing [sun] will be [for] 7 times, like the light of 7 days, in the day that Jehovah binds up the breakdown of his people and heals even the severe wound resulting from the stroke by him.
26 And the understandings of false religion must become like the understandings of true religion; and the powerful understandings of the true religion will last for 7 times, 7 years, like the light of 7 days, (each of which is a year long) in the 7 year long last 'day' (which is coincident with the 'day' of the big slaughter above, since this is a day of streaming people responding to this 7 year light) in which Jehovah binds up the breakdown of the JWs and heals even the severe wound resulting from their disfellowshipping (excommunication) on 1994Tammuz30. This 7 year long day ends with the end of the big slaughter, i.e. at the end of Armageddon on 2008Elul15. So it began 7 years earlier in 2001Elul. The Twin Towers fell on 2001Elul19 which was September 11th 2001.

27 Look! The name of Jehovah is coming from far away, burning with his anger and with heavy clouds. As for his lips, they have become full of denunciation, and his tongue is like a devouring fire.
27 Look! The reputation, authority and status of Jehovah arises from a place a long way away (heaven). His heart is burning with his anger and with heavy clouds. As for his lips, they have become full of denunciation, and his tongue is like a devouring fire. (For mankind has not made the proper effort to understand his book for 2000 years. No we have built nuclear bombs, we have walked on the moon, we have sequenced the DNA of mankind we have invented computers which can perform trillions of operations per second programmed with millions of lines of code, but there was not one line of the bible code of the holy book, on which our very lives depend, that we properly understood. We have served our own egos and our own desires very well, through them we have served Satan very well, but we have not served God who gave us both our ego and our desires, and Satan, very well at all).

28 And like an overflowing torrent, His breath shall divide to the neck, to sift the nations with the sieve of vanity, and a misleading bridle on the jaws of the peoples.
28 And his spirit is like a flooding torrent that reaches clear to the neck, to swing the nations to and fro with a separating judgmental sieve of worthlessness/destruction for those who fall through it; and a bridle that causes one to wander about/astray will be in the jaws of the peoples who are not his own.

29 you people will come to have a song like that in the night that one sanctifies oneself for a festival, and rejoicing of heart like that of one walking with a flute to enter into the mountain of Jehovah, to the Rock of Israel.
29 But you people, the loyal JWs, will come to have a song like that in the night that one sanctifies oneself for a festival, and rejoicing of heart like that of one walking with a flute to enter into the administration of FDS4, the mountain of Jehovah, the Rock of Israel.

30 And Jehovah will certainly make the dignity of his voice to be heard and will make the descending of his arm to be seen, in the raging of anger and

the flame of a devouring fire [and] cloudburst and rainstorm and hailstones.
30 And Jehovah will certainly make the dignity of his voice to be heard and will make the descending of his fighting arm to be seen, in the raging of anger and the flame of a devouring fire [and] cloudburst and rainstorm and hailstones.

31 For because of the voice of Jehovah Assyria will be struck with terror; he will strike [it] even with a staff.
31 For because of the voice of Jehovah the rotten new covenant saints (who are now the big enemy of God's true people) will be struck with terror; he will strike the evil slave of Matthew 24 even with the authority of FDS4.

32 And every swing of his rod of chastisement that Jehovah will cause to settle down upon [Assyria] will certainly prove to be with tambourines and with harps; and with battles of brandishing he will actually fight against them.
32 And every swing of his rod of chastisement that Jehovah will cause to settle down upon [them] will certainly prove to be with tambourines and with harps; and with battles of brandishing he will actually fight against them.

33 For his Topheth is set in order from recent times; it is also prepared for the king himself. He has made its pile deep. Fire and wood are in abundance. The breath of Jehovah, like a torrent of sulphur, is burning against it.
33 For his destructive incinerator is set in order from recent times; it is also prepared for the sanctified and now defiled members of the evil slave himself. He has made its pile deep. Fire and wood are in abundance. The breath of Jehovah, like a torrent of sulphur, is burning against it.

Isaiah 30 Decoded Second Presence Account Symbolism

1 Woe to the stubborn sons of the new covenant in the JWs, is the utterance of Jehovah, [those disposed] to act on advice, but not advice that came from me; and to manufacture a cover up, but not with my spirit, in order to add sin to sin;
2 those who are setting out to go down to the UN having deliberately ignored the word of God with which they are fully familiar, to take shelter in the UN security council and to take refuge in the protection of the UN!
3 And the UN security council must become even for you men a reason for shame, and the refuge in the protection of the UN a cause for humiliation.
4 For Jesus' princes have come to be in the UN General Assembly itself, and his own envoys participate in UN NGO conferences.
5 Every one will certainly become ashamed of a people that bring no benefit to one, that are of no help and bring no benefit, but are a reason for shame and also a cause for reproach.
6 The pronouncement against the apostate ruling groups of the WSS (the Negeb desert with no food and no accepted water baptism): Through the administration of the Wicked and Sluggish Slave of Matthew 25, an administration of distress and hard conditions, of the lion and the leopard growling, of the viper and of Satan himself, on the shoulders of mature congregations they carry their understandings, and on the backs of those

trying to maintain a discredited water baptism they carry their food. In behalf of JWs loyal to God they will prove of no benefit.
7 And the UN are mere vanity, and they will help simply for nothing. Therefore I have called this one: Rahab (the prostitute of Jericho, because the UN is quick to form meaningless unions) but they will do nothing whatsoever to help the Watchtower (in fact they will sit still when the Watchtower is attacked - and they will eventually attack it themselves just as the Egyptians under Pharaoh Necho attacked Josiah in 608 BC).
8 Now come, write the first presence fulfilment of the account symbolism upon a tablet with them, and inscribe a further second presence fulfilment of the account symbolism even in a book using the same set of words, that it may serve for a future day in the first presence of the Christ, for a witness to time indefinite in the second presence of the Christ.
9 For it is a rebellious people the JWs, untruthful sons, the new covenant saints, sons who have been unwilling to hear the law of Jehovah;
10 who have said to the ones seeing the true bible code in the JWs, 'You must not literally interpret', and to the ones decoding accounts, 'You must not decode anything concrete for us. Speak to us diplomatically, decode deceptively. Say things like: 'The end of the world is very soon' and 'we are in the time of the end of the time of the end', but do not tell them that Armageddon is in 2008 and starts on March 23rd.
11 Turn aside from the way; deviate from the path. Pay attention to us (who are deranged spiritual toddlers) rather than to the Holy One of Israel who created the whole universe and wrote the bible and created love etc. etc.
12 Therefore this is what the Holy One of Israel has said: In view of your rejecting of this word, and [since] you men trust in defrauding and in what is devious and you support yourselves on it,
13 therefore for you this error will become like a broken girder about to fall down, like bulge in a highly raised wall, the breakdown of which may come suddenly, in an instant. You know the house of the fallen FDS3 is going to be destroyed, it is just a matter of time.
14 And one will certainly break it as in the breaking of a large jar of the potters, crushed to pieces without one's sparing [it], so that there cannot be found among its crushed pieces a fragment of earthenware with which to rake the fire from the fireplace or to skim water from a marshy place. When FDS3 goes, there will be no part of the administration left at all, there will not even be left two people having a coffee break. (Let his lodging place become desolate - Acts 1:20)
15 For this is what the Sovereign Lord Jehovah, the Holy One of Israel, has said as regards your future salvation from his punishment: By coming back (from the Watchtower to God in FDS4) and resting from the physical works required by FDS3 (which is now the WSS), which are not required by God, you people will be saved. Your mightiness will prove to be simply in keeping undisturbed and in trustfulness. Not in door to door ministry service or frequent meeting attendance. But you were not willing.

16 And you proceeded to say: No, but on the great understandings of the Watchtower we shall flee Armageddon! That is why you will flee not Armageddon, but the Watchtower. And on swift [horses] we shall ride! That is why those pursuing you in FDS4 will show themselves to have greater understandings than you.
17 1,000 new covenant saints will repent on account of the rebuke of one, Gordon; on account of the rebuke lasting for the final 5 years of the second presence from 1999Elul to 2004Elul you will flee from FDS3 until only one new covenant saint is left, like a mast on the top of a mountain and like a sign on a hill.
18 And therefore Jehovah will keep in expectation of showing you favor, and therefore he will rise up to show you mercy, once you have fled. For Jehovah is a God of judgment. Happy are all those keeping in expectation of him.
19 When the very people approved by God will rule over you, you will by no means weep. He will without fail show you favor at the sound of your outcry; as soon as he hears it he will actually answer you.
20 And Jehovah will certainly teach you people with distress and feed you with oppression; yet your Grand Instructor will no longer hide himself, and your eyes must become [eyes] seeing your Grand Instructor through the true bible code.
21 And your own ears will understand the current meanings of the scriptures written millennia ago saying: This is the way. Walk in it, you people, in case you people should go to the right or in case you should go to the left.
22 And you people must defile the respectability of your Governing body, your Bethelites (head office guys), your Elders. You will scatter them. Like a menstruating woman, you will say to them: Mere dirt!
23 And God will certainly accept the baptism you then give to new disciples, and the spiritual food, the bible understandings, will be very up-building. Your flock will be taught in a non oppressive atmosphere.
24 And your evangelisers will be given top class bible understandings, worked on and refined by unpretentious honest and industrious lovers of God (who do not regard themselves as being anything special or as having any sort of exclusivity on the holy spirit or on correct bible interpretation).
25 And in every false religion and in every secular oganisation there must come to be streams of courageous decisive enlightened people heading for the LWs, and groups of less motivated believers hiding within these religions and secular organisations, in the 7 year long last 'day' of the big slaughter of mankind within which the TWIN TOWERS fall.
26 And the understandings of false religion must become like the understandings of true religion; and the powerful understandings of the true religion will last for 7 times, 7 years, like the light of 7 days, (each of which is a year long) in the 7 year long last 'day' (which is coincident with the 'day' of the big slaughter above, since this is a day of streaming people responding to this 7 year light) in which Jehovah binds up the breakdown of the JWs and heals even the severe wound resulting from their disfellowshipping

(excommunication) on 1994Tammuz30. This 7 year long day ends with the end of the big slaughter, i.e. at the end of Armageddon on 2008Elul15. So it began 7 years earlier in 2001Elul. The Twin Towers fell on 2001Elul19 which was September 11th 2001.

27 Look! The reputation, authority and status of Jehovah arises from a place a long way away (heaven). His heart is burning with his anger and with heavy clouds. As for his lips, they have become full of denunciation, and his tongue is like a devouring fire. (For mankind has not made the proper effort to understand his book for 2000 years. No we have built nuclear bombs, we have walked on the moon, we have sequenced the DNA of mankind we have invented computers which can perform trillions of operations per second programmed with millions of lines of code, but there was not one line of the bible code of the holy book, on which our very lives depend, that we properly understood. We have served our own egos and our own desires very well, through them we have served Satan very well, but we have not served God who gave us both our ego and our desires, and Satan, very well at all).

28 And his spirit is like a flooding torrent that reaches clear to the neck, to swing the nations to and fro with a separating judgmental sieve of worthlessness/destruction for those who fall through it; and a bridle that causes one to wander about/astray will be in the jaws of the peoples who are not his own.

29 But you people, the loyal JWs, will come to have a song like that in the night that one sanctifies oneself for a festival, and rejoicing of heart like that of one walking with a flute to enter into the administration of FDS4, the mountain of Jehovah, the Rock of Israel.

30 And Jehovah will certainly make the dignity of his voice to be heard and will make the descending of his fighting arm to be seen, in the raging of anger and the flame of a devouring fire [and] cloudburst and rainstorm and hailstones.

31 For because of the voice of Jehovah the rotten new covenant saints (who are now the big enemy of God's true people) will be struck with terror; he will strike the evil slave of Matthew 24 even with the authority of FDS4.

32 And every swing of his rod of chastisement that Jehovah will cause to settle down upon [them] will certainly prove to be with tambourines and with harps; and with battles of brandishing he will actually fight against them.

33 For his destructive incinerator is set in order from recent times; it is also prepared for the sanctified and now defiled members of the evil slave himself. He has made its pile deep. Fire and wood are in abundance. The breath of Jehovah, like a torrent of sulphur, is burning against it.

Hopefully the above will persuade the reader that we are not just guessing that Isaiah 30 refers to the Twin Towers. We are not speculating wildly, we have done the research, we have decoded the whole account in the old and the new meanings.

52 Then he said to them: That being the case, every public instructor, when taught respecting the kingdom of the heavens, is like a man, a householder, who brings out of his treasure store things new and old (Matthew 13).

From these fully decoded meanings we can state categorically that Isaiah 30 does refer to the fall of the Twin Towers last year. So now let us bring you up to speed with God's book, so that you can understand how the words of a Hebrew prophet spoken/written over 2700 years ago, in the 8th century BC refer to things you see on the news today in the 21st century.

[1] The accurate translation of the true words of Isaiah 30, spoken or written over 2700 years ago.

The direct literal translation from the original Hebrew is:

25 And he will be on every of mountain high and on every of hill being lofty, streams, ditches of waters in day of slaughter great in which to fall towers
26 And he will be 7 times like light of 7 days on day of to bind up Jehovah namely bruise of people of him and wound of infliction of him he heals (New International Version Hebrew English Old Testament adapted from the Hebrew using Ben Davidson's Hebrew and Chaldee Lexicon).

The New Revised Standard Bible reads:

25 On every lofty mountain and every high hill there will be brooks running with water on a day of the great slaughter when the towers fall
26 Moreover, the light of the moon will be like the light of the sun, and the light of the sun will be sevenfold, like the light of 7 days, on the day when the Lord binds up the injuries of his people and heals the wounds inflicted by his blow

J. P. Green's Literal translation reads:

25 And on every high mountain, and on every high hill, shall be rivulets lifted up, streams of water, in a day of great slaying, when towers fall.
26 And the moonlight shall be like the light of the sun. And the sun's light shall be sevenfold, as the light of seven days, in the day of binding up, Jehovah *binding* the break of His people, and healing the wound of His blow (Green LITV)

So how do we know that the Hebrew Text from which this is translated (the BHS version of the Masoretic text, the codex Leningrad B19a which is in Leningrad) is an accurate representation of Isaiah's words?

Well, it just so happens that the dead sea scrolls, which were found in the last century and date to before Christ had a complete version of the book of Isaiah. And this version of Isaiah, although over 1,000 years older, agreed extremely closely with the BHS Hebrew text (which dates from 1008 AD). The BHS is the basis of most modern bible translations of the old testament. The new testament was written in Greek.

So mankind has a copy of the book of Isaiah which is over 2,000 years old and which translates as above. The Reader is invited to buy the New International Version Hebrew English Old Testament published by Zondervan, which contains the Hebrew text, and a not particularly good but very literal translation into English. You are further invited to buy Ben Davidson's Analytical Hebrew and Chaldee Lexicon, which translates every word of the BHS Hebrew old testament very accurately. In this way you can check the whole deal thoroughly for yourself. Because let us face it, the consequences of the premise of this book being correct are monumental!

[2] The Prophetic Principle

Before we start please ask yourself the following two questions:

Am I cleverer than God, can I find mistakes in his work that he has overlooked?

Is Stephen Spielberg an order of magnitude better than God at telling stories?

Put these two together and the question then is basically: How could such a clever God write such a dumb book?

Why is it so ambiguous? Why does it go in for irrelevant detail and miss out vital explanations, facts and dates?

The answer is that God is hiding his astonishingly powerful sacred secrets in the seemingly irrelevant and trivial and repetitive mundane details of bible accounts. God is hiding vital explanations, facts and dates in each account by employing a symbolic code within the scriptures. One aspect of this code is that every scripture (which contains a repeated non trivial word or phrase) has a further meaning, a second meaning, a second fulfilment.

For full details of this principle please see chapter [18]

[3] The Bible is Written in a Code

22 For there is nothing hidden except for the purpose of being exposed; nothing has become carefully concealed but for the purpose of coming into the open (Mark 4).
17 For there is nothing hidden that will not become manifest, neither anything carefully concealed that will never become known and never come into the open (Luke 8).
2 But there is nothing carefully concealed that will not be revealed, and secret that will not become known (Luke 12).

3 if, moreover, you call out for understanding itself and you give forth your voice for discernment itself,
4 if you keep seeking for it as for silver, and as for <u>hid treasures</u> you keep searching for it,
5 in that case you will understand the fear of Jehovah, and you will find the very knowledge of God (Proverbs 2).

As usual St. Paul explains the whole deal:

7 But we speak God's wisdom in a sacred secret, the hidden wisdom, which God foreordained before the systems of things for our glory.
8 This [wisdom] not one of the rulers of this system of things came to know, for if they had known [it] they would not have impaled the glorious Lord.
9 But just as it is written: Eye has not seen and ear has not heard, neither have there been conceived in the heart of man the things that God has prepared for those who love him.
10 For it is to us God has revealed them through his spirit, for the spirit searches into all things, even the deep things of God.
11 For who among men knows the things of a man except the spirit of man that is in him? So, too, no one has come to know the things of God, except the spirit of God.
12 Now we received, not the spirit of the world, but the spirit which is from God, that we might know the things that have been kindly given us by God.
13 These things we also speak, not with words taught by human wisdom, but with those taught by [the] spirit, as we combine spiritual [matters] with spiritual [words].
14 But a physical man does not receive the things of the spirit of God, for they are foolishness to him; and he cannot get to know [them], because they are examined spiritually.
15 However, the spiritual man examines indeed all things, but he himself is not examined by any man (1 Corinthians 2)

The things prepared for those that love God are the hidden meanings of the scriptures. Hidden in a symbolic code which God is revealing to mankind through us.

At this point the reader is most likely asking questions like:

[1] Why didn't the Pope get this?

[2] Why doesn't the federal council of churches of America know about this?

[3] Why didn't some seemingly pious monks in some remote monastery get this?

[4] Who are these Lord's Witnesses guys?

[5] Why didn't any church get this code at some point in the last 2,000 years?

The simple answers to the above questions are:

[1]   The Pope is plainly a Pharisee, seeking as he does the glory of men rather than the glory of God. You can tell this just from his wonderful outfits. And Pharisees are blind. Jesus said of them:

5 All the works they do they do to be viewed by men; for they broaden the [scripture-containing] cases that they wear as
safeguards, and enlarge the fringes [of their garments].
6 They like the most prominent place at evening meals and the front seats in the synagogues (Matthew 23).

[2]   God does not go in for democracy. He has one true religion with one true leader. He does not operate via a multi-headed committee. God created no beast with two heads (except a rare kind of serpent apparently).

[3]   Jesus was not a monk and neither were any of his original disciples.

[4]   We are people with no status at all in the eyes of men or women. The very criterion that the true God has always used to confer status on men and women in his eyes. He chose the smelly fishermen of Galilee to confer his divinely elegant wisdom to the perfumed Pharisee of Jerusalem, did he not?

[5]   The angel Gabriel said to the prophet Daniel, referring to the whole bible:

9 And he went on to say: Go, Daniel, because the words are made secret and sealed up until the time of [the] end (Daniel 12).

The time of the end began in 1991Shebat (1991January/February) when the writer of this book first worked out the date of the end as being Nisan14 (March 21) 2008. He did this from the prophecy of the Exedenic Times - see www.truebiblecode.com/understanding132.html

If you are persuaded more by Status than you are by Logic, and let us face it the overwhelming majority of men and women are, which is why Pharisees (glorious looking religious leaders) are so successful, then bear this fact in mind. Sir Isaac Newton, who was voted the most influential mind of the last millennium, believed that the bible was written in a code, and spent almost half of his life trying to decode it and to deduce the date of Armageddon from it. The reason that you the reader are unaware of this spiritual side of Sir Isaac Newton, is that the Churches of Newton's day persecuted anyone who served God by attempting to work out what the bible might mean. So a lot of Newton's work (Observations on the prophecies Daniel and the Revelation of St. John etc) was published either anonymously or after he died or both. A few hundred years earlier, it was a criminal offence punishable by death to own a bible translated into English!! The date Newton calculated for Armageddon was 1948 (Isaac Newton - Michael White). He deduced that the bible was in a code because he knew that the God of galactic creation was perfect and he knew that the bible was inspired by him and was therefore also perfect. Yet the literal meaning of the bible did not manifest God's perfection. So he deduced that there was another meaning, a hidden meaning which did manifest this perfection, because perfection is a trade mark of all of God's work.

Newton believed that every man owed it as a debt of gratitude to God to make a thorough search and analysis of the scriptures to attempt to understand them. Just as he believed that every man should make a thorough search and analysis of the physical world in gratitude for the gift of our intelligence and our reasoning capabilities and in gratitude for the Bible and the physical Universe in which we live.

If you do not think that God created the universe then listen to this famous story involving Halley the atheist (who discovered the comet) and Newton:

Halley walked into Newton's room in Cambridge university and there in front of him was an Orrery (which is a mechanical model of the Solar System). Halley asked Newton: Who made this great device? Newton thought for a moment and then answered: Nobody. Halley said: Do not be unreasonable, Isaac, someone must have made it. Newton retorted: If you know for a fact that this Orrery had a maker, then why do you not know for a fact that the universe itself, of which this Orrery is merely a poorly constructed copy, also had a maker?

Dear reader, do not be like naive Eve. Do not be fooled by status. Eve was sold on the possibility of her becoming like God, a huge increase in her status. She then sold Adam on sexual desire, which is why they needed fig leaves after the experience. The world has not changed, we are just more sophisticated, but we make precisely the same mistakes. Sisters, pursue love more than you pursue status. Brothers pursue love more than you pursue sexual desire. Brothers and sisters, if you seek first the Kingdom of God you will have more status than you can possibly imagine added to you, not that you will be interested much in it, and you will be fully satisfied in his kingdom.

16 You are opening your hand and satisfying the desire of every living thing (Psalm 145).

Psalm 145 is a prophecy about the Kingdom of God, because our current desires, many of which are destructive, are in no way being satisfied.

For the whole story on the bible code please visit chapter [18].

[4] Dates in the bible are stated in terms of the Biblical Lunar Calendar

Please visit chapter [4] of the Basic Bible Understandings section.

[5] The bible prophesies that the battle of Armageddon starts on 2008Nisan16 (March 23rd 2008) and ends 150 days later on 2008Elul15 (August 20th 2008).

We have 8 different proofs of the date of Armageddon from the bible code. And each proof uses a different calculation. The web pages quotes are all section of www.truebiblecode.com.

[1] The Midst Prophecy (understanding100.html, understanding16.html - see section 16 of this book)
[2] The Exedenic Times (understanding31.html, understanding133.html)
[3] The Corresponding ransom of Jesus for Adam (understanding16.html)
[4] The 10 Times of Pharaoh's Times (understanding31.html)
[5] The 10 horns and 7 heads of the Beast of Revelation 13 (see below)

[6] The 1.1 million men of the registration of Israel by Joab (understanding40.html)
[7] The heat wave from the South wind and the cloud rising in the Western parts (see below)
[8] The UN accepted the JWs as an NGO on January 28 1992, 4600 solar days of Daniel 8 before 1290 lunar days of Daniel 12 before the last day of this system, the end of the world, 2008Nisan14 (March 21st 2008) (understanding247.html)

Armageddon from the Gulf War and the UN

We will prove two simple ones here. The wild beast of Revelation 13 is the UN - see (understanding158.html for the full story). It has 10 horns representing 10 years of power over mankind and it has 7 heads representing 7 years of headship over mankind. It is unarguable that the UN currently has power over mankind. This power began at the end of the Gulf War, when the UN established itself (through US and to a much smaller extent UK fire power) as the ultimate military power on the planet. The power reign of the UN in New Biblical Lunar Calendar years (which start in the Hebrew month of Elul - for reasons outside the scope of this booklet) therefore ran from 1991Elul (the first NBLC year after the Gulf War) until 2001Elul. The 7 years of headship then run from 2001Elul to 2008Elul which is the end of Armageddon. The problem with this interpretation is that at the time of writing the UN is the political head only of Afghanistan (by virtue of the Bonn agreement) and not of the rest of the World. But we expect and prophesy (not in God's name, but with our best understanding of God's word) that the UN will expand its security council to 10 permanent members on the Hebrew date of 2002Heshvan19/20 (October 29/30/31 2002). These 10 member nations will accept a reduced veto over the activities of the UN. The reduced veto will give the UN headship over each of the 10 permanent member nations. At that time the US/UK world power, which is the 7th biblical king of the world, will be fully 'conquered' by the UN, the 8th biblical king of the world. The UN will become the political head of the world, because the UN will be able to tell the US and the UK what to do, and neither country will be able to veto it any longer in areas where the veto is lost. However the UN became the 8th Biblical King of the World on July 12th 002, when the US acceded to the jurisdiction of the UN International Criminal Court.

Armageddon from the heat wave of Luke 12

54 Then he went on to say also to the crowds: When you see a cloud rising in western parts, at once you say, 'A storm is coming,' and it turns out so.
55 And when you see that a south wind is blowing, you say, 'There will be a heat wave,' and it occurs.

56 Hypocrites, you know how to examine the outward appearance of earth and sky, but how is it you do not know how to examine this particular time? (Luke 12).

Well dear reader... Do you know how to examine this particular time? This kind of question is called a Reader Question. It is a question asked by the holy spirit of the reader of the bible. This is how one examines this time...

In 1918 on Nisan16 in the BLC the first tranch in the second presence of 16,000 new covenant saints were resurrected as angels. (see www.truebiblecode.com/understanding164.html). The are symbolised by a rising cloud because Jesus ascended to heaven in a cloud before the eyes of his disciples.

9 And after he had said these things, while they were looking on, he was lifted up and a cloud caught him up from their vision (Acts 1).

12 And they heard a loud voice out of heaven say to them: Come on up here. And they went up into heaven in the cloud, and their enemies beheld the (Revelation 11).

The ascension of the first group of new covenant saints of the second presence, started Nisan 16, 1918 with their resurrection and ended on 1918Iyyar25 with their entry into heaven. This is the 'cloud rising in western parts'. The 'heatwave' is Armageddon, which is identified as following from a South wind. But South is 90 degrees or one quarter of a circle away from West. But the circle has 360 degrees because the biblical lunar calendar, the original calendar of mankind, has 360 days, so we can equate 90 degrees to 90 days, or relate a quarter of a circle to a quarter of an orbit of the earth around the sun. The two events are separated by a quarter of a cycle. The Word symbolic meaning of a bible account always makes a substitution for a time period such as 90 days. Typically the substitution is a day for a year. A period of 360 years rather than 360 days is called a 'Prophetic Time'. If we make this typical substitution then we get a time period of a quarter of a Prophetic Times or 90 years between the resurrection and Armageddon. This puts Armageddon at 2008 on Nisan16. But this is the first day of Armageddon (March 21st).

Granted the substitution of a day for a year seems artificial at first sight. But it is very common in Word symbolic interpretations and is in fact a Principle of the Code - see www.truebiblecode.com/code.html#c10 - The Times Principle. The Jehovah's Witnesses are familiar with it in the case of Daniel 4 as are all Christian religions who accept that the coming as King of Christ during the second presence is 2520 years or 7 Prophetic Times after the fall of the Kingdom of Judah.

[6] The phrase '7 times' means '7 years' of the biblical lunar calendar in the bible

14 But the two wings of the great eagle were given the woman, that she might fly into the wilderness to her place; there is where she is fed for a time and times and half a time away from the face of the serpent (Revelation 12).

Where 'times' is obviously in the plural (since Greek has no dual number as Hebrew does). But earlier in the same chapter we read:

6 And the woman fled into the wilderness, where she has a place prepared by God, that they should feed her there a thousand two hundred and sixty days (Revelation 12).

In the actual vision, (but not in it's symbolic meaning) the two periods are the same period and so we are being told by holy spirit that the phrase 'a time, times and half a time' is 1260 days of the BLC (Biblical Lunar Calendar), which is 3.5 lunar years of 360 days. But a year is a time, a cycle, of the earth around the sun. So 3.5 years is 3.5 times. So 3.5 times is 1260 days. So 7 times is 2520 days which is 7 BLC years. In general n times is 360n days.

[7] Conclusion

Nobody disputes the physical significance of the Twin Towers Tragedy. The purpose of this book has been to prove that the spiritual significance of this disaster is in fact greater even than the physical significance. The destruction of the Twin Towers and the subsequent and unprecedented unity of world leaders in their 'co-alition against terror' is the most significant political re-organisation of mankind since the Tower of Babel was abandoned. Because knocking down the two divided towers of the World Trade Centre resulted in and symbolised a worldwide political unification which will result in a big mess and a massive destruction (like ground zero was). Whereas God's prevention of the building of the one tower of Babel and the separation of all the languages of mankind in the day of Nimrod as recorded in Genesis 11 resulted in and symbolised a worldwide political division.

Here is the perspective politically. Every nation knows that commercial monopolies are dangerous and must be policed very carefully. In the UK we have a monopoly and mergers commission, in the US there is the Department of Justice, which has the job of policing monopoly abuse by large corporations. But it is most obvious that a worldwide political monopoly is far more powerful and therefore far more dangerous than a worldwide commercial monopoly. Microsoft, for example can dominate software unfairly, but a worldwide political monopoly can dominate every law of every country unfairly.

For the EU to attempt to police Microsoft, is therefore the height of Hypocrisy. The EU is a far more dangerous monopoly than Microsoft, in fact it is unscriptural and unnatural for a people who speak French to attempt to rule a people who speak English or vice versa in any way at all. God created all of the different languages in order to protect mankind against the ambitions of megalomanic politicians, who not satisfied with control of an entire nation, seek control of an entire continent or even control of the whole world. Men are not able to cope with such huge power - they become corrupt. More corrupt than Microsoft or Getty Oil, or any large commercial monopoly could ever become. If the reader has ever met a politician when he is not in power, he will often find a well motivated reasonable and sound positive man. But once that politician gains power, then he all too often undergoes a horrendous metamorphosis. Abraham Lincoln said:

'Nearly all men can stand adversity, but if you want to test a man's character, give him power'

The EU should have remained the trading agreement that it was initially represented as being, the EEC, rather than the obscene and corrupt political monopoly that it has now become. The UN should remain a police force and a judge of erring governments and corrupt dictators, a social service and a security service for the world. It should not become a worldwide political monopoly. But guess what it is going to become?

Babel is reversed. We can now all speak the same language and reach each other within 24 hours. The world is one village, and what that means is, we are going to get one mayor.

What has protected mankind against abusive conquering totalitarian regimes and against an even more rapid progress towards self annihilation for over 4,000 years has been worldwide political division, enforced by large scale geography and by a multiplicity of language. Today we have overcome both of these protections. But we have failed to gain the wisdom necessary to live without them. So the majority of mankind (in fact 75% of mankind) will now annihilate themselves within the next 7 years. But the God who created these protections will step in at the very last minute, actually half way through Armageddon itself, and save those of us (25% of mankind) who can find it in our hearts to show him a little gratitude.

[1] Millions of years of human fossils reconciled with Genesis at last !

'Science without religion is lame; religion without science is blind.' - Albert Einstein

This section is designed to be read in conjunction with www.truebiblecode.com.

The Conflict between Fundamental Christians and Archaeologists

In the past the Archaeologist's view of man's ancient history over millions of years and the account of it in Genesis, spanning a time scale of either 7 'days' or of 77 generations from Adam to Jesus, have been viewed as conflicting, as contradictory and as mutually exclusive. We (the Lord's Witnesses) had previously taken the view that all 'History' before the flood was rubbish, in order to justify our acceptance of the Genesis account.

The argument of the Archaeologist has been that man has indeed been around for hundreds of thousands of years and so Genesis is nonsense. The argument of the fundamental Christian has been that Genesis is true word for word and that human archaeology must therefore be nonsense.

And he made out of one [man] every nation of men, to dwell upon the entire surface of the earth, and he decreed the appointed times and the set limits of the dwelling of [men] (Acts 17:26).

But we have now found out that these two histories are not actually contradictory at all, in fact they fit together perfectly. We will find out that Adam's sin did not only condemn his sons, it also saved his species, Homo Sapiens, and was the beginning of civilisation as we know it today.

Therefore I ask, Did they stumble so that they fell completely? Never may that happen! But by their false step there is salvation to people of the nations, to incite them to jealousy (Romans 11:11).

This scripture, in the literal meaning, applies to the physical Jews and the Gentiles. But the principle that the error of a chosen race leads to salvation for the rest of us applies also to Adam and his sons, as we shall see.

Human History

First we take a quick tour of ancient human history. The Cambridge Encyclopedia of Human Evolution (CEHE) & World Prehistory (Scarre & Fagan), more or less agree on the following Early Humans Table:

Type of Man	Height (metres)	Brain (cc)	Period years (before present)
Homo Habilis (small)	1	500 - 650	2 - 1.6 million
Homo Habilis (large)	c. 1.5	600 - 800	2.4 - 1.6 million
Homo Erectus	1.3 - 1.5	750 - 1250	1.8 million - 300,000
Archaic Homo Sapiens	?	1100 - 1400	400,000 - 100,000
Neanderthals	1.5 - 1.7	1200 - 1750	150,000 - 30,000
Modern man (cro magnon) Homo sapiens	1.6 - 1.85	1200 - 1700 (a bit smaller)	130,000 - now

It is not known how these changes occurred. It is presumed that the changes were for evolutionary advantage. Neanderthal and modern man coexisted for a long time. It is not known whether they could interbreed. It is thought that they could. It is not known why Neanderthals died out 30,000 years ago. The correlation with the Monrose Hypothesis is astounding - see [234].

Prehistoric Man's Achievements

The Cambridge Encyclopedia of Human Evolution (CEHE) and the Cultural Atlas of Mesopotamia (CAM) and World Prehistory have the following dates for Animal & Cereal domestication:

Domesticated	Wild progenitor	First Domestication Approx BC (CAM)	First Domestication approx BC (CEHE)
Dog	Wolf	11,000	10,000
Cereals	Wild Cereals	8,000 (WP)	8,000 (WP)
Goat	Bezoar Goat	8,500	7,000
Sheep	Asiatic mouflon	8,000	7,000
Cattle	Aurochs (extinct)	7,000	6,000
Pig	Boar	7,500	6,000
Horse	Wild Horse	4,000	4,000 For Riding
Camel	Camel	3,000	3,000 For Riding
Cat	Cat	7,000	3,000
Chicken	Jungle Fowl	6,000 (China)	2,000

If truly all Dogs descend from the wild wolf, as is currently believed then the gene pool of the wolf is unbelievably large, encompassing the Bull Terrier, the Chihuahua, the Poodle, the Great Dane, the Rottweiler and the Beagle. These modern dogs cannot possibly have evolved by random mutations away from the wolf in a mere 12,000 years. On the contrary, It is a known fact that they were selectively bred by man from the gene pool of the wolf. If indeed individual species do have this much genetic flexibility, then Darwin's comparatively minor Finch differentiation observations must all have been manifestations of this built in species capability rather than the result of evolution from random mutations over eons of time - see [221].

Genesis tells us that Adam would have in subjection: **every living creature that is moving upon the earth** (Genesis 1:28). This would include Horses and Camels for riding. So this command was fulfilled right on time, because Adam was born in 4027 BC - see [16].

Human Tool Advancement

Metallurgy table:

Radio Carbon Date	Bristlecone Pine - Dendro Date	Egyptian	Mesopotamian (Babylonian)	Aegean (Greece)	Balkan	France	UK
1200-1600	1500-2000					Bronze	Bronze
1600-2000	2000-2500					Copper	Copper
2000-2400	2500-3000	Bronze	Bronze	Bronze	Bronze		
2400-2800	3000-3500	Copper					
2800-3200	3500-4000			Some Copper			
3200-3700	4000-4500		Copper		Some Copper forging		
3700-4150	4500-5000		Some Copper		Some Copper		
Before 4150	Before 5000	Stone	Stone	Stone	Stone	Stone	Stone

The earliest scientifically documented hot working, annealing of copper is 4,000 BC in western Russia. The earliest scientifically accepted forging, casting, is in the Gumelnitsa culture of Troy. Now in standard Radio carbon dating this culture started between 4000 BC and 3300 BC (Before Civilisation, Renfrew p108,190-192). With dendrochronological recalibration from bristlecone pine it's 700 years earlier.

The Copper age, or Chalcolithic age generally starts in 4,500 BC. In Canaan, the modern day Israel and Palestine, the copper industry began to be developed from 4300 to 3300 (Genesis - Feyerick). It would have started with cold working of copper nuggets, then progressed to hot working, then smelting, then casting. Genesis relates that:

As for Zillah, she too gave birth to Tubal-cain, the forger of every sort of tool of copper and iron. And the sister of Tubal-cain was Naamah (Genesis 4:22).
Crudely speaking, this chap was around at the right time to be the father of hot forging of metals.

Historical Estimates of World Population

Year	World Population in Millions
-10000	4
-8000	5
-5000	5
-4000	7
-3000	14
-2000	27
-1000	50
-500	100
-200	150
1	170
200	190
400	190
500	190
600	200
700	210
800	220
900	240
1000	265

Table from: McEvedy, Colin and Richard Jones, 1978, Atlas of World Population History, Facts on File, New York, pp. 342-351.

The Post Adam Population boom

Genesis dates Adam as being born in 4027 BC - see [16]. Ancient History has it that in Nagada, 15 miles south of Thebes in Egypt, in 4000BC, little hamlets spaced around 1 km apart grew enough food to support around 100 people/square km. By 3600BC a walled town with cemeteries stood in the heart of Nagada with rectangular mud brick dwellings and larger more palatial residences. Many inhabitants were non farmers. They were traders, officials and artisans who lived in permanent towns. This was all made possible by improved farming which supported around 1000 people/square km. They cleared trees, removed dense grass, built dykes, dug drainage canals and did many of the things that modern farmers do today, from a standing start 400 years earlier (Ancient Civilisations - Scarre & Fagan p94). Cambridge Ancient History and Genesis - Feyerick, put this advance as occurring in 3500BC, so the whole process was from 3700 to 3300BC in this Chronology.

These things show that the scripture in Genesis:

When men started to <u>grow in numbers</u> on the surface of the ground, and daughters were born to them, then the sons of the true God began to notice the daughters of men, that they were good looking (Genesis 6:1,2).
refers to the first true population boom of mankind.

'Man', 'The Man' and the bible code

We read in Genesis 1:26 about 'man', we then read in Genesis 1:27 about 'the man'. This may seem like a trivial distinction to make, until one remembers that 'the God' is Jehovah, the one true God, whereas 'god' can be any angel in bible terminology:

No man has seen God at any time; the only-begotten god who is in the bosom [position] with the Father is the one that has explained him (John 1:18).

The only begotten God is Jesus. He was seen, but the God is Jehovah, who cannot be seen (if you are a Trinitarian do not worry at this stage, you can still believe that 'the God', whoever he is, is different from the angels who are merely 'gods'). Jesus is a God in the sense that all angels are Gods, this being the sense of John 10 below and Psalm 82:

**The Jews answered him: We are stoning you, not for a fine work, but for blasphemy, even because you, although being a man, make yourself a god.
Jesus answered them: Is it not written in your Law: I said: You are gods. If he called 'gods' those against whom the word of God came, and yet the Scripture cannot be nullified** (John 10:33).

I myself have said: You are gods, And all of you are sons of the Most High (Psalm 82:6).

Moses explains:
For Jehovah your God is the God of gods and the Lord of lords, the

God great, mighty and fear-inspiring, who treats none with partiality nor accepts a bribe (Deuteronomy 10:17).

Paul explains fully:
For even though there are those who are called "gods," whether in heaven or on earth, just as there are many "gods" and many "lords," there is actually to us one God the Father, out of whom all things are, and we for him; and there is one Lord, Jesus Christ, through whom all things are, and we through him (1 Corinthians 8:5,6).

So keeping this fine distinction in mind, we propose that just as 'the God' is a different being from all of the other gods with the generic title of 'god', so 'the man', who was Adam, was a different being from all of the other Homo sapiens around at the time of the creation of Adam who have the generic title of 'man'. Now the exact Hebrew Interlinear translation of Genesis 1:26,27 is as follows:

Let us make man in our image according to our likeness (Genesis 1:26).

אדם man

בצלמנו in our image

כדמותנו according to our likeness

Where ב means 'in' and כ means 'as', and the root צלם means: Shade, shadow, image, likeness, and the root דמה means: Likeness.

And God proceeded to create the man in his image, in God's image he created him, male and female he created them (Genesis 1:27).

האדם the man

בצלמו in his image

בצלם אלהים in image of God.

If you are reading this from the web and the above is not Hebrew then you need to download the SPTiberian Hebrew font!! To fully interpret these two verses we are going to use some of the bible code. We appreciate that the reader may not be familiar with this code as yet, since it is meant to be studied after the Basics section of this website/book has been fully read. But the more adventurous among you can take a peek at this stage by following the links if they desire. If not then do not worry, the flavour can still be fully ascertained even from the literal meaning as follows:

So 'man' was created by 'us' in 'our image' according to 'our likeness', an image of several beings, but 'the man' was created by 'God' in God's image, an image of one being, not in 'our image' and not according to any likeness. This is precisely the distinction that we have just made above. Namely, 'man' is generic, made by a plurality of Gods, and made in the image of a plurality of Gods, 'our image', whereas Adam, is unique, made by God himself and made in the image of the one and only God, Jehovah. So 'man' stands for mankind, which was Homo sapiens, Cro-magnon man, and 'the man' stands for the one off Adam.

One of the ways in which Adam was created in God's image, rather than in 'our image' which is the image of the angels, is that he was the first of a new type of man and there was only one of him, just as God was the first spirit being and initially there was only one of him.

Applying the Code to Genesis 1:26,27

We are effectively applying the Designations Principle of the code to 'man' and 'the man'. Two different designations for one creation in the literal meaning, refers to two creations in the symbolic meaning, one of which is actually the creation of Adam, the literal meaning. Next we apply the Omission Principle, because 'man' is said to be both in an image and in a likeness, whereas 'the man' is said to be only in an image. This principle states:

> If an account contains an obvious and glaring omission, then the further fulfillment of the account involves this omission.

So the greater meaning of this account, which relates not to the creation of Adam, but to the creation of Homo Sapiens, is the creation 'in our likeness'.

Next we apply the Immediate Repetition Principle to the wonderful phrase:

And God proceeded to create the man in his image, in God's image he created him, male and female he created them (Genesis 1:27).

Here we have three successive repetitions of the concept of the creation of man, so there are three creations here. These three are:

The man in his image	Adam the human
In God's image he created him	Adam's associated angel, he was born again when he was born, God blew his spirit of life into two nostrils, two receptacles for the spirit of life, two souls, human and angelic
Male and female he created them	Homo Sapiens

And Jehovah God proceeded to form the man out of dust from the ground and to blow into his <u>nostrils</u> the breath of life, and the man came to be a living soul (Genesis 2:7).

We appreciate that we haven't covered what it is to be born again as yet, if you wish to jump there then see [190]. However, the first and the third successive repetition in the table above are sufficient to establish that there were two types of men around at the advent of Adam. Adam, before his fall, was a closer representation of God, being made in his image, than man was, who was made in his likeness. Adam was the spitting image of God whereas man was the wannabe. As regards the last Adam, Jesus:

He is the image of the invisible God, the firstborn of all creation (Colossians 1:15).

He is the reflection of [his] glory and the exact representation of his very being, and he sustains all things by the word of his power; and after he had made a purification for our sins he sat down on the right hand of the Majesty in lofty places (Hebrew 1:3).

It is even so written: The first man Adam became a living soul. The last Adam became a life-giving spirit (1 Corinthians 15:45).

Adam was the first human to be called 'man' by God in the literal meaning of Genesis (notwithstanding the symbolic meaning of 'man' in the account), and he was the first human to be created 'ready born again' as it were, with an associated angel. This being a declaration in advance of his spirituality. In fact God waited until Homo Sapiens was ready to become spiritual and then he introduced Adam. This is the 2001 movie concept.

The full picture is given by the whole of verses 26-28:

And God went on to say: Let us make man in our image, according to our likeness, and let them have in subjection the fish of the sea and the flying creatures of the heavens and the domestic animals and all the earth and every moving animal that is moving upon the earth.

And God proceeded to create the man in his image, in God's image he created him; male and female he created them.

Further, God blessed them and God said to them: Be fruitful and become many and fill the earth and subdue it, and have in subjection the fish of the sea and the flying creatures of the heavens and every living creature that is moving upon the earth (Genesis 1:26-28).

'Man' is not blessed, and is not commanded to fill the earth and does not have in subjection every living creature that is moving upon the earth. But Adam and Eve are blessed, and commanded to fill the earth, and have in subjection every living creature, which would include 'man'. This was a prophetic blessing (as they all are). The sons of Adam did fill the earth, the modern humans (cro magnon man, or homo sapiens sapiens) had only produced around 5 -7 million by the time of Adam. So now please view Adam and his sons like Abraham and his sons. They existed alongside Homo Sapiens, just as the Jew existed alongside the Gentile, just as modern Homo Sapiens existed alongside Neanderthal man!

This is the book of Adam's history. In the day of God's creating Adam/man he made him in the likeness of God.

Male and female he created them. And he blessed them and called their name Man in the day of their being created (Genesis 5:1,2).

The literal meaning refers simply to Adam and Eve. But in the symbolic meaning, we have a repetition of the day of creation. Applying the Repetition Principle, there is a greater 'day of creation', than the actual day when Adam was created. This day is the 6th creative day, when Mankind (pre-adamic man) was created. 'Male and Female' in verse 2 are the creation of pre-adamic man in the symoblic meaning. However from the literal meaning we know that God only called mankind 'man' (the Hebrew word for 'man' is 'Adam') at the creation of Adam.

The covenant for the salvation of both adamic and pre-adamic man, was made by Enoch (we think).

How fast could Adam and Eve Reproduce ?

Assume that the typical lifespan of a daughter of Eve was 900 years, and her first child was at around 75 years old.

Assume that there were 100 year generations, 10 daughters per generation, 20 children per generation, for the first three generations from 75 to 375, then only 5 daughters per generation for the next generation 375 to 475, then no further children.

We know that Eve gave birth to Cain in 3992Shebat and Abel in 3990Tishri - see [41]. So we take her first 100 year generation as starting in 3990 approx. They all lived up to 960 years.

Years	3990	3890	3790	3690	3590	3490	3390	3290	Total
Eve		10	10	10	5	0	0	0	35
Gen2			100	100	100	50	0	0	350
Gen3				1,000	1,000	1,000	500	00	3,500
Gen4					10,000	10,000	10,000	5,000	35,000
Gen5						100,000	100,000	100,000	300,000
Gen6							1,000,000	1,000,000	2,000,000
Gen7								10,000,000	10,000,000

Grand Total of daughters = 12,338,885

Grand total of sons and daughters = 24,000,000 possible in 3300 BC !!

McEvedy and Jones have 14 million for 3000 BC, but 7 million of these would have been Homo Sapiens.

Vegetarians amongst Omnivores

Now we know that modern man was an omnivore and that he wore clothes. But as regards Adam in the garden we know that he was naked and not ashamed and we read:

And God went on to say: Here I have given to you all vegetation bearing seed which is on the surface of the whole earth and every tree on which there is the fruit of a tree bearing seed. To you let it serve as food (Genesis 1:29).

So Adam and Eve were to be vegetarians, both inside and outside the garden since their food was on the surface of the whole earth. This is also an implied prophecy that they will leave the garden. For why give them food outside it if they will always be inside it?

Now God had already formed all of the animals outside the garden, before man, as described in Genesis 1. Not only that but Homo sapiens himself had named them and painted them on walls of caves and domesticated some of them by the time of Adam's appearance. So why do we read in Genesis 2:

And Jehovah God went on to say: It is not good for the man to continue by himself. I am going to make a helper for him, as a complement of him.

Now Jehovah God was forming (imperfect tense in Hebrew) **from the ground every wild beast of the field and every flying creature of the heavens, and he began bringing them to the man to see what he would call each one; and whatever the man would call it, each living soul, that was its name** (Genesis 2:18,19)?

It is because these animals were being created after Adam! They were the first souls that God created in the garden to keep him company before Eve. They were Edenic animals, new creations, which were also vegetarian, because God had already said:

And to every wild beast of the earth and to every flying creature of the heavens and to everything moving upon the earth in which there is life as a soul I have given all green vegetation for food (Genesis 1:30).

This would bind the Edenic animals, but the exedic animals were already eating each other (as were some of the exedic humans!) These are the same animals that we will find in the Kingdom of God about which Isaiah prophesied:

For here I am creating new heavens and a new earth; and the former things will not be called to mind, neither will they come up into the heart (Isaiah 65:17).

The wolf and the lamb themselves will feed as one, and the lion will eat straw just like the bull; and as for the serpent, his food will be dust. They will do no harm nor cause any ruin in all my holy mountain, Jehovah has said (Isaiah 65:25).

This has a literal meaning, that the lion, presently a carnivore will be a vegetarian like the bull. Now we know that these vegetarian animals have already been created because God is resting from his creative works. So they must have been created already. So there were two types of animals coexisting at one point in history, the Kingdom animals and the current animals. It is not hard to see that these were the ones decreed to eat green vegetation in the garden of Eden. They never left the garden however.

So now we can understand the full meaning of Adam's prophetic words uttered when God brought Eve to him:

This is at last bone of my bones and flesh of my flesh (Genesis 2:23).

Homo sapiens was bone of his bone, since he shared a common skeleton with Adam. But Eve was flesh of his flesh as well. Indefinitely living flesh at that time.

Both of them had no interaction with the outside world before Adam's sin because they were not ashamed to be naked, whereas the rest of mankind wore clothes because they were ashamed to be naked. Incidentally they were not ashamed to be naked because they did not know sexual desire in the garden - see [2]. As regards the men outside Eden, we have the scriptures:

Whereas angels, although they are greater in strength and power, do not bring against them an accusation in abusive terms, [not doing so] out of respect for Jehovah.

But these [men], like unreasoning animals born naturally to be caught and destroyed, will, in the things of which they are ignorant and speak abusively, even suffer destruction in their own [course of] destruction (2 Peter 2:11,12).

Yet these [men] are speaking abusively of all the things they really do not know; but all the things that they do understand naturally like the unreasoning animals, in these things they go on corrupting themselves (Jude 10).

Adam's release from Eden

The effect of Adam's release from Eden upon mankind was monumental. Having achieved virtually nothing other than the domestication of sheep the creation of small farming villages with no administrative structure, the making of some stone and bone tools and the battering of some copper nuggets in the previous 100,000 years we now absolutely explode upon the planet.

Within just 1000 years of his expulsion (in 3993Nisan - see [16], [31]), in fact whilst Adam was still alive (he died in 3097 aged 930 years see - Genesis 5:3,4) we had built cities with large bureaucracies, learned how to write, invented the wheel, domesticated the horse, forged all sorts of alloys, started worshipping in temples and doubled our population from around 7 million to around 14 million!!

At the end of the early Chalcolithic period, then let us say 5000 BC, we find that throughout the greater part of the Near East, all the requirements for the birth of civilisation were present. Villages, Market towns (eg: Catal Huyuk West, over 1300 ft in diameter)...Nevertheless, the expected birth of civilisation did not take place. It was delayed for nearly another millenium and a half, and when it did come, it was not in the areas which had hitherto been most prominent, but in the dismally flat lands of S. Iraq (Mesopotamia) and a little later in Egypt. Areas which until then had been of little or no importance. Why was this so? (The Dawn of Civilisation - Sunday Times 1961).

We will now show that all of this happened as a result of Adam!

It is apparent from the above that it all happened after Adam who was born in 4027Tishri. We will now see confirmation that Writing, the Wheel and the first City all came along after 3500 BC...

First Writings Table:

The appearance of writing marks the end of the prehistoric period and the beginning of the historic period.

Nation	Date of first writings found	Source
Mesopotamia (Uruk IVb)	3500 BC	Cambridge Ancient History Vol1 Part 1 p226-228.
Egyptian Hieroglyphics	3000 BC	Genesis - Feyericks
Chinese	2500 BC	Ancient Civilisations - Scarre & Fagan

The Wheel:

The solid wheel was invented around 3000BC (The Dawn of Civilisation - Sunday Times 1961) and the spoked wheel around 2000BC (Cambridge Ancient History Vol 1 part 1).

The First City:

Today we define a city (in the West) as a town with a cathedral in it. The very first City in the World is known to be Eridu in Mesopotamia, it contained man's first temple. The Summerian King List (SKL), a rectangular clay tablet, an early historical document still in existence today, details 5 cities in

Mesopotamia from which 8 kings ruled before the flood. The first of these is said to be Eridu. It says:

When Kingship was lowered from heaven, the kingship was in Eridu. Eridu, Alulim king and reigned 28,800 years/days/units. Algalar reigned 36,000 units. Two kings reigned its 64,800 units. I drop Eridu, its kingship to Badtibira was carried......

Badtibira had three kings reigning for 43,200 units, 28,800 units and 36,000 units.

Then Larak had one king reigning for 28,800 units.

Then Sippar had one king reigning for 21,000 units.

Shuruppak, Ubartutu became king and reigned 18,600 units. One king reigned 18,600 units.

Five cities were they, 8 kings reigned there 241,200 units. The flood swept thereover. After the flood had swept thereover when kingship was lowered from heaven, the kingship was in Kish.

The Cambridge Ancient History (Vol1 Part 1 p330), confirms that Eridu was the first town to become a city, by which is meant that it had an elite ruling class of administrators who were not farmers, it was not a farming co-operative. Cities have overall Mayors and local councils basically. 'Ancient Civilisations' dates this City at 3700 BC and we quote:

The Eridu temples underline the key role of religion in the formation of the first cities. Temples dedicated to patron deities formed a focus of community attention and identity and also became powerful economic institutions, owning large areas of land. The end result was a kind of state religion (Ancient Civilisations p53).

The Dawn of Civilisation (Sunday Times 1961) states:

About 3500 BC a temple was built in Eridu which was to be the classic prototype for the monumental architecture to come. All that remains of it today is the gypsum plastered limestone platform.

All of this came after Adam, and as we shall see, the big boom in civilisation occurred first in the low plain below the garden of Eden, Mesopotamia. We now compare Genesis with Mesopotamian history, geography and mythology with some help from David Rohl (Legend, the Genesis of Civilisation - highly recommended - see [book]).

The Garden of Eden

Now there was a river issuing out of Eden to water the garden, and from there it began to be parted and it became, four heads.

The first one's name is Pishon; it is the one encircling the entire land of Havilah, where there is gold.

And the gold of that land is good. There also are the bdellium gum and the onyx stone.

And the name of the second river is Gihon; it is the one encircling the entire land of Cush.

And the name of the third river is Hiddekel; it is the one going to the east of Assyria. And the fourth river is the Euphrates (Genesis 2:10-14).

We know that the Euphrates (Perath) and the Tigris (Hiddekel) are the two great rivers of Mesopotamia. So Eden was an area near to Mesopotamia, and the Garden itself was an area within Eden. Now from Eden we have 4 head waters, or 4 sources of rivers.

David Rohl has shown that the Euphrates and the Tigris have their head waters in the Lake Van and Lake Urmia region in the Iranian highlands between Kurdistan and Armenia. Now just east of this region are two rivers which flow into the Caspian Sea, the Araxes and the Uizhun. The Araxes (Greek name) is called today the Araks or the Aras. Reginald Walker discovered that during the 8th Century AD some pieces of this river were called the Gaihun. He then discovered that 19th Century Persians referred to it as the Jichon - Aras. In fact early Victorian bible dictionaries and commentaries mention the Gihon-Aras (Easton's bible dictionary). But this crucial data has been overlooked recently. Near the Araxes North of the modern town of Tabriz, is a mountain ridge called: 'The Mountain of Cush'. Whereas the Gihon was said to encircle the entire land of Cush. So we now have three of the 4 rivers of Eden.

Walker identified the Uizhun as the only possible candidate for the Pishon by a process of elimination (there were no other rivers around). But David Rohl has gone one better. He has pointed out that there is a place on the southern shore of lake Urmia currently called Pisdeli, that used to be called Uishteri. With this linguistic flexibility we get the Puizhun, which is close enough to the Pishon.

This kind of thing is similar to London, Londres, Londinium etc, or indeed to the case of 'Ornan' of 1 Chronicles 21:18 the man whom David purchased the site of Solomon's temple from (It is now the big Mosque in Jerusalem), who is called 'Araunah' by Samuel in 2 Samuel 24:18.

As a further proof that the Uizhun is the Pishon: We know that the Pishon encircles the land of Havilah where there is gold. Now this river flows past a village called Zarshuyan, which means 'gold washing', indicating panning for gold in the river, and where there was a gold mine around 1500 years ago.

The Land of Nod

If we go east of Eden we should end up in Nod:

With that Cain went away from the face of Jehovah and took up residence in the land of Nod to the East of Eden (Genesis 4:16).

So even after leaving the garden, Adam's family was still near to the face of Jehovah, which actually means that they were still his people, and still worshipping him.

If you go further East towards the Caspian Sea you find the districts of Upper and Lower Noqdi. Several villages here are called Noqdi, and one is called Noadi. The suffix '-i' means belonging to (c.f. Pakistani, Israeli).

The Temple at Eridu

David Rohl in 'Legend' compares the Sumerian Adapa Epic to the Genesis account of Adam's fall:

Adapa was the first great Sage who introduced the worship of the Gods to mankind. He was the high priest of Ea's shrine at Eridu. One day he went into the sea in his boat where he was caught in a storm. Angry with the elements Adapa cursed the South Wind, breaking his wing. As a result the wind did not blow for seven days. This change in the natural order of things was noticed by Anu, god of heaven, and he sent for Adapa in order to punish him. Before the priest of Eridu reached heaven he was warned by Ea that he would be offered the bread and water of death which he must refuse. When Adapa finally arrived in heaven he explained that his curse upon the South Wind was in retaliation for the sinking of his boat by the storm. Once Anu realised what had transpired he was sympathetic to the priest of Eridu and offered him the ultimate gift - the bread and water of eternal life. But of course Adapa refused the priceless gift of the gods and returned to the earth to die a mortal's death.

This is quite obviously a Satanic counterfeit of the fall of Adam. This sort of deception is typical of Satan. With some spiritual knowledge one can see right into this deception.

Adapa	Adam
Breaking his wing	Losing his associated angel
Ea	Jehovah
Anu	Satan
South Wind	Holy Spirit

59

When Moses asked God what his name was he replied:

'**Eyah asher Eyah**' which means' **I am who I am**' or '**I am who is Eyah**'

So Ea, was Jehovah, who is 'I am' in Hebrew.

The South Wind is the holy spirit, and God was walking in the Garden in the breezy part of the day when he called for Adam.

Ea is blamed by the account as deceiving Adam into losing his everlasting life. When it was Satan who deceived Eve into losing her everlasting life, and Adam who knowingly lost his without any deception. Here Anu, who is Satan, is depicting himself to be more merciful and sympathetic than God (vomit, vomit).

But the account shows that Adam was the high priest of Ea at Eridu. (Satan always mixes the truth with the lie, he gets credibility from the truth so that he can sell the lie better). Obviously he was the *first* high priest of Ea there. As regards this name of God, Ea, which was made known to Moses, we read:

And to Seth there also was born a son and he proceeded to call its name Enosh. At that time a start was made of calling on the name of Jehovah (Genesis 4:26).

So Mankind knew God to be Ea at the time of the birth of Enosh the grandson of Adam (Enosh means 'mortal man' - so Adam had accepted his penalty and was calling on God in repentance). The emergence of a plethora of temples and associated cities, at and after Eridu, proves that there was at least one original and true temple of worship. For no one makes forgeries in the absence of an original.

Enki

The first temple at Eridu was dedicated to Enki, which means 'Lord of the earth'. Enki was also the God of the watery Abyss, Abzu (Legends - David Rohl). Enki was also a son in the Atrahasis Epic:

Nammu the goddess of the primeval ocean says to her son:

Oh my son (Enki) rise from your bed… and work your wisdom! Fashion servants of the gods in their own likeness..

Enki then gathers together all the 'good and princely craftsmen' and replies:

Oh my mother, the creature whose name you uttered shall exist. (instructions to the craftsmen): Attribute to it the likeness of the gods. Mix the heart of the clay which is over the abyss. The good and princely craftsmen will work the clay...Ninmah (the goddess of birth) will attribute to it the mould of the Gods - it is man.

So Enki is a son, who gathers all the good and princely craftsmen, i.e. the loyal angels, and organises the making of man in the image of the Gods. Now Enki has the same consonants and the same first letter as Enoch. And Enoch was Michael - see [305], who is the angel of the abyss:

They have over them a king, the angel of the abyss. In Hebrew his name is Abaddon, but in Greek he has the name Apollyon (Revelation 9:11).

Michael the archangel organises all of the loyal angels. But not only this, he rises from a bed after he dies, for he was Jesus - see [14b]. The Hebrew word for dust, is 'aphar' which also means clay. So now we have Adam as the high priest of Jehovah in the temple dedicated to Enoch in the first city Eridu. Of course Michael had no mother, being the first born and only begotten son of God, the first angel created. The concept of a goddess arose when the daughters of Adam, who were daughters of God through Adam, started mixing with homo sapiens after Eden. To homo sapiens who had only just domesticated the sheep, and presumably was only living for around 100 years. Adam and his children who were living nearly 1,000 years were immortal gods. This is the origin of all mythology we suggest. For Adam and his children were sons of God, but Homo sapiens were intelligent creations who initially were animalistic and without spirituality, but later developed it.

Now Adapa means 'the wise'. In the British Museum, on tablet W-20030, there is a list of 7 antedeluvian kings (6 of which correspond with the Sumerian King List - the 7th might have been coregent i.e in another city which was allied to the lead city.) They each have an associated sage, an apkallus. These look like sons of Adam, because wisdom is what they brought to mankind.

The Sage of the first king in the SKL (Sumerian King List), the first king of Eridu was called Uan-adapa, who might well have been Adam, except that Adam was dead before he became king if we take the units in the SKL as days. So we guess Uan-adapa was a descendant of Adam. The Sage of the 2nd last of the 8 preflood kings (Enmenduranna/Enmeduranki) was called Utuabzu. This chap is traditionally said not to have died and been buried but to have been taken up to heaven. But this is what happened to Enoch. And Abzu, means abyss, whereas Enoch/ Enki was Lord over the abyss. Now Utuabzu was not Enoch because Enoch was transferred in 3040, aged 365 years, much too early for the 2nd last preflood king to have him as a sage. But Utuabzu is being used as a Satanic counterfeit of Enoch here.

Enoch was born in 3405. Michael would not have possessed him until after the age of procreation, 65+. So after 3340 we have the possibility of a temple to do with Enki. The date for the urbanization of Eridu is around 3500.

Now Enoch was transferred so as not to see death in 3040BC. But if we take the 241,200 units of time in the Sumerian King List as being days (and there is no other sensible unit of time to take them as) we find that it's 670 years of 360 days each. Also every reign of the first 8 kings in the SKL is divisible by 360 except the last two which are divisible by 120, or thirds of a year, which indicates that the Sumerians had 3 seasons. The ancient calendars of mankind all had 360 days in the year - see [90], as does the Biblical Lunar Calendar - see [4]. The longest reign of the 8 Kings is 120 years, this is short for a son of Adam. The average reign was 84 years, which is long for a man if he was not a son of Adam and if he was living 120 years max. Now the bible dates the year of the flood as 2371 BC - see [16]. If we count back from the year of the flood 2371Tishri (September/October) - 2370Elul (August/September), 670 years we end up in 3041Tishri to 3040Elul. If we count the years inclusively, then we end up in 3040Tishri - 3039Elul the year in which Enoch ascended to heaven:

And Enoch lived on for 65 years. Then he became father to Methuselah. And after his fathering Methuselah Enoch went on walking with the [true] God 300 years. Meanwhile he became father to sons and daughters.
So all the days of Enoch amounted to 365 years.
And Enoch kept walking with the [true] God. Then he was no more, for God took him (Genesis 5:21-24).

By faith Enoch was transferred so as not to see death, and he was nowhere to be found because God had transferred him; for before his transference he had the witness that he had pleased God well (Hebrews 11:5).
For the chronology of the sons of Adam - see [96]. The ancient Hebrew year ran Tishri (September/October) to Elul (August/September). Did Enoch appoint Alulim king in his last year or did Alulim take over on the ascension of Enoch/Enki, after he was out of the way?

The other Enoch in Genesis and Eridu or Irad

Cain had intercourse with his wife, and she became pregnant and gave birth to Enoch. Then he engaged in building a city and called the city's name by the name of his son, Enoch. Later there was born to Enoch Irad (Genesis 4:17,18 NWT).

At first sight this looks like Cain built a city called Enoch. But Cain had already prophesied his own future saying:

I must become a wanderer and a fugitive on the earth and it is certain that anyone finding me will kill me (Genesis 4:14).

It is hardly likely that such a recluse who was exiled to wandering around Nod would build a city. The Hebrew actually says:

And he knew Cain, namely wife of him, and she became pregnant and she bore namely Enoch and he was building city and he called name of the city as name of son of him, Enoch. And he was born to Enoch, namely, Irad (Genesis 4:17,18 NIVHEOT ammended).

It is not linguistically clear whether Enoch is the subject or object here. So Enoch could well be the subject of the sentence, the city builder, in which case the City would be called as 'Irad'. The Hebrew word for city is 'Ir' עיר the Sumerian is 'Uru', 'Eri', 'Ur' (English Urban) in various dialect spellings (David Rohl - Legends).

But Eridu has the same consonants as Irad, and both names start with the word for 'city' in their respective languages. So Eridu could be the Sumerian of Irad צרד.

Now the Hebrew for first is: אחד pronounced 'Achad'. So the Hebrew for 'first city', or 'city first' would be: Irachad. This would easily shorten to Irad, in fact try saying Irachad a few times!

So Eridu is looking very much like Irad. As David Rohl would then say: Have we now reconciled the first city of Archaeology with the first city of Genesis ?

So it was the sons of Adam and their wisdom that turned a prehistoric man, into what we are today. They built cities, they tamed animals, they invented the wheel and writing, they forged metals and they fought wars, they worshipped the one true God and they worshipped several false Gods. For the purpose of a fake is to mask the original.

Tubal Cain and Metal forging

As regards forging metals, the second city in the Sumerian King List is called Badtibira, which means 'Settlement of the metal worker' (David Rohl - Legends). Now the 7th in line from Cain was called Tubal Cain.

As for Zillah she too gave birth to Tubal Cain the forger of every sort of tool of copper and iron (Genesis 4:22).

Tubal is from the root: יבל meaning 'to flow'. Forging involves heating up a metal until it flows! And Cain comes from a root meaning 'to forge'. So Tubal

Cain is a flow-forger. One suspects that these forged metals were used as weapons. The second city in the SKL, Badtibira, the 'settlement of the metal worker' may have defeated the first city, Eridu, using weapons made by this metal worker. Who was this unique singular metal worker? Tubal Cain looks like an outstanding candidate.

In fact since Abel's blood was crying out to God from the field it is possible that Cain stabbed him with something that he forged. But Tubal Cain appears to have started off not only the bronze age but also the iron age!

Noah

David Rohl has introduced a new chronology of Mesopotamia based on the first regnal year of Ammisaduga being 1419 BC (see Legends). With this Chronology every post flood ruler in the Sumerian King List ruled after 2371 BC. Then we have Tablet 15833 in the British Museum. This records transactions between temple herds and mentions the name of the god Shuruppak. It is dated to 2500 BC (Ancient Civilisations - Scarre & Fagan p55). But Shuruppak was the last city in the Sumerian King list, to rule over Mesopotamia before the flood, through King Ubartutu. So since false worship took a while to re-establish after the flood, and since we have no evidence of the city of Shuruppak being rebuilt after the flood, we can say that the flood was after 2500 BC.

The Gilgamesh (Sumerian) Flood Epic

Ea, the clever prince, was under oath with them (the gods) so he repeated their talk (of the flood) to the reed house: Reed house, reed house! Wall, wall! Hear Oh reed house, understand oh wall! Oh man of Shuruppak, son of Ubartutu, tear down the house and build a boat!

Then Utnapishtim, was instructed by Ea to build an ark which he did. Then the flood came and when it subsided he let out a dove then a swallow then a raven, and the ark finally came to rest on mount Nimush where he sacrificed to the gods. Then God said:

Hitherto Utnapishtim has been but a man, but now Utnapishtim and his wife shall be as the gods. In the distance, at the mouth of the rivers, Utnapishtim shall dwell.

So Utnapishtim/Noah was Ubartutu's son. So Ubartutu was Lamech. Now Lamech died aged 777 years in 2376 BC, 5 years before the flood. He was the last King of Shuruppak according to the SKL (Sumerian King Legends).

The Mesopotamian flood myth has Ziusudra, the Noah hero figure gaining: breath eternal, like a God. A reasonable assessment for a man who lived 950 years:

So all the days of Noah amounted to nine hundred and fifty years and he died (Genesis 9:29).
Whilst his sons after the flood were living 480 years max between Arpachshad and Peleg, and then 240 years max after Peleg - check it out in Genesis 11.

How fast could Noah's daughters procreate ?

Assume: 480 year max humans, who could start procreating at 40 (c.f. Genesis 11).

Assume: 40 year generations, 8 daughters and 8 sons in 40 years, for the first 4 generations, then no more.

After the flood the first children arrived in 2369 (say 2370). 3 breeding pairs say (Shem, Ham, Japheth and wives).

Year	2330	2290	2250	2210	2170	2130	2090	2040	Total
Mrs Shem	8	8	8	8	0	0	0	0	40
Gen2		64	64	64	64	0	0	0	256
Gen3			512	512	512	512	0	0	2,048
Gen4				4096	4096	4096	4096	2560	16,384
Gen5					32,768	32,768	32,768	32,768	131,072
Gen6						262,144	262,144	262,144	786,432
Gen7							2,097,152	2,097,152	4,194,304
Gen8								16,777,216	16,777,216
Total									21,907,752

But there were three breeding pairs to start with so by 2050 there could have been: 65,733,102 daughters of Noah and: 131,466,204 children of Noah in all. (Noah was still alive then!)

This is 5 times McEvedy & Jones' estimate of 27 million as a world population at 2000 BC. Over 20 million children in under 330 years !

The first Semitic Dynasty, (Dynasty of the sons of Shem) Akkad, started in 2334 BC (Genesis - Feyericks). This was 35 years after Shem's first son Arpachshad was born - a bit early but reasonable.

[3] The Bible and its Translations

This section is designed to be read in conjunction with www.truebiblecode.com.

The Old Testament was originally written in Hebrew and the New testament was originally written in Greek. The Hebrew Text of the old Testament that is used as the basis of most English translations today is the BHS, the Biblia Hebraica Stutgartensia. The 3 main Greek Texts used as the basis of most English translations today are the United Bible Societies 3rd corrected Edition/Nestle Aland 26th Edition (Alexandrine Manuscript), The Hodges and Farstad Majority text, and the Wescott & Hort Greek Text. These Hebrew and Greek Texts are considered to be the closest to the original Hebrew and Greek texts which we no longer possess.

We do possess many complete Hebrew and Greek texts of the bible. The BHS is based mainly on the Codex Leningrad B19A which is in the Leningrad State Public Library, dated at 1008 CE (AD). The Greek texts are based on the Vatican 1209 (B) manuscript in the Vatican City, Rome, dating from the 4th Century CE (AD), the Sinaitic manuscript, in the British Museum, dating from the 4th Century CE and the Alexandrine Manuscript, in the British Museum, dating from the 5th century CE, among others.

FJA Hort (Wescott & Hort) a Cambridge Greek Scholar said:

> The great bulk of the words of the New Testament stand out above all discriminative processes of criticism, because they are free from variation, and need only be transcribed...the words in our opinion still subject to doubt, can hardly amount to more than a thousandth part of the whole testament.

So the differences between the various Greek manuscripts are minor, certainly in the literal meaning of the bible. The dead sea scrolls, discovered last century contain the whole book of Isaiah dated to before Christ. This version of the book of Isaiah in the scrolls is almost identical to the BHS version in the Codex Leningrad which dates around 1200 years later. Since there is no obvious reason to suppose that the scribes responsible for the Codex Leningrad did a more accurate job on Isaiah than they did on any other book, we can be confident that the BHS is a good representation of the original Hebrew text.

With the recent discovery of the True Bible Code, *not* the Old Testament only ELS 'code' of Eli Rips and Michael Drosnin, but the symbolic code of the whole bible. And with a better understanding of the literal meaning of the bible, it may be possible to improve our determination of which Codices are the more accurate. To the extent we have done this so far we have found that the Alexandrine Manuscript is the best, possibly even - 'the one'.

So for the reasons above, or alternatively from one's faith that if God can create the universe and mankind, then he can ensure that a book is properly copied for a few thousand years. We assume that the the BHS and the UBS 3rd edition text and the Hodges and Farstad Majority text and the Wescott & Hort text are all good enough for our purposes of understanding the bible and decoding it. For if God can preserve a seed, a blood line, from Eve to Mary to Jesus, uncorrupted for over 4,000 years, then he can certainly preserve a book, uncorrupted from the time of Jesus until today, a period of under 2,000 years.

Bibles

The most accurate non-interlinear English translations that we have seen are the New World Translation, published by the Watchtower and J. P. Green's Literal Version (Downloadable from this site). Neither is perfect, but they are both very good efforts in all the circumstances. The former being the work of many men and the latter the work of more or less one man! To find out how to get your hands on a NWT see - Help. The most common bibles in use today are the King James Version or the New King James Version in the UK, and the Revised Standard Version or the New Revised Standard Version in the US. The King James is largely based on the Tyndale Bible, which was first printed in 1535 whilst the author, William Tyndale, was in prison for his effrontery. The very first English translation of the holy scriptures was completed by John Wycliffe in 1382. William Tyndale based much of his work on the translation of Wycliffe, and was killed by the state as a result of laws past at the insistence of the Church for his efforts. At Tyndale's death he cried:

Lord, open the King of England's eyes!

3 years later, he did, and the church commissioned his fellow workers to produce the first state sanctioned translation, the Geneva Bible. For a fuller account of this - see [History of the English Bible]. So the Church did to Tyndale through the English state, what the Sanhedrin, the Pharisees, the Jewish religious leaders, did to Jesus, through the Roman state of that time. And for the same reason - they wanted to play God themselves before their flocks.

The best way to stop religious leaders playing God is to fully inform the congregation directly of his purposes. It is to teach them to understand the bible for themselves without having to ask their priest for guidance. This is one of the purposes of this website, which we hope will be worthy of the great efforts and sacrifices made just to have the book in our language at all. There is quite obviously no point in reading a bible in a foreign tongue, and yet, even when it is read in one's mother tongue it is still written in a foreign language, a symbolic language, a coded symbolic language, the language of the true bible code. The reason that the KJV and the RSV are so popular is that the state religions such as the Church of England etc, have adopted these translations. But they are by no means the best translations available.

The ultimate solution to the problem of English translations is to get a Hebrew and a Greek Interlinear Bible. These give you the original language text, with a very literal word for word translation under each original Hebrew or Greek word, on the line below. Hence they are called Interlinear Bibles. We recommend a visit to amazon.com (unfortunately) and a title search for "Greek Interlinear" and "Hebrew Interlinear", they have a good range of Interlinear bibles and they claim to ship within 24 hours! The best ones in our opinion are:

The New International Version Hebrew English Old Testament   - Kohlenberger
The New Greek English Interlinear New Testament - Brown and Comfort

Others worth getting are:

The Kingdom Interlinear Translation of the Greek Scriptures, published by the Watchtower.
The NIV interlinear Greek English New Testament, by Marshall, published by Zondervan.
The Greek New Testament According to the majority text, Zane C. Hodges & Arthur L. Farstad, published by Nelson.

Having obtained these, if you wish to see even further then you will need a Hebrew and a Greek Bible Lexicon. These books give the precise grammatical make up of each Hebrew or Greek word in the bible, and all of their possible meanings. There are useful and not so useful Lexicons. In our opinion the best two are:

The Analytical Hebrew and Chaldee Lexicon - Ben Davidson
The Analytical Lexicon to the Greek New Testament - William Mounce

In this way you can get at the original meaning of the bible without becoming an ancient languages scholar.

We quote from a mixture of the NWT, the DV (below), Green's Literal Translation (GLT) and various interlinear bibles in this site/book.

The Decoders Version

The reader, it is hoped, will soon grasp that the bible is written in a symbolic code. This extra meaning necessitates a new translation. Hitherto, the less linguistically strict translations, such as the KJV and the RSV and the NIV (New International Version) have attempted to bring out the full literal meaning of the bible with a kind of explanatory translation style, which puts things in a modern idiom and in a context for a modern reader. This can and usually does destroy the symbolic meaning.

What is therefore needed is a translation which preserves both the literal meaning and the symbolic meaning.

Interlinear bibles more or less do this, but are not written in such a way that the reader would wish to commit important scriptures to memory. For example:

Let he who is without sin cast the first stone at her (John 8:7 KJV - ish)
The one sinless of you first upon her let him throw stone (John 8:7 Greek Interlinear - Kingdom Interlinear Bible)

Obviously the Interlinear format of John 8:7 is not something one can easily remember. Incidentally, if as some believe, these words were not spoken by Jesus, then Gordon for his part would like to know who did say them so that he can follow him.

So we need a code preserving translation, a code transparent translation, which is also comfortable for modern man to read. Such a translation will need the following features:

[1] It must preserve singulars and plurals in the original language as singulars and plurals in the translation

[2] It must use the same unique English word for every incidence of the same unique Greek word if possible

[3] It must translate prepositions conjunctions and articles uniquely and faithfully

[4] Any explanatory words, which do not appear in the original language must be marked as such

We are currently working on such a translation, the Decoders Version. In the DV, all numbers, whether cardinal (greater than one) or ordinal (greater than second) are represented numerically. So that the feeding of the five thousand, for example, is now the feeding of the 5,000. The thirty second year of Artxerxes is now the 32nd year of Artaxerxes. The bible, being possibly the only history book with almost no relevant dates in it (in the literal meaning), has these dates encoded in terms of numbers of shekels, sheep, camels etc. So these numbers are important and they are more easily recognised in numerical form.

It is also worth getting the electronic version of the NWT, because one can search for every incidence of the word: 'helper' for example, or of the phrase 'founding of the world' or of the word 'mystery'. Please do these searches in this translation! You will find out some very interesting things. For advice on how to get Watchtower publications without being ensnared by them - see [Help].

Downloadable and Online Bibles and Books

www.njcnews.org/bible/bible.html (King James Version)
www.theology.edu/software/rsv95.zip (Revised Standard Version).
www.ccel.org (Loads of early Christian Literature, Bible Dictionaries and reference material)

We have compiled a short list of recommended books in the [books] section of this site, from which you can also order this website as a book. We have also put up Josephus, Easton's Bible Dictionary, Green's Literal Translation etc on our [download] page from which you can download this entire site for offline browsing and printing out sections for closer examination.

[4] The Biblical Lunar Calendar (BLC)

This section is designed to be read in conjunction with www.truebiblecode.com.

The bible is a book which contains prophecy. It is a book of past events which symbolically represent future events. Prophecy is statements about events which are going to occur in the future. One cannot understand when in the future the events are going to occur until one knows how the bible expresses times and dates. So we need to know what sort of calendar the bible uses.

All the chronology in the bible, the dates, the days, months and years, are expressed in terms of the Biblical Lunar Calendar. This Calendar which was used in the day of Noah is the same calendar that was used by all ancient civilisations. It has 12 lunar months each of 30 days. The Egyptians used this type of calendar up to around the 8th Century BC, the Chinese used it up to around the 4th Century BC. When Rome was founded by Romulus, a 360 day calendar was being used - see Ancient Calendars. Sir Isaac Newton stated:

All nations, before the just length of the solar year was known, reckoned months by the course of the moon, and years by the return of winter and summer, spring and autumn; and in making calendars for their festivals, they reckoned thirty days to a lunar month, and twelve lunar months to a year, taking the nearest round numbers, whence came the division of the ecliptic into 360 degrees. (Anderson, Robert. *The Coming Prince*. London: Hodder & Stroughton, 1894.)

The truth about the biblical 360 day year as mentioned by Newton was quoted by Sir Robert Anderson in his book, *The Coming Prince*, page 68. This was not a new discovery by Sir Isaac Newton in the late 1600's or by Sir Robert Anderson in 1895. It was clearly discussed in detail by the Christian, Julias Africanus in his Chronology within his explanation of the fulfillment of Daniel's Seventy Weeks, written about A.D. 240. www.direct.ca/trinity/360day.html

The Biblical Lunar Calendar Timetable

Position in year	BLC name of month	Modern Calendar Equivalent
First	Nisan	March/April
Second	Iyyar	April/May
Third	Sivan	May/June
Fourth	Tammuz	June/July
Fifth	Ab	July/August
Sixth	Elul	August/September
Seventh	Tishri	September/October
Eighth	Heshvan	October/November
Ninth	Chislev	November/December
Tenth	Tebeth	December/January
Eleventh	Shebat	January/February
Twelfth	Adar	February/March

The first month of the year started in the spring after the Jewish exodus from Egypt in 1513 BC, and it started in the Autumn (in the months of Tishri) before the Exodus. Jews today still celebrate the new year on Tishri 1 (but this is according to the modern Hebrew Calendar which is slightly different from the Biblical Lunar Calendar). We have designed a Calendar Converter Program which converts the modern calendar (Gregorian) into the Biblical Lunar Calendar for dates from 2000 BC to 3000 AD. You can download it free - see **BLC calendar converter.**

Technical Calendar stuff

Lunar calendars start the year at a new moon, or a full moon, which is taken as the beginning of a lunar month. A true lunar month is around 29.5 days long, because the moon takes 29.5 days to orbit the earth (29 days, 12 hours 44 minutes and 3 secs according to current astronomy or 3 and a third seconds according to the current Hebrew Calendar). We currently use a Solar calendar which starts the new year after a complete orbit of the earth around the sun. Such an orbit takes almost precisely 365.25 days. This period is around 12.4 lunar months. The Greeks, the Babylonians and the ancient Hebrews all operated lunar calendars before Christ. In 46 AD, Julius Caesar issued a decree changing the Roman calendar from Lunar to Solar. The resulting Julian calendar, based on the calculations of Sosigenes, had 365 days in each year and a leap year every 4th year with 366 days. It had 12 months whose lengths exactly fitted the year. In 1582 AD this calendar had become ten days out, since the true solar year is a bit longer than 365.25 days, (making it not much better than a lunar calendar by then as regards seasons starting at the correct time). So Pope Gregory XIII abolished October 5th to October 14th, in that year, and he abolished leap years in century years, unless such years were divisible by 400. This Gregorian calendar is the one in use today.

We supply a free Calendar converter program, which converts Gregorian dates into Biblical Lunar Calendar dates (and vice versa) for the period from 1999BC until 2999AD. You can down load it from the web site.

The biblical lunar calendar had 12 months in each year. The bible writers adopted the Babylonian names of these months during and after the period when the Jews were deported from Israel to Babylon by Nebuchadnezzar II, the King of Babylon (reigned 604 - 562 BC). These months were:

Position	Post Babylonian Exilic Name	Pre Babylonian Exilic Name	Solar Calendar Equivalent
First	Nisan	Abib	March/April
Second	Iyyar	Ziv	April/May
Third	Sivan		May/June
Fourth	Tammuz		June/July
Fifth	Ab		July/August
Sixth	Elul		August/September
Seventh	Tishri	Ethanim	September/October
Eighth	Heshvan	Bul	October/November
Ninth	Chislev		November/December
Tenth	Tebeth		December/January
Eleventh	Shebat		January/February
Twelfth	Adar		February/March

Let there be an observing of the month of Abib, and you must celebrate the passover to Jehovah your God, because in the month of Abib

Jehovah your God brought you out of Egypt by night (Deuteronomy 16:1).

This month will be the start of the months for you. It will be the first of the months of the year for you....you may pick from the young rams or from the goats. And it must continue under guard until the 14th day of this month...and you must eat it in haste. It is Jehovah's passover (Exodus 12: 2-11).

The Passover is still celebrated by Jews today and is in late March/Early April, on Nisan14. It occasionally coincides with 'Good Friday' (well, statistically every 7 years). Of course it coincided in 33 CE, when Jesus was killed, since Jesus was killed on the Jewish Passover, he being the greater Passover lamb.

In the 1st month, that is, the month Nisan (Esther 3:7).
In the month of Ziv, that is, the 2nd month (1 Kings 6:1).
In the 3rd month, that is, the month of Sivan (Esther 8:9).
In the lunar month of Ethanim in the festival, that is, the 7th month (1 Kings 8:2).
In the lunar month of Bul, that is, the 8th month (1 Kings 6:38).
On the 4th [day] of the 9th month, in Chislev (Zechariah 7:1).
In the 10th month, that is, the month Tebeth (Esther 2:16).
On the 24th day of the 11th month, that is, the month Shebat (Zechariah 1:7).

In the 1st month, that is, the month Nisan, in the 12th year of King Ahasuerus, someone cast Pur, that is, the Lot, before Haman from day to day and from month to month, [to] the 12th, that is, the month Adar (Esther 3:7).

1 Kings was written before and Esther and Zechariah were written during or after the 70 year Babylonian exile of Judah (586 to 516 BC - see later).

And he proceeded to burn the house of the [true] God and pull down the wall of Jerusalem; and all its dwelling towers they burned with fire and also all its desirable articles, so as to cause ruin. Furthermore, he carried off those remaining from the sword captive to Babylon, and they came to be servants to him and his sons until the royalty of Persia began to reign, to fulfill Jehovah's word by the mouth of Jeremiah, until the land had paid off its sabbaths. All the days of lying desolated it kept sabbath, to fulfill seventy years (2 Chronicles 36:19-21).

The remainder of the names of the months can be deduced from Josephus (the Jewish historian) or the Talmud or current Jewish calendars. The post Babylonian exilic names were the month names used in Babylon.

In the 600th year of Noah's life, in the second month, on the 17th day of the month, on this day, all the springs of the vast watery deep were broken open and the flood gates of the heavens were opened (Genesis 7:11).

And the waters began receding from off the earth, going and receding, and at the end of 150 days the waters were lacking. And in the seventh month, on the 17th day of the month, the ark came to rest on the mountains of Ararat (Genesis 8:3,4).

When the waters are lacking the Ark would run aground, so from this we deduce that 5 months was 150 days, so there were 30 days in each Biblical Lunar Calendar (BLC) month. If all the months were the same length.

**You will eat, not one day nor two days nor five days nor ten days nor twenty days,
but up to a month of days,** until it comes out of your nostrils and it has become a loathing to you, just because you rejected Jehovah, who is in your midst, and you went weeping before him, saying: Why is it that we have come out of Egypt? (Numbers 11:19,20).

So he dwelt with him a month of days (Genesis 29:14).

And he continued to reign for a lunar month of days (2 Kings 15:13).

So a month of days was a specific number of them. So all months had the same length (30 days). The BLC therefore has 12 months each of which is 30 days long. So it spans 360 days. But there are 365.25 days in the Solar year. Furthermore 12 lunar cycles only take 354 days since each cycle is 29.5 days long. So we have a problem at the end of each year where the thirteenth lunar cycle is starting around 11 days (365 - 354) early with respect to the Solar calendar. The way the Hebrews dealt with this, was that sometimes the next year did indeed start with the next lunar month, and other times it skipped a month, or rather the previous year had another month added. This month was called Veadar, or 'second Adar'. The 14th month then became the first of the new year. The Modern Jewish calendar adds a 13th month every 3rd, 6th, 8th, 11th, 14th, 17th & 19th years in a 19 year cycle. The first new moon and the first full moon of the 19th lunar year occur on the same solar day that they did in the first lunar year. This is not how the ancient Hebrews did it however. They added an extra month only when the 14th day of that month was not in spring, in the sense that it did not start after the day of the vernal equinox.

The bible defines the 12 months of the year as follows:

As for the sons of Israel by their number, the heads of the paternal houses and the chiefs of the thousands and of the hundreds and their officers that were ministering to the king in every matter of the divisions of those that came in and that went out month by month <u>for all the months of the year</u>, each division was 24,000.
Over the first division of the first month there was Jashobeam the son of Zabdiel, and in his division there were 24,000.
Some of the sons of Perez the head of all the chiefs of the service groups were for the first month.
And over the division of the second month there was Dodai the Ahohite with his division, and Mikloth was the leader, and in his division there were 24,000.
The chief of the 3rd service group for the third month was Benaiah the son of Jehoiada the chief priest, and in his division there were 24,000. This Benaiah was a mighty man of the 30 and over the 30; and [over] his division there was Ammizabad his son.
The 4th for the 4th month was Asahel, Joab's brother, and Zebadiah his son after him, and in his division there were 24,000.
The 5th chief for the 5th month was Shamhuth the Izrahite, and in his division there were 24,000.
The 6th for the 6th month was Ira the son of Ikkesh the Tekoite, and in his division there were 24,000.
The 7th for the 7th month was Helez the Pelonite of the sons of Ephraim, and in his division there were 24,000.
The 8th for the 8th month was Sibbecai the Hushathite of the Zerahites, and in his division there were 24,000.
The 9th for the 9th month was Abi-ezer the Anathothite of the Benjaminites, and in his division there were 24,000.
The 10th for the 10th month was Maharai the Netophathite of the Zerahites, and in his division there were 24,000.
The 11th for the 11th month was Benaiah the Pirathonite of the sons of Ephraim, and in his division there were 24,000.
The 12th for the 12th month was Heldai the Netophathite, of Othniel, **and in his division there were 24,000** (1 Chronicles 27:1-12).

There was no ministering recorded for any 13th month. So presumably there was actually no ministering in the 13th month (Veadar). In non (lunar) leap years (years with no 13th month or intercalary month) the last 5/6 days of Adar are coincident with the first 5/6 days of Nisan (because 12 lunar cycles are 354.36707 days, and 12 BLC months are 360 days). Adar25/26, the $355/6^{th}$ day of the year, is Nisan1 in the next year, and Adar30 is Nisan5/6 in the new year. Likewise in the case of Solomon's food:

And Solomon had twelve deputies over all Israel, and they provided the king and his household with food. It would devolve upon each one to provide the food one month in the year (1 Kings 4:7)

As for the courtyard that is outside the temple. Cast it clear out and do not measure it, because it has been given to the nations, and they will trample the holy city underfoot for 42 months. And I will cause my two witnesses to prophesy a thousand two hundred and sixty days dressed in sackcloth (Revelation 11:2,3)

This period of 42 months is 42 months all of which are one of the 12 months above. In other words if it started in Nisan then it ended in Tishri, 3 years and 6 months later. There is no 13th month mentioned anywhere in the bible explicitly. In fact there would have been 43 lunar months in the period of 42 BLC months. Likewise, if the period of 1260 days started on Nisan18 it would end on Tishri18 three years later. In fact there may well have been 1240 or 1280 true days between these two BLC dates, separated by 1260 BLC days, each one of which is in a 30 day BLC month.

To apply bible prophecy to dates today we need to know when each first month of the lunar year starts. We need to know Nisan1 for each year. The modern Jews calculate it so that Nisan14 is on or after March 26th. This is because they start the year on Tishri 1 and are effectively choosing this month with reference to the Autumn equinox. The early Christian Churches calculated it so that the Passover, Nisan14, is on or after March 21st, the date they chose for the Vernal Equinox, when day and night are precisely the same length, see: www.ozramp.net.au/~sanhub/godstime.htm

Comments from Anatolius, Bishop of Laodicea, [c.230-c.280] are confirmatory of what has already become very evident. Nor is this an opinion confined to ourselves alone. For it was also known to the Jews of old and before Christ, and it was most carefully observed by them. And this may be learned from what Philo, and Josephus, and Musaeus have written; and not only from these, but indeed from others still more ancient, namely, the two Agathobuli, who were surnamed the Masters, and the eminent Aristobulus, who was one of the Seventy who translated the sacred and holy Scriptures [i.e., the Septuagint] of the Hebrews for Ptolemy Philadelphus [285-246 B.C.] and his father, and dedicated his exegetical works on the law of Moses to the same kings. These writers, in solving some questions which are raised with respect to the Exodus, say that all alike ought to sacrifice the Passover after the vernal equinox in the middle of the first month" (Ante-Nicene Fathers, (Eerdmans, 1986), Vol 6, The Paschal Canon of Anatolius of Alexandria, III, p. 147).

Norm Womersley and Orest Solyma have produced the clearest explanation we have seen (from Appendix B of the web page above - altered)

The 1st day of the lunar month is a new moon, therefore the full moon occurs on the 14th-15th of the month. A lunar month is 29 days 12 hours 44+ minutes long.

The first month, Abib or Nisan (in the northern hemisphere; Jerusalem as the focus Psalm 122; 135:19-21; Zechariah 14:1-4; Revelation 21:2-3), is the beginning of the sacred year when the days start to get longer. Some barley is ready for harvesting (Leviticus 23:10; Ruth 1:22; 2:23; 2Samuel 21:9), but reaping may continue as late as August in higher altitudes. Wheat and rye are still immature in spring (Exodus 9:31,32). This season must coincide with the Vernal Equinox, which causes seasonal change and crop development not vice versa. The 20th-21st March is the turn from winter to summer of a solar year (Genesis 1:14). Biblically, it is the start of the summer season (Genesis 8:22; Psalm 74:17).

Passover is an 8 day feast, including Unleavened Bread, a day, or a meal (Matthew 26:17; Ezekiel 45:21; Numbers 9:6; Luke 22:15). Included is the Lord's Supper on the 14th Nisan, the Night to be Much Observed on the 15th Nisan, (i.e., 14th-15th at the time of a full moon), followed by the Wave-Sheaf Offering (God's acceptance of the resurrected Christ), both set during the Days of Unleavened Bread, and with the seventh day of Unleavened Bread being 21st Nisan. The full moon of Passover must be the first full moon and after the new moon nearest to the Vernal Equinox, i.e., nearest to March 20th-21st.

This calculation wherein the Passover is the first 14th day of a lunar month to fall on or after the day of the vernal equinox is the way that God stipulated things should be done after the Exodus:

And Jehovah now said to Moses and Aaron in the land of Egypt: This month will be the start of the months for you. It will be the first of the months of the year ....you may pick from the young rams or from the goats. And it must continue under guard until the 14th day of this month...and you must eat it in haste. It is Jehovah's Passover (Exodus 12: 2-11).

And it will certainly occur that from new moon to new moon and from sabbath to sabbath all flesh will come in to bow down before me, Jehovah has said (Isaiah 66:23).

God was stipulating that Nisan, the Passover month, the month in which the Jews left Egypt, was to be the anchor month for the lunar calendar (whereas before this it was Tishri). This month is synchronised to the Solar calendar, to the seasons, through the spring equinox which defines the beginning of the spring and harvesting half of the year. Basically the Passover is the first 14th day of a lunar month where this day is actually in spring (which starts after the Hebrew day of the vernal equinox).

Before the exodus from Egypt Josephus tells us that the first month of the year was Tishri:

The catastrophe happened in the 600th year of Noah's rulership, in what was once the second month, called by the Macedonians Dius, and by the Hebrews Marsuan (Marheshvan or Heshvan), according to the arrangement of the calendar which they followed in Egypt. Moses, however appointed Nisan, that is to say Xanthicus, as the first month for the festivals, because it was in this month that he brought the Hebrews out of Egypt. He also reckoned this month as the commencement of the year for everything relating to divine worship. But for selling and buying and other ordinary affairs he preserved the ancient order (Jewish Antiquities Book I).

In the six hundredth year of Noah's life, in the second month, on the seventeenth day of the month, on this day all the springs of the vast watery deep were broken open and the floodgates of the heavens were opened (Genesis 7:11).

The bible shows that the agricultural year, which was the fiscal year in what was an agricultural economy, started in the seventh month, Tishri:

And you will carry on your festival of weeks with the first ripe fruits of the wheat harvest, and the festival of ingathering, at the turn of the year (Exodus 34:22).

Also the festival of the harvest of the first ripe fruits of your labours, of what you sow in the field, and the festival of ingathering at the outgoing of the year, when you gather your labour from the field (Exodus 23:16).

The festival of booths you should celebrate for yourself seven days when you make an ingathering from your threshing floor and your oil and winepress (Deuteronomy 16:13).

So the turn and outgoing, meaning beginning, of the agricultural year was the seventh month. The ingathering of all the crops is obviously a good end to an agricultural year. The modern Jews celebrate their new year on Tishri1. This day was the start of the agricultural or secular year. Since the bible does not introduce this new year as a new concept, one can deduce that this was the one being used before the change to Nisan for the sacred new year as mentioned above (Exodus 12:2-11).

To calculate which day Nisan14 is we need to know when the new and full moons are around March 21st for the last 6,000 years. There is a great website for this at: http//sunearth.gsfc.nasa.gov/eclipse/phase/phasecat.html written by Fred Espenak of Nasa. He uses Gregorian dates on and after

1582 October 15th, which was the first day after the ten days from October 5
to October 14 inclusive, that the Pope abolished. He uses Julian dates
before October 5th that year, as mankind did.

```
Moon Phase Table (accurate to 1 minute)
Year        New Moon        First Quarter      Full Moon         Last Quarter

1991
         Feb 14  17:32     Feb 21  22:58     Feb 28  18:24     Mar  8  10:34
         Mar 16  08:12     Mar 23  06:03     Mar 30  07:17     Apr  7  06:47
1992
         Mar  4  13:23     Mar 12  02:35     Mar 18  18:17     Mar 26  02:30
         Apr  3  05:02     Apr 10  10:05     Apr 17  04:42     Apr 24  21:40
1993
         Feb 21  13:05     Mar  1  15:46     Mar  8  09:46     Mar 15  04:17
         Mar 23  07:15     Mar 31  04:09     Apr  6  18:43     Apr 13  19:38
1994
         Feb 10  14:31     Feb 18  17:48     Feb 26  01:16     Mar  4  16:54
         Mar 12  07:06     Mar 20  12:15     Mar 27  11:10     Apr  3  02:55
1995
         Mar  1  11:49     Mar  9  10:12     Mar 17  01:26     Mar 23  20:10
         Mar 31  02:10     Apr  8  05:34     Apr 15  12:09 p   Apr 22  03:18
1996
         Feb 18  23:31     Feb 26  05:51     Mar  5  09:23     Mar 12  17:15
         Mar 19  10:46     Mar 27  01:30     Apr  4  00:08     Apr 10  23:35
1997
         Feb  7  15:06     Feb 14  08:57     Feb 22  10:26     Mar  2  09:37
         Mar  9  01:15     Mar 16  00:06     Mar 24  04:45     Mar 31  19:37
1998
         Feb 26  17:26     Mar  5  08:41     Mar 13  04:34     Mar 21  07:39
         Mar 28  03:14     Apr  3  20:19     Apr 11  22:23     Apr 19  19:53
1999
         Feb 16  06:40     Feb 23  02:44     Mar  2  06:59     Mar 10  08:43
         Mar 17  18:49     Mar 24  10:18     Mar 31  22:49     Apr  9  02:53
2000
         Mar  6  05:18     Mar 13  06:59     Mar 20  04:44     Mar 28  00:23
         Apr  4  18:13     Apr 11  13:30     Apr 18  17:41     Apr 26  19:32
2001
         Feb 23  08:22     Mar  3  02:03     Mar  9  17:23     Mar 16  20:47
         Mar 25  01:23     Apr  1  10:49     Apr  8  03:22     Apr 15  15:32
2002
         Feb 12  07:42     Feb 20  12:03     Feb 27  09:17     Mar  6  01:26
         Mar 14  02:04     Mar 22  02:29     Mar 28  18:25     Apr  4  15:30
2003
         Mar  3  02:36     Mar 11  07:15     Mar 18  10:35     Mar 25  01:52
         Apr  1  19:19     Apr  9  23:40     Apr 16  19:36     Apr 23  12:19
2004
         Feb 20  09:20     Feb 28  03:24     Mar  6  23:16     Mar 13  21:02
         Mar 20  22:43     Mar 28  23:48     Apr  5  11:04     Apr 12  03:47
2005
         Feb  8  22:29     Feb 16  00:15     Feb 24  04:54     Mar  3  17:37
         Mar 10  09:12     Mar 17  19:18     Mar 25  21:00     Apr  2  00:51
2006
         Feb 28  00:32     Mar  6  20:15     Mar 14  23:35     Mar 22  19:10
         Mar 29  10:16     Apr  5  12:01     Apr 13  16:41     Apr 21  03:28
2007
         Feb 17  16:14     Feb 24  07:56     Mar  3  23:16     Mar 12  03:55
         Mar 19  02:43     Mar 25  18:16     Apr  2  17:15     Apr 10  18:04
2008
         Mar  7  17:14     Mar 14  10:45     Mar 21  18:39     Mar 29  21:48
         Apr  6  03:55     Apr 12  18:31     Apr 20  10:24     Apr 28  14:13
```

The times above are GMT. The Hebrew day is taken as starting at 6pm in Jerusalem. But Jerusalem is 2 hours ahead of GMT. So the Hebrew day starts at 4pm GMT. So in the case of 2008, the Hebrew day which starts at 4pm on March 7th has the new moon. But this does not make it the first day of the new lunar month. Because new moons are only visible at night and are not generally visible to the naked eye until around 18 to 48 hours after they occur.

So we need to know how long after a new moon occurs one has to wait in Jerusalem before one can actually see it. The record for a human first seeing a new moon is 15.5 hours after it occurred, but visibility depends upon a lot of factors. However in the middle east, Jerusalem, at a mid northern latitude (31:47 North), and a reasonable altitude (820 metres above sea level or 2700 feet), at the time near the vernal equinox, is well placed in this regard see: http://aa.usno.navy.mil/AA/faq/docs/islamic.html

Obviously, the visibility of the young lunar crescent depends on sky conditions and the location, experience, and preparation of the observer. Generally, low latitude and high altitude observers who know exactly where and when to look will be favored. For observers at mid-northern latitudes, months near the spring equinox are also favored, because the ecliptic makes a relatively steep angle to the western horizon at sunset during these months (tending to make the Moon's altitude greater).

Mind you the first passover was in Egypt ! The new moon's visibility in Jerusalem largely depends on the rotational position of the earth. Normally at some place on the earth the new moon will be visible around 18 to 24 hours after it occurs. But it can obviously take the globe up to 24 hours to rotate until Jerusalem reaches this position. This combines with other factors to mean that the period between occurrence and visibility in the once holy city can be anything from 18 to 48 hours. It is possible to calculate when the moon will first become visible in Jerusalem: Mooncalc 5.2 by Dr. Monzur Ahmed ('Monz') seems to do this fairly well and is very easy to use. It is advertised on the South African Astronomical Observatory site at: http://www.saao.ac.za/sky/vishome.html and you can download it from: http://www.starlight.demon.co.uk/mooncalc . Of course the best way to find this out is to go there with your binoculars on the day of the new moon itself. I am sure that someone is doing this already.

The spring equinox does not occur on March 20/21 every year in the Julian calendar, which mankind used before 1582, because it does not track the solar year properly. So one needs to convert the Julian date to the Gregorian date to find out when the vernal equinox is. This can be done with the Calendar Converter at: www.mollis-ltd.demon.co.uk/CalendarApplet.htm .

But the vernal equinox is not always on March 21st even in the Gregorian calendar. It occurs when the apparent longitude of the Sun is zero degrees. This can occur as early as March 19th or as late as March 21st. Furthermore the day when day and night are observed to have the same length is dependent on the latitude of the observer, occurring typically two or three days early i.e. around March 17th for an observer at 40° North latitude, see: http://aa.usno.navy.mil/AA/faq/docs/equinoxes.html (London is 52° North and Jerusalem is 32° North). So visibility is not a good guide to when spring occurs. But since the Passover involves harvested fruit and a spring lamb, it must occur on a true spring day independent of observation.

The first true day of spring is the first full day after the vernal equinox. There are astronomical tables of vernal equinoxes for the various years that we can look up, for example see: http://www.geocities.com/Athens/3116/eqindex.html . The vernal equinoxes from 1991 to 2008 fall as follows:

Year	Day	Hour
1991	21	03:02
1992	20	08:48
1993	20	14:41
1994	20	20:28
1995	21	02:15
1996	20	08:03
1997	20	13:55
1998	20	19:55
1999	21	01:46
2000	20	07:35
2001	20	13:31
2002	20	19:16
2003	21	01:00
2004	20	06:49
2005	20	12:33
2006	20	18:26
2007	21	00:07
2008	20	05:48

So we can now make an exact definition of the date of the first day of the Hebrew year as follows:

Definition: The first day of Nisan, the first lunar month of the year, is the first Hebrew day in that year which is not more than 12 days before the day of the vernal equinox on which a new moon occurs visibly in Jerusalem.

Definition: The vernal equinox occurs when the apparent longitude of the Sun is zero degrees

Definition: A new moon is deemed to become visible 30 hours after it occurs, and is only visible in Jerusalem between 6pm and 6am local time, unless true observation data or accurate calculated data is available.

This means that the Passover, Nisan14, is always in spring, i.e. the day starts after the vernal equinox. Putting all of this together we can now work out the dates of the Passover from 1991 to 2008 as follows. The Passovers in 2000 and in 2008 are particularly interesting (JT is Jerusalem Time, Visibility in Jerusalem is from Mooncalc 5.2). Our Gregorian/BLC Calendar converter program [download] uses the above definition. It takes the Vernal Equinox as occurring on the Hebrew day starting at 6pm JT on March 20th for dates before 1991 and the true vernal equinox dates for 1991 to 2008. It uses mooncalc 5.2 for more accurate data for the visibility of the new moon in Jerusalem for passovers from 1884 to 2008 only. But in general we have found it to be accurate to the day or one day out at most back to 2000 BC - see [100].

Year	New moon GMT	Delay to 1st visible night mooncalc 5.2	Visible in Jerusalem after 6pm on	Nisan1 starts at 6pm JT on	Vernal Equinox Day & GMT	Vernal Equinox Day & JT	Nisan14 starts at 6pm JT on
1991	March 16 08:12	32 hours	March 17	March 17	March 21 03:02	March 21 05:02	March 30
1992	April 3 05:02	35 hours	April 4	April 4	March 20 08:48	March 20 10:48	April 17
1993	March 23 07:15	32 hours	March 24	March 24	March 20 14:41	March 20 16:41	April 6
1994	March 12 07:06	32 hours	March13	March 13	March 20 20:28	March 20 22:28	March 26
1995	March 31 02:10	38 hours	April 1	April 1	March 21 02:15	March 21 04:15	April 14
1996	March 19 10:46	29 hours	March 20	March 20	March 20 08:03	March 20 10:03	April 2
1997	March 9 01:15	38 hours	March 10	March 10	March 20 13:55	March 20 15:55	March 23

1998	March 28 03:14	36 hours	March 29	March 29	March 20 19:55	March 20 21:55	April 11
1999	March 17 18:49	21 hours	March 18	March 18	March 21 01:46	March 21 03:46	March 31
2000	March 6 05:18	34 hours	March 7	March 7	March 20 07:35	March 20 09:35	March 20
2001	March 25 01:23	38 hours	March 26	March 26	March 20 13:31	March 20 15:31	April 8
2002	March 14 02:04	37 hours	March 15	March 15	March 20 19:16	March 20 21:16	March 28
2003	April 1 19:19	45 hours	April 3	April 3	March 21 01:00	March 21 03:00	April 16
2004	March 20 22:43	41 hours	March 22	March 22	March 20 06:49	March 20 08:49	April 4
2005	March 10 09:12	30 hours	March 11	March 11	March 20 12:33	March 20 14:33	March 24
2006	March 29 10:16	29 hours	March 30	March 30	March 20 18:26	March 20 20:26	April 12
2007	March 19 02:43	37 hours	March 20	March 20	March 21 00:07	March 21 02:07	April 2
2008	March 7 17:14	22 hours	March 8	March 8	March 20 05:48	March 20 07:48	March 21

In 2000, the Passover day starts on March 20th. This would be impossible if we simply assumed like the churches do, that the vernal equinox was on March 21st. Nearly all the Christian churches, the Jews and the Jehovah's Witnesses celebrated the Passover on the wrong day in 2000 (if the above is correct). If you are a new covenant saint, an anointed remnant, you were warned to please celebrate this on the evening of March 20th in the proper way see - 1994Nisan3 [E]. A good way to test our Passover definition is to apply it to the Passover of 33Nisan14, since we know that this was on the day before the sabbath:

After the Sabbath, when it was growing light, on the first day of the week, Mary Magdalene and the other Mary came to view the grave (Matthew 28:1)

Then the Jews, since it was the preparation, in order that the bodies might not remain upon the torture stakes on the Sabbath, (for the day of that Sabbath was a great one), requested Pilate to have their legs broken and them taken away (John 19:31).

A great sabbath was a sabbath in a festival that was also the weekly sabbath, it was a double sabbath. So Jesus died on Friday afternoon. Since the Jews celebrate the Sabbath on Friday 6pm to Saturday 6pm, and this one thing they have right. So 33Nisan14 started on Thursday. The vernal equinox can be obtained from:

http://riemann.usno.navy.mil./AA/data/docs/SpringPhenom.html . The situation was as follows:

JULIAN CALENDAR

Year	New moon GMT	New moon Jerusalem time JT : GMT + 2	Time delay available until 6am March 21	Nisan1 starts at 6pm JT on	Vernal Equinox Day & GMT	Vernal Equinox Day & JT	Nisan14 starts at 6pm JT on
33	March 19 10:36	March 19 12:36	41:24 hours	March 20	March 22 03:00	March 22 05:00	April 2 (Thursday)

Year	New Moon	First Quarter	Full Moon	Last Quarter	Delta T (some error measure)
33	March 19 10:36	March 26 10:28	April 3 14:47	April 11 03:41	02h37m

GREGORIAN CALENDAR

Year	New moon GMT	New moon Jerusalem time JT : GMT + 2	Time delay available until 6am March 19	Nisan1 starts at 6pm JT on	Vernal Equinox Day & GMT	Vernal Equinox Day & JT	Nisan14 starts at 6pm JT on
33	March 17 10:36	March 17 12:36	41:24 hours	March 18	March 20 03:00	March 20 05:00	March 31 (Thursday)

So Jesus made the new covenant with his disciples at the last supper on the Thursday night and he was impaled on the Friday, and died at about the ninth hour, which is 3pm Friday April 1 Gregorian.

And about the ninth hour Jesus called out with a loud voice saying: Eli, Eli lama sabachthani? That is: My God, my God, why have you forsaken me? (Matthew 27:46).

He said it twice brothers and sisters see - The Repetition Principle of the code. Even in his agony he was a prophet.

To check that 33April3 Julian, was 33April1 Gregorian, which was Friday, visit: http://riemann.usno.navy.mil./AA/data/docs/SpringPhenom.html and www.mollis-ltd.demon.co.uk/CalendarApplet.htm Isn't the internet amazing!!

It is quite a complicated puzzle. But it is worth doing because Jesus commanded his brothers to celebrate the first new covenant and to:

keep doing this in remembrance of me (Luke 22:19).

One cannot commemorate the Last Supper any old day of the year. In fact, there is no religious festival instigated by God in the bible that did not have an appropriate day for it which God himself chose. One should commemorate the Last Supper, and take holy communion, therefore, on the day that God chose for Jesus to celebrate it on. If instead you celebrate it when it is convenient to you then you have become Cain, offering not what God has determined is suitable for you but what you have determined is suitable for God. The day God choose for the last supper was the Passover, which occurred once a year under the law of Moses. For the Last Supper is the greater Passover, and Jesus is the greatest Passover lamb.

For indeed Christ, our Passover, has been sacrificed (1 Corinthians 5:7).

For Jesus was the lamb of God (according to John the baptist), the Passover lamb of God. But now a second new covenant has been made between God and the writer see - The New Earthly Covenant, the messenger of this new covenant, through Jesus and through Abraham. Because you do not need *two* emblems, wine and bread, to symbolise *one* covenant. This covenant is for a further passover, the passover of Armageddon, wherein a great crowd of some half a billion people, the firstborn human sons of the Kingdom of God, are saved along with some others see - The Kingdom of God and the Great Crowd. It was made on a date determined by the BLC in 2000. And finally we have realised that a greater Passover means a second calendar change. The New Biblical Lunar Calendar (which began on 1992Elul1) is the same as the BLC except that the year starts in Elul, the last month of Armageddon, the month when the greatest passover ends.

[5] How Ages & Reigns are Counted

This section is designed to be read in conjunction with www.truebiblecode.com.

Before the Jews left Egypt (in 1513 BC - see [101]) the Hebrew calendar year used to start in the month of Tishri (August/September) see - BLC. After they left Egypt as recounted in the book of Exodus, the Hebrew calendar year was changed by a command from God. (Being God he can do this sort of thing):

Jehovah now said to Moses and Aaron in the land of Egypt:
This month will be the start of the months for you. It will be the first of the months of the year for you.
Speak to the entire assembly of Israel, saying, 'On the 10th day of this month they are to take for themselves each one a sheep... And it must continue under safeguard by you until the 14th day of this month, and

the whole congregation of the assembly of Israel must slaughter it between the two evenings (Exodus 12:1-6).

This was the first Passover festival which occurs on Nisan14. The new calendar year started in the month of Nisan (March/April - Spring) for Sacred things (Religious festivals etc) and Tishri (August/September - Autumn) for farming or economic or secular things or fiscal things in what was an agricultural economy. In particular Land Sabbath years, which occurred every 7th year and were a fallow period for the whole nation for that whole year, were still taken as running from Tishri to Tishri. So it is not immediately apparent whether ages and reigns should be calculated in years starting in Nisan or Tishri. Here are the scriptures which provide the answer:

And it came about in the four hundred and eightieth year after the sons of Israel came out from the land of Egypt, in the fourth year, in the month of Ziv, that is, the second month, after Solomon became king over Israel, that he proceeded to build the house to Jehovah (1 Kings 6:1).
Ziv, was Iyyar (April/May), the month after Nisan.

Accordingly he started to build in the second month on the second [day], in the fourth year of his reign (2 Chronicles 3:2).
This scripture also refers to Solomon's temple. So the second month of the fourth year of Solomon's reign was Iyyar. So the first month was Nisan, the preceding month, see - BLC, so reigns are measured from Nisan. When Hezekiah became king, he cleansed the temple from Nisan1 to Nisan16, and so was unable to hold the passover on Nisan14, since the temple was not clean at that time. So he held it on Iyyar14, 30 days later. We read:

Hezekiah himself became king at the age of 25 years, and for 29 years he reigned in Jerusalem. And his mother's name was Abijah the daughter of Zechariah.
And he kept doing what was right in Jehovah's eyes, according to all that David his forefather had done.
He himself, in the first year of his reigning, in the first month, opened the doors of the house of Jehovah and began to repair them (2 Chronicles 29:1-3).

Thus they got started on the first [day] of the first month at sanctifying, and on the 8th day of the month they came to the porch of Jehovah; so that they sanctified the house of Jehovah in 8 days, and on the 16th day of the first month they finished (2 Chronicles 29:17).

However, the king and his princes and all the congregation in Jerusalem resolved to hold the passover in the second month; for they had not been able to hold it at that time, because not enough priests,

on the one hand, had sanctified themselves and the people, on the other hand, had not gathered themselves to Jerusalem (2 Chronicles 30:2,3).

So the first month of his reigning, i.e. the first month of his first regnal year, was Nisan. King Ahasuerus of Persia, whilst he was also king of Babylon, measured his reign from Nisan as well:

In the first month, that is, the month Nisan, in the twelfth year of King Ahasuerus, someone cast Pur, that is, the Lot (Esther 3:7).

It is apparent from the above that the first month is always Nisan in the context of reigns of kings of Israel and elsewhere.In fact the decree that Nisan should be the first month (Exodus 12:2) would logically apply to everything unless otherwise stated. And only in the case of Land Sabbaths is there a statement that Tishri should be the first month of the year. So we take ages and reigns as counting from Nisan to Nisan.

The bible counts years in the form: **The ninth year of Hoshea the King** (2 Kings 18:10). We count them currently as the 1999th year after the birth of Christ (although he was actually born on Tishri 10th 2BC (see [41]). The biblical count has several problems. Suppose for example that on Nisan1 in a certain year there is no king, because he died in the previous month and everybody is fighting over who will succeed him. Then we have no way of referring to what year we are in! Or suppose King [a] died on Nisan1 and his successor King [b] was enthroned on Nisan 2. Then that year would be the last regnal year of King [a] for the whole year, because once the year is named, a thing which occurred on Nisan1, it could not be renamed. For king [b], this year is called the accession year, and the next year is called his first regnal year. Actually the cut off point might have been the passover, Nisan14, rather than Nisan1. Hence we see:

In the third year of the kingship of Jehoiakim the king of Judah, Nebuchadnezzar the king of Babylon came to Jerusalem and proceeded to lay siege to it (Daniel 1:1).

The word that occurred to Jeremiah concerning all the people of Judah in the fourth year of Jehoiakim the son of Josiah, the king of Judah, that is, the first year of Nebuchadrezzar the king of Babylon (Jeremiah 25:1).

Incidentally Nebuchadnezzar and Nebuchadrezzar were the same chap, known as Nebuchadnezzar II (604 - 564 BC). He appears to be a king in the 3rd year of Jehoiakim, before his first regnal year, which was the 4th year of Jehoiakim. This could have been because the third year of Jehoiakim which was 605 BC (Nisan to Nisan) was his accession year, the year in which he became king, but his predecessor, Nabopolassar, his dad, was still reigning at the beginning of the year and so he got the regnal year rather than his son. Or it could have been because he was inferior coregent with his dad Nabopolassar in the last few years of his father's reign. This means that although Nebuchadnezzar was king along with his father, the regnal years were all counted only to his father.

Likewise with ages, if you were born in Tishri 39 BC you became one year old in Nisan 38 BC, and the year 38 BC was your first year. This is totally counter intuitive to the modern way of counting, in which as we know, you would be anything from 6 months to 18 months old during 38 BC and you would only be in your first year until Tishri 38BC. The concept of being one year old all the way through your first year is ludicrous in our counting system. However Noah managed this feat:

In the 600th year of Noah's life, in the second month, on the 17th day of the month, on this day, all the springs of the vast watery deep were broken open and the flood gates of the heavens were opened (Genesis 7:11).

And Noah was six hundred years old when the deluge of waters occurred on the earth (Genesis 7:6).

And Noah son of 600 year and the flood he was waters upon the earth (Genesis 7:6 NIVHEOT New International Version Hebrew English Old Testament).

In year of 600 year to life of Noah, in the month the second, in 17th day to the month in the day the that, they burst all of springs of great deep and floodgates of the heavens, they were opened (Genesis 7:11 NIVHEOT).

So Noah was 600 years old in the 600th year of his life!

Basically the Hebrew baby became one year old on the first Nisan1 of his life, and remained one year old until the second Nisan1 of his life whereupon he became two years old. Although in Noah's day (born in 2971 BC, died in 2021 BC), since years counted from Tishri (August/September) to Tishri, before the Exodus from Egypt (in 1513 BC - see [101]), one became one year old on the first Tishri1 of one's life, and remained such until the second Tishri1 of one's life.

[5a] There is a God

'Newton showed his Orrery to Halley the atheist, who was charmed with the contrivance, and asked the name of the maker: Nobody, was the ad hominem retort'

The implication being that if Halley could believe that no one had made the Solar System, then why would he find it hard to believe that no one had made the Orrery, which was a poor model of the Solar System, vastly inferior in design?

Putting this another way: If Halley the atheist, knew for a fact that someone had made the Orrery, the naive model of the universe in Isaac Newton's room, then why did he not know that someone had made the Solar System itself, something which was a lot more complicated and involved a lot more design work than the model?

The answer of course is that Halley would have known that someone had made the Solar System if his heart had allowed his brain to think as freely in the case of the reality as it obviously did in the case of the model.

But Halley's heart was not without fear of the implications and the ramifications that the existence of a God might have on him personally. For atheists do not allow themselves to think freely because they fear the consequences. And actually the same is true of many believers, who make themselves idolaters of their chosen belief system out of fear of the implications of what may be the truth. Mankind just throws his reason away when it comes to God and the bible. This book/website will hopefully show the reader what happens if one retains at least some of ones power of reason in these matters. Newton for his part very rarely threw away his reason. Perhaps he read and understood this verse of the bible:

30 You must love the Lord your God with your whole heart and with your whole soul and with your whole mind and with your whole strength (Mark 12:30).

And perhaps now the reader can truly understand the meaning of the famous words of Jesus Christ:

8 Blessed are the pure in heart for they shall see God (Matthew 5:8).

The existence of order in the universe implies the existence of an orderer. Random chance cannot create sustained order. An orderer is an intelligence with power. We know that mankind did not create the ordered universe. So we can deduce that there is a powerful non human intelligence that created it. This is a matter of logic. So we know that there is a creator. In fact the second law of thermodynamics which basically states that whatever you do you create more chaos, or that chaos always increases, proves that there was an orderer to start with. Which means there was a creator, a God, this orderer. The big bang was perfect order in some sense, it must have been a seed with all of the information neccessary for the entire universe, the most ordered creation ever.

Descartes said: I think therefore I am

The intelligent man says: I think therefore I was created by an intelligence

How many computers, devices with some limited intelligence, did random chance ever create?

Evolution vs. creation

This debate is covered more fully in section [221].

The first thing to say is that evolution is not a fact. It is rather a theory, which was first postulated by Charles Darwin. He observed little birds, Finches, which 14 different types of beak on the Galapagos Islands. He then returned home in his ship called the Beagle and thought nothing much of it. However once he was back in Cambridge he spoke to John Gould, an ornithologist, a bird expert, who told him that these 14 differing beaked birds were in fact in 14 different species (breeding groups). This changed everything for Darwin. He then proposed that the differing environmental conditions on the different islands had lead to the changes in these Finches and to these 14 new species developing. He then generalised this to cover the origin of all species on the earth as a result of environmental pressure, a force which he termed natural selection. This was his theory on the 'Origin of the Species'.

The definition of 'Species' used in Darwin's day was: Breeding Group, a group of animals who could breed with each other.

In this way these species were a partition of nature, dividing all living things into breeding groups. So John Gould was telling him that these 14 differing finches, with different beaks could not interbreed with each other.

The whole of Darwin's theory was based on this assertion from John Gould. But how would John Gould know whether these Finches could or could not breed with each other? We don't even know whether they can or cannot interbreed today !!

But we do know that Beagles and Poodles and Bull Terriers can breed with Alsatians and Great Danes and Labradors. And these dogs are animals which differ in a lot more than merely their mouths. In fact all dogs are known to be descended from the Wolf (Canis Lupus), because they are all in the same species and can all interbreed. This being the case we find it very hard to believe that these Finches cannot breed with each other - unless they breed with their beaks that is.

In fact if Darwin had only looked at the species which his ship was named after, he would surely have realised that John Gould was likely to have been mistaken !!

So Darwin's theory is based upon an unproved and probably false assertion from John Gould. When will someone put these 14 types of Finch together and see what chicks result? Why has this not occurred to date ??

We propose that Darwin was correct in his deduction that the different environments of the islands lead to the 14 different types of beak, but that Gould was guessing and he was wrong. All of these Finches were still your basic Finch species, not withstanding their finely tuned new beaks. We propose that the same enormous genetic flexibility built into the Wolf as is manifested in the various breeds of Dog, was also built into the Finch as is manifested in the various types of beak. In the case of Dogs the selection was human, by their breeders, in the case of Finches, the selection was natural, by their environments.

Who created God?

This begs the question: Who created God? a question of the type: who baptised John the baptist? The bible ' answers' as follows:

You are my witnesses, is the utterance of Jehovah: even my servant whom I have chosen, in order that you may know and have faith in me, and that you may understand that I am the same One. Before me there was no God formed, and after me there continued to be none (Isaiah 43:10).
The name 'Jehovah', is a best fit pronounciation from the 4 Hebrew letters: יהוה. It means: 'He who causes to become', i.e. the creator. His name appears thousands of times in the Hebrew Scriptures.

You are worthy, Lord, even our God, to receive the glory and the honour and the power, because you created all things, and because of your will they existed and were created (Revelation 4:11).

God is a spirit, but not necessarily a spirit creature, for he was not necessarily created. The above scripture implies that God's will existed before all creation occurred, which could logically imply that God himself was not created, we ourselves do not know. But what we do know is that God created space and time. He is the creator of everything:

God is a Spirit, and those worshipping him must worship with spirit and truth (John 4:24).

He has a character like the angels do and like humans do, he gets happy and sad, angry and relaxed:

According to the glorious good news of the happy God, with which I was entrusted (1 Timothy 1:11)
And Jehovah felt regrets that he had made men in the earth, and he felt hurt at his heart (Genesis 6:6).
Therefore this is what the Sovereign Lord Jehovah has said: I will also cause a blast of windstorms to burst forth in my rage, and in my anger there will occur a flooding downpour, and in rage there will be hailstones for an extermination (Ezekiel 13:13).
And Jehovah began to smell a restful odor, and so Jehovah said in his heart: Never again shall I call down evil upon the ground on man's account, because the inclination of the heart of man is bad from his youth up; and never again shall I deal every living thing a blow just as I have done (Genesis 8:21).

He has a character like ours, like that of Jesus to be precise, this is a meaning of:

Let us make man in our image according to our likeness (Genesis 1:26).

We do not want to oversimplify things here. If God was not created then how did he come into existence? Well one answer is that he has always been in existence. The sense in which this is meant is not that given any amount of time in the past he was always around before that time. It is rather that he himself created time. So the question: Was there anything before God? has the answer: No, because there was actually no 'before', since God created time. We cannot pretend to understand this very much but it is the best we can do right now.

This much we do know: Humans are limited both by space and by time. Angels are limited by time alone and not by space, and God is limited by neither. All humans who are saved by God, through Jesus, will eventually become angels and escape the confines of space. It is conceivable that some or all of us may also escape the confines of time at some point. This could only happen if we had developed a character good enough for this purpose, and perhaps we can never do this, we do not know. Actually it is more likely that we will always need God so we will never get such a character. Perhaps being outside time defines God in some way?

Bible Prophecy

One can also deduce the existence of God from knowledge that appears in the bible that no human could have had at the time:

There is one who is dwelling above the circle of the earth, the dwellers in which are as grasshoppers, the one who is stretching out the heavens just as a fine gauze, who spreads them out like a tent in which to dwell (Isaiah 40:22).

He is stretching out the north over the empty place, Hanging the earth upon nothing (Job 26:7).
So we have a circle of the earth hung upon nothing. Pretty good seeing as the earth was believed flat for 2,000 years after Isaiah and gravity was discovered 3,000 years after Job.

One can also deduce his existence, or at least the existence of non human intelligence, from the prophecies and fulfilments in the bible. For example:

[a] Daniel 8 prophesied the rise of the Greek world power through Alexander the Great (see Daniel 8)

[b] Both Revelation and Daniel prophesy that the UN will have world wide power in the last ten years of this system, from 1998 to 2008 (see Daniel 7, Daniel 8, Revelation 13, Revelation 14). This is already fulfilled.

[c] Jeremiah in chapter 51 prophesied before 586AD when Jerusalem fell, how the city of Babylon would fall to the Medes, who would damn up the rivers to gain access to the city. They did this in 539AD. He also prophesied that it would eventually become piles of stones which would never be inhabited again, which it is today.

There is a devastation upon her waters and they must be dried up (Jeremiah 50:38).

Therefore the haunters of the waterless regions will dwell with the howling animals, and in her ostriches must dwell. And she will never more be dwelt in, nor will she reside for generation after generation (Jeremiah 50:39).

Jehovah has aroused the spirit of the kings of the Medes, because it is against Babylon that his idea is, in order to bring her to ruin (Jeremiah 51:11).

And Babylon must become piles of stones (Jeremiah 51:37).
Saddam Hussein was reported to have desired to rebuild Babylon, which is in modern Iraq, just before the Gulf War. He was stopped from doing this fairly comprehensively.

[d] Jesus prophesied in 33 AD about the temple in Jerusalem that not a stone would be left upon a stone. This is precisely the destruction that occurred in 70 AD under the Roman general Titus.

However, Jesus said to him: Do you behold these great buildings? By no means will a stone be left here upon a stone and not be thrown down (Mark 13:2).

[e] God said through Ezekiel over 600 years before Christ that the city of Tyre would become a shining crag and never be rebuilt:

For this is what the Sovereign Lord Jehovah has said: Here I am bringing against Tyre Nebuchadrezzar the king of Babylon from the north, a king of kings, with horses and war chariots and cavalrymen and a congregation, even a multitudinous people...And I will make you a shining, bare surface of a crag. A drying yard for dragnets is what you will become. Never will you be rebuilt; for I myself, Jehovah, have spoken, is the utterance of the Sovereign Lord Jehovah (Ezekiel 26:7..14).
Today it is a shining crag that has never been rebuilt.

There are around 300 prophecies which Jesus fulfilled personally as a human in his first century ministry. Someone somewhere has calculated that the chances of his doing this if there were no God are basically zero. Here are a few of the more famous ones with their fulfilments:

Prophecy: **My God, my God, why have you left me? [Why are you] far from saving me, [From] the words of my roaring?** (Psalm 22:1).
Fulfilment: **About the ninth hour Jesus called out with a loud voice, saying: Eli, Eli, lama sabachthani? that is: My God, my God, why have you forsaken me?** (Matthew 27:46).

Prophecy: **He committed himself to Jehovah. Let him provide him with escape! Let him deliver him, since he has taken delight in him!** (Psalm 22:8)
Fulfilment: **He has put his trust in God; let him now rescue him if he wants him, for he said: I am God's Son** (Matthew 27:43).

Prophecy: **They apportion my garments among themselves, And upon my clothing they cast lots** (Psalm 22:18).
Fulfilment: **Therefore they said to one another: Let us not tear it, but let us determine by lots over it whose it will be. This was that the scripture might be fulfilled: They apportioned my outer garments among themselves, and upon my apparel they cast lots. And so the soldiers really did these things** (John 19:24).

Prophecy: **And you, O Bethlehem of Ephrath, the one too little to get to be among the thousands of Judah, from you there will come out to me the one who is to become ruler in Israel, whose origin is from early times, from the days of time indefinite** (Micah 5:2).
Fulfilment: **After Jesus had been born in Bethlehem of Judea in the days of Herod the king, look! astrologers from eastern parts came to Jerusalem** (Matthew 2:1).

Prophecy: **Therefore Jehovah himself will give you men a sign: Look! The maiden (virgin/unmarried woman) herself will actually become pregnant, and she is giving birth to a son, and she will certainly call his name Immanuel** (Isaiah 7:14).
Fulfilment: **But after he had thought these things over, look! Jehovah's angel appeared to him in a dream, saying: Joseph, son of David, do not be afraid to take Mary your wife home, for that which has been begotten in her is by holy spirit.
She will give birth to a son, and you must call his name Jesus, for he will save his people from their sins.
All this actually came about for that to be fulfilled which was spoken by the Lord through his prophet, saying:
Look! The virgin will become pregnant and will give birth to a son, and they will call his name Immanuel, which means, when translated, 'With Us Is God'** (Matthew 1:20-23).

[6] What is a Soul? What is your spirit ?

This section is designed to be read in conjunction with www.truebiblecode.com.

Here are some scriptures which help us to precisely define this rather nebulous concept:

It is sown a physical body, it is raised up a spiritual body. If there is a physical body, there is also a spiritual one.

It is even so written: The first man Adam became a living soul. The last Adam became a life-giving spirit (1 Corinthians 15:44,45).

For the word of God is alive and exerts power and is sharper than any two-edged sword and pierces even to the dividing of soul and spirit, and of joints and [their] marrow, and [is] able to discern thoughts and intentions of [the] heart (Hebrews 4:12).

This is why the Father loves me, because I surrender my soul, in order that I may receive it again.

No man has taken it away from me, but I surrender it of my own initiative. I have authority to surrender it, and I have authority to receive it again. The commandment on this I received from my Father (John 10:17,18).

The soul that Jesus surrenders and gets back is his angelic body. Because he certainly will not get back the body that was impaled/crucified. He is not going to walk around again in that one again because it has been used to ransom Adam, and anyway it wasn't even his in the first place, he took it from Joseph and Mary's son at his baptism as we shall see in section [14b].

Everyone touching a corpse, the soul of whatever man may die, and who will not purify himself, has defiled Jehovah's tabernacle, and that soul must be cut off from Israel. Because the water for cleansing has not been sprinkled upon him, he continues unclean. His uncleanness is still upon him (Numbers 19:13).

The Soul here is the physical body. So now we have seen that the soul can either be a physical body or an angelic body. So we can therefore deduce that the soul is the body, be it physical or angelic. The soul is therefore the life carrying vehicle. So now, at last, we can understand the famous scripture:

And do not become fearful of those who kill the body but cannot kill the soul; but rather be in fear of him that can destroy both soul and body in Gehenna (Matthew 10:28).

The 'soul' here means the angelic body, and 'body' means physical body. When a man dies, his life can only continue in an angelic body, his second soul, God can kill this body, man cannot.

And he should not come to any dead soul. For his father and his mother he may not defile himself (Leviticus 21:11).

So the soul is the life carrying vehicle, it is either a human or an angelic body. The soul (any type of body) contains the spirit:

His spirit goes out, he goes back to his ground; In that day his thoughts do perish (Psalm 146:4).

The spirit, on the other hand, is your character, it is 'you'. Things get confusing when one realises that an angelic body is a spirit body and an angel is a spirit creature, sometimes referred to as a 'spirit'. But to spell things out unequivocally:

All creatures are spirits within souls.

A human is a spirit within a physical soul

An angel is a spirit within a spiritual soul.

[7] The Ransom of Jesus for Adam

This section is designed to be read in conjunction with www.truebiblecode.com.

This section has been partially covered in the section - A Quick Introduction to the Bible. But is included here as a stand alone item. It's like a certain mathematics professor at Cambridge used to say jokingly referring to Cauchy's Theorem: You can never have too many proofs of this fundamental theorem.

Adam ate the fruit from the tree of the knowledge of Good and Bad. And today we certainly have that knowledge in abundance. The penalty for this sin was stated by God as:

But as for the tree of the knowledge of good and bad you must not eat from it, for in the day you eat from it [as regards] **dying you will die** (Genesis 2:17).

This is quite obviously a prophecy that Adam will eat from it. Eve recited this penalty to Satan saying:

But as for [eating] of the fruit of the tree that is in the middle of the garden, God has said: You must not eat from it, no, you must not touch it that you do not die.

They both ate from this tree and they both died. But neither died on the literal day that they ate. On the other hand the world was not created in 6 literal days. It was created is 6 very large equal time periods 'days' or 'epochs'. Like Queen Victoria's 'day'. Each creative day may have been millions of years long if our current dating methods are correct (although, in fact, they are not, the speed of light has changed in each creative day - see [234]). So the 'day' that 'Adam' who stands for 'Adam and his progeny' eat from this tree is the entire period during which humans die. This period has an end, as any time period does hence the famous scripture:

97

And he will wipe out every tear from their eyes, and death will be no more, neither will mourning nor outcry nor pain be anymore. The former things have passed away (Revelation 21:4).

Whilst we take in this knowledge of Good and Bad, i.e. whilst we learn at school right from wrong, we die dying, i.e. we age and die (or in Hebrew idiom as regards dying, we die). But in the next system, the 1,000 year kingdom of God, after Armageddon, we, Adam's sons, do not die dying. We do not age and only some of us die (those who do not learn). So the 'day' referred to in Genesis 2:17, is this system from Adam's sin until we stop dying at the end of the 1,000 year kingdom, this is the 7th creative day of Genesis 1, during which God rests from his creative works.

When Adam and Eve were thrown out of the Garden we read:

22 And Jehovah God went on to say: Here the man has become like one of us in knowing good and bad, and now in order that he may not put his hand out and actually take [fruit] also from the tree of life and eat and live to time indefinite,--
23 With that Jehovah God put him out of the garden of Eden to cultivate the ground from which he had been taken (Genesis 3:22,23).

This is an omission symbolism. Adam was thrown out in order that he could not eat from the tree of life, the tree of knowledge is conspicuously absent from God's words. So we deduce that he (him and his progeny) were still able to eat from that tree outside the garden.

The ground from which he had been taken in symbolic terms is pre-adamic man! see [1].

So Adam had a death penalty pronounced on him, but God gave him a stay of execution long enough for his to procreate and create what is now the entire human race, through Noah. Although Adam was not the only human around at his creation, for Homo Sapiens had been around for a long time before Adam turned up, see - Millions of years of human fossils reconciled with Genesis at last!

So we, his sons, live today only because of this stay of execution on Adam's death sentence. Now Adam can only pass on to his children the life that he himself has. This life is subject to a death sentence. So we all have the same life that he had, life subject to a death sentence. So we are all under the very same death sentence. Paul explains:

12 That is why, just as through one man sin entered into the world and death through sin, so also death spread to all men because they had all sinned. For until the Law, sin was in the world, but sin is not charged against anyone

when there is no law (Romans 5:12,13).

This scripture is saying that death spread to all men through one man, Adam. This death is not due to the personal sins of each man, because we are told that sin is not charged where there is no law, and most men are not under any law. So the sin that we all carry is the unpaid sin of Adam. It is this which is the cause of our death. The death of course is physically as a result of our ageing bodies which fall apart today after a maximum of 120 years (a limit that came into force during the life of Moses who lived 120 years to the day - see [235]). Adam's sin has been paid for today by Jesus, but Adam is still dead, since the ransom has not yet been applied to Adam himself. But at the time that Adam's children were born, the sin was still unpaid, these children inherited the death sentence of Adam, which sentence is entirely executed through their ageing bodies. We are victims of this sentence through our bodies today, notwithstanding the ransom of the Christ.

Please realise that we age and die due to the sin of Adam, not due to our own sin. Charles Manson, Jack the ripper, Osama Bin Laden, Hilter, and all of the other lying and murdering sons of Adam have not broken God's law, because they were none of them under God's law. It is even possible if they truly have obeyed their consciences that they may be resurrected - this is a matter for God, not for man. But only the true people of God are under God's law, and these one's do not suffer physical death today for breaking it. On the contrary they suffer expulsion from God's true people. So there is no man who by his own works, be they exemplary or not quite so exemplary, can either condemn himself or save himself. We have all died due to Adam, independent of our works. But at Armageddon the situation is different. If one obeys one's conscience, if one loves God or, and we say or, if one loves the true people of God (without joining them), or if one joins the true people of God then one may be saved by this integrity or by this love or by this faith respectively:

14 For whenever people of the nations that do not have law do by nature the things of the law, these people, although not having law are a law to themselves.
15 They are the very ones who demonstrate the matter of the law to be written in their hearts, while their conscience is bearing witness with them and, between their own thoughts, they are being accused or even excused.
16 This will be in the day when God through Christ Jesus judges the secret things of mankind, according to the good news I declare (Romans 2:14-16).

40 And in reply the king will say to them, 'Truly I say to you, To the extent that you did it to one of the least of these my brothers, you did it to me (Matthew 25:40).

At this point the writer must point out that Spirituality involves the use of multi step thought processes, not single step thought processes (which are in general animalistic). For example the statement: Well, if Jesus truly had paid the penalty for Adam then no one would be dying today and Adam would be alive! Is false and results from a single step thought process. It is a good question to ask. But God wants us to thinks about the answer, not to jump to a one step animalistic instinctive reaction conclusion. There is more than one step in God's plan for the salvation of Adam and his sons. Peter and Jude refer to this lack of spirituality as follows:

12 But these [men], like unreasoning animals born naturally to be caught and destroyed, will, in the things of which they are ignorant and speak abusively, even suffer destruction in their own [course of] destruction (2 Peter 2:12).

10 Yet these [men] are speaking abusively of all the things they really do not know; but all the things that they do understand naturally like the unreasoning animals, in these things they go on corrupting themselves (Jude 10).

The Big Deal

Adam, before he sinned, had an indefinitely lasting human body, and had judicial life, in other words he was not under a death sentence. This means that he had an associated angel in heaven with his name on it. He was born again when he was born if you like - see [190]. Every one who has judicial life is an angelic son of God. Adam had two souls at his birth, the indefinitely lasting human soul and the angelic soul.

Had Adam procreated before he sinned, then his children would likewise have had indefinitely lasting non ageing human bodies and judicial life (associated angelic bodies). This does not defy God's principle that: Since we have free will, we have to demonstrate some loyalty and gratitude before he grants us everlasting life. A principle which is not explicitly stated, but is implicit in all of his dealings with his sons, and is obvious. Because Adam died and any one of his sons could likewise have died. In fact the judicial condition of man in the Garden of Eden is the judicial condition of man on the earth during the 1,000 year Kingdom of God. After 2008, all of us who are on the earth will have indefinitely lasting human bodies and some of these (those who have been baptised in holy spirit) will also have associated angels.

But Adam sinned before he procreated so he passed on instead a death sentence through our ageing bodies. But Jesus, at the time of Adam's sin, stepped in with an oath, saying that he himself would pay for this sin with his soul. This agreement is the master covenant between God and Jesus through which all men are saved:

5 For there is one God, and one mediator between God and men, a man, Christ Jesus (1 Timothy 2:5).

There are many sub-mediators between God and man. There was Abraham, Moses, etc, but all of their covenants were dependant on the master covenant between God and Jesus, that he should ransom Adam. So no man covenants with God without going through Jesus. This master covenant we call the Angelic Ransom Covenant or the ARC.

Now our God cannot lie, and neither should his sons. He takes his sons at their word. So once Jesus (who was the angel Michael) had given his word, then God treated him as if he had already ransomed Adam. This meant that the Fatherhood rights that Adam had before he sinned now belonged to Michael, who was bound by agreement to pay for them with his life.

So what Adam was no longer able to give us, namely and indefinitely lasting human body and judicial life is manifested by having an associated angelic body, Jesus was now able to give us instead. Hence the prophet declares:

6 For there has been a child born to us, there has been a son given to us; and the princely rule will come to be upon his shoulder. And his name will be called Wonderful Counselor, Mighty God, Eternal Father, Prince of Peace. (Isaiah 9:6).

Adam is our temporary father, the father of our current bodies. Jesus is our eternal father, the father of our indefinitely lasting human bodies (for those of us who get them) actually through Abraham, via a 'water baptism' and the father of our angelic bodies, our judicial life, through the new covenant, the newer covenant and through various other pre and post-abrahamic covenants, via a spirit baptism, which is a washing in the blood of the sub-mediator of the relevant covenant.

But Jesus does not just adopt anyone. No, there are adoption procedures for sons of the true God, and these are what many of the covenants in the bible are about.

So the above is why we all die and how we are all saved. It is a simple matter of Fatherhood. God says:

Look! All the souls to me they belong. As the soul of the father so likewise the soul of the son, to me they belong (Ezekiel 18:4).

God owns Adam's soul, this being the penalty for his sin. Adam will get his soul back just before the end of the 1,000 year Kingdom of God.

But God knew that Adam would sin and he wants to adopt all of us as his sons and daughters. He wants us all to be saved:

For God loved the world so much that he gave his only-begotten Son, in order that everyone exercising faith in him might not be destroyed but have everlasting life (John 3:16).

So having set a price on the redemption of Adam, as an indefinitely long living human soul and an angelic soul, God paid the price himself with his only begotten son, Jesus, who wasn't a son of Adam and therefore wasn't under a death penalty himself.

[The] **Lord is not slow respecting his promise, as some people consider slowness, but he is patient with you because he does not desire any to be destroyed but desires all to attain to repentance** (2 Peter 3:9).

The scriptures describe this ransom as follows:

For there is one God, and one mediator between God and men, a man, Christ Jesus, who gave himself a corresponding ransom for all--[this is] what is to be witnessed to at its own particular times (1 Timothy 2:5,6).

For just as in Adam all are dying, so also in the Christ all will be made alive (1 Corinthians 15:22).

The ransom was simple, it was soul for soul as stipulated in the Law of Moses in the case of damages:

And in case men should struggle with each other and they really hurt a pregnant woman and her children do come out but no fatal accident occurs, he is to have damages imposed upon him without fail according to what the owner of the woman may lay upon him; and he must give it through the justices.

But if a fatal accident should occur, then you must give soul for soul, eye for eye, tooth for tooth, hand for hand, foot for foot, branding for branding, wound for wound, blow for blow (Exodus 21:22-25).

And in case a man strikes any soul of mankind fatally, he should be put to death without fail.

And the fatal striker of the soul of a domestic animal should make compensation for it, soul for soul.

And in case a man should cause a defect in his associate, then just as he has done, so it should be done to him.

Fracture for fracture, eye for eye, tooth for tooth; the same sort of defect he may cause in the man, that is what should be caused in him.

And the fatal striker of a beast should make compensation for it, but the fatal striker of a man should be put to death (Leviticus 24:17-21).

No son of Adam can offer his soul to God as a ransom for Adam because that soul is already given to the heavenly court, owned by God, as is Adam's soul. This is not because God visits the sins of Fathers on to their sons, it is because Adam had all of his children *after* the death penalty was incurred. So his children are owned by the maker of the penalty, the judge, God. It is purely a question of timing.

However a man who is not a son of Adam can ransom Adam, by giving up his soul. Of course the soul must not be under any death penalty, so it must be free from sin at the time of it's offering. In Jesus' case this meant that he had to obey the law of Moses. Something that no other man was able fully to do. This was a rather more difficult test than obeying the law of the tree in the garden. But there again Jesus was a rather more experienced test pilot.

From a legal standpoint, Adam's sons who do not get a resurrection are not saved by Jesus' ransom because they die before this ransom is applied to Adam. They just die too early. But once the ransom is applied to Adam himself, then none of his sons can die due to Adam's sin. At this point God would be unrighteous if Adam's sons continued to exist in ageing dying bodies. In fact Adam is ransomed and resurrected into the Kingdom of God on earth, the second Eden, last of all humans, sometime after 2882 CE, see - Resurrection Timetables for the Kingdom of God. This is one meaning of:

And, look! there are those last who will be first, and there are those first who will be last (Luke 13:30)

Adam, the first 'man' to be born, is resurrected last.

The next question is: Fine, well then all of these Christians who have been adopted as sons of the eternal father Jesus, through his rights, due to his ransom, why do they die?

The answer is that they are adopted subject to various conditions. The conditions hitherto have been that they themselves die not judicially, since they are under no death sentence, but sacrificially on behalf of other humans. They then get resurrected afterwards with everlasting life. It is a multi level ransom. So they are ransomed but the benefit of the ransom to them is delayed until after their death, because they agree to die a sacrificial death like Jesus did. The apostle St. Paul explains this:

Or do you not know that all of us who were baptized into Christ Jesus were baptized into his death? (Romans 6:3).

So they are baptised into a sacrificial death with everlasting life afterwards. They get the same deal that Jesus got in this respect.

[8] The Kingdom of God and the Great Crowd

'Whoever will introduce into public affairs the principles of Christianity will change the face of the world' - Benjamin Franklin

This section is designed to be read in conjunction with www.truebiblecode.com.

This is the Kingdom that Jesus preached about and that we all pray for in the Lord's prayer:

Our father which art in heaven
Hallowed be thy name
Thy kingdom come (Matthew 6:9,10 King James Version)

There is no point in praying for it to come if you do not know what it is. It also helps to know when it actually does come! Jesus gave his disciples and us the signs of the times in Matthew 24, to alert us to the general period in which it would come. He gave them in answer to the questions below:

While he was sitting upon the Mount of Olives, the disciples approached him privately, saying: Tell us, when will these things be, and what will be the sign of your presence and of the conclusion of the system of things? (Matthew 24:3).
Just that one word 'privately' and that demand 'Tell us' shows that only his disciples will know when these things will be. So being blunt, if only we know when these things will be, then only we are his disciples at this time. Although in truth, many Christians have recognised that the signs of the times are currently being exhibited. Part of his answer was:

And this good news of the kingdom will be preached in all the inhabited earth for a witness to all the nations; and then the end will come (Matthew 24:14).
The 'end', in the largest meaning of this scripture, is the end of 'this system of

things', which obviously is the start of the next system of things. And the next or coming system of things is the Kingdom of God.

He said to them: Truly I say to you, There is no one who has left house or wife or brothers or parents or children for the sake of <u>the kingdom of God</u> who will not in any way get many times more in this period of time, and in the <u>coming system of things</u> everlasting life (Luke 18:29,30).

Paul describes the order of events as follows:

For just as in Adam all are dying, so also in the Christ all will be made alive.
But each one in his own rank: Christ the firstfruits, afterward those who belong to the Christ during his presence.
Next, the end, when he hands over the kingdom to the God and Father, when he has brought to nothing all government and all authority and power (1 Corinthians 15:22-24 NWT adapted from Greek).

So we have a resurrection of those who belong to Christ during his presence, a presence which occurs just before the end of this system of things. Then we have 'the end' when Jesus hands over the Kingdom, which is removed from Satan, to his father God, thereby starting the kingdom of God. Armageddon is the battle wherein Jesus brings to nothing all government and all authority and power of this system of things. This is called 'the end of the world' but it isn't the end of the planet and neither is it the end of life on the planet. It is rather then end of the present system of things, a system very much in the hands of Satan. A politically incorrect statement to make, but of course we are not politicians we are Christians, and the Christian position, one of truth and insight is laid out by St. Paul, as usual:

If, now, the good news we declare is in fact veiled, it is veiled among those who are perishing, among whom the <u>god of this system of things</u> has blinded the minds of the unbelievers, that the illumination of the glorious good news about the Christ, who is the image of God, might not shine through (2 Corinthians 4:3,4).

The God of this system of things is Satan. He is 'the ruler of the world' for Jesus said, just before he died:

I shall not speak much with you anymore, for the ruler of the world is coming. And he has no hold on me (John 14:30).

But this ruler will be chucked out:

Now there is a judging of this world; now the ruler of this world will be cast out (John 12:31).

In fact he is locked up for the entire duration of the kingdom of God, as we shall see below. His deposing and incarceration is immediately before the battle of Armageddon.

So the end of the world, is the end of *his* world, not the end of the planet. It is the end of the current system of things, a system which started at the founding of the world. The founding of the world was the start of the 7th creative day of Genesis, when God rested from his creative works:

For we who have exercised faith do enter into the rest, just as he has said: So I swore in my anger, They shall not enter into my rest, although his works were finished from the founding of the world (Hebrew 4:3).
God's last creative act was to make some clothes for Adam and Eve at the time of their sin:

And Jehovah God proceeded to make long garments of skin for Adam and for his wife and to clothe them (Genesis 3:21).
This scripture is literally true, God did make them both clothes. But it also has a greater meaning, a cryptic meaning, a Times crossword meaning. He made them new bodies that lasted a long time, 930 years in the case of Adam, a very long garment of skin! Whereas in the Garden of Eden, Adam had an indefinitely long garment of skin! A body that did not age. So Adam's sin was the founding of the World, the beginning of the current system of things. And the God of this system of things, the ruler of this world is Satan. This is how Satan was able to offer all the kingdoms of the world to Jesus, if he would perform one act of worship to him:

**So he brought him up and showed him all the kingdoms of the inhabited earth in an instant of time.
And the Devil said to him: I will give you all this authority and the glory of them, because it has been delivered to me, and to whomever I wish I give it.
You, therefore, if you do an act of worship before me, it will all be yours.
In reply Jesus said to him: It is written, It is Jehovah your God you must worship, and it is to him alone you must render sacred service** (Luke 4:5-8).
Jesus did not say, who are you kidding? He knew that Satan did have these kingdoms to give. Having received them at the founding of the world. But Jesus was not interested in status, and did not want to be first lieutenant to a lying murderer. He was interested in love, for his father and for his brothers. He was down there not for his benefit but for our benefit. A concept that Satan cannot accept, because by doing so he would condemn himself. But he did accept it when Jesus died. And he condemned himself, committing suicide whilst demonically possessing Judas. But God resurrected him!

It is of course a huge realisation that Satan is the god of this system of things and the ruler of the world. And we appreciate that if this concept is new to the reader it may cause some serious consternation. But remember that Satan can only act within prescribed limits set by God. God is the referee here, and Satan is just a very dirty team captain, he is not the head of FIFA (although some might disagree). But he does have a lot of supporters.

God only allows Satan's continued existence and authority in order that we can learn from him without having ourselves to become like him. But nonetheless the world is the Titanic and Satan is the captain, and God is the iceberg, but Jesus is the lifeboat. However in his case it will not be the rich ones who get in first, whilst the poor are locked in below, in fact quite the reverse. Anyone and everyone who wants to get in and be saved will be, and the rich, because they falsely believe that they have got it made already, will, in general find it harder to leave their comfort zone. They can be trapped by their own physical success. Come on guys, wake up!! In fact the scripture says, and Jesus himself quoted it to his home synagogue:

So the scroll of the prophet Isaiah was handed him, and he opened the scroll and found the place where it was written:
Jehovah's spirit is upon me, because he anointed me to <u>declare good news to the poor</u>, he sent me forth to preach a release to the captives and a recovery of sight to the blind, to send the crushed ones away with a release, to preach Jehovah's acceptable year.
With that he rolled up the scroll, handed it back to the attendant and sat down; and the eyes of all in the synagogue were intently fixed upon him.
Then he started to say to them: Today this scripture that you just heard is fulfilled (Luke 4:17-21).

So when Jesus was asked by Pontius Pilate, are you a King? God's firstborn son replied:

My kingdom is no part of this world. If my kingdom were part of this world, my attendants would have fought that I should not be delivered up to the Jews. But, as it is, my kingdom is not from this source (John 18:36).
Whereas his apostle John said:

Furthermore, the world is passing away and so is its desire, but he that does the will of God remains forever (1 John 2:17).
So the world passes away to make room for the Kingdom of God. It was Eve's desire for Satan's status that kicked off 'The World', and Adam's desire for Eve's body kicked off death. But this new Kingdom of God is the final whistle on the World. And the end of the Kingdom of God is the final whistle

on death. Here we have the first and the second Eden, the problem, and the resolution. 'The World' is the period between the two. The World is the primary school, the Kingdom of God is the secondary school. And although the Kingdom of God will have much more glory that the World ever had, the scripture remains saying:

For God so loved the world that he gave his only-begotten son, in order that everyone exercising faith in him might not be destroyed but have everlasting life (John 3:16).
Everlasting life in the Kingdom of God and thereafter.

What will the Kingdom of God be like?

To see what this kingdom will be like we have the prophecy of Isaiah 65:

For here I am creating a new heavens and a new earth...no more will there come to be a suckling a few days old from that place, neither an old man that does not fulfill his days, for one will die as a mere boy although a hundred years of age. And as for the sinner, although a hundred years of age he will have evil called down upon him (Isaiah 65:17-20)

This is very carefully worded. Babies and old men will not die during this kingdom, but sinners will. In other words people will not die of old age, and they will not die of illness, sickness, frailty, but they may die due to sin. Humans of 100 years old will be considered boys and will die not of old age but for life abusing sins. 'New heavens' does not mean a new physical universe, it means rather a new heavenly rulership for men. A new set of angels ruling over us.

And they will certainly build houses and have occupancy, and they will certainly plant vineyards and eat their fruit. They will not build and someone else have occupancy, they will not plant and someone else do the eating. For <u>like the days of a tree</u> will the days of my people be (Isaiah 65:21,22).

Trees can live for thousands of years (The sequoia tree lives for 2,000). There will be no economic slavery in this kingdom. A man will taste the fruits of his own labour himself. These are just a few words of prophecy but they describe one hell of a kingdom (if you'll pardon the metaphor). The apostle Peter says of this kingdom:

For you know this first, that in the last days there will come ridiculers with their ridicule, proceeding according to their own desires and

saying: Where is this promised presence of his? Why, from the day our forefathers fell asleep [in death], all things are continuing exactly as from creation's beginning.

For, according to their wish, this fact escapes their notice, that there were heavens from of old and an earth standing compactly out of water and in the midst of water by the word of God; and by those [means] the world of that time suffered destruction when it was deluged with water.

But by the same word the heavens and the earth that are now are stored up for fire and are being reserved to the <u>day of judgment and of destruction of the ungodly men</u>.

However, let this one fact not be escaping your notice, beloved ones, that one day is with [the] Lord as 1,000 years and 1,000 years as one day.

[The] Lord is not slow respecting his promise, as some people consider slowness, but he is patient with you because he does not desire any to be destroyed but desires all to attain to repentance.

Yet [the] Lord's day will come as a thief, in which the heavens will pass away with a hissing noise, but the elements being intensely hot will be dissolved, and earth and the works in it will be discovered.

Since all these things are thus to be dissolved, what sort of persons ought you to be in holy acts of conduct and deeds of godly devotion, awaiting and keeping close in mind the presence of the day of Jehovah, through which [the] heavens being on fire will be dissolved and [the] elements being intensely hot will melt!

But there are new heavens and a new earth that we are awaiting according to his promise, and in these righteousness is to dwell (2 Peter 3:3-13).

So just as the earth was destroyed by the flood of Noah, and in fact the heavens were changed then too, because the demons who had come down to the earth to procreate with the women before the flood, were thrown into Tartarus:

Certainly if God did not hold back from punishing the angels that sinned, but, by throwing them into Tartarus, delivered them to pits of dense darkness to be reserved for judgment.
And he did not hold back from punishing an ancient world, but kept Noah, a preacher of righteousness, safe with seven others when he brought a deluge upon a world of ungodly people (2 Peter 2:4,5).

This new heavens after the flood, was the second heaven, the second rulership over the sons of Adam.

Likewise both the current heavens and earth will be destroyed by the fire. Also since Peter refers to the Lord (a term which can mean either God or Jesus, but here means God) as not being slow respecting his promise, it is apparent that a day has been set when these things will occur. Now Peter refers to a day of judgement, and then says that a 'day' to God is a 1,000 years. From which we deduce that the day of judgement, the judgement day is 1,000 years long. The destruction of the ungodly men by fire is Armageddon and this battle kicks off the 1,000 year judgement day. We have already seen from Isaiah 65 above that people will die only due to their sins in the Kingdom of God, so the kingdom of God is a day of judgement. But the confirmation of the length of this Kingdom, and the fulfilment of both Isaiah 65 and these words of Peter is seen by the Apostle John in his visions of Revelation 20 and 21:

The Kingdom of God lasts for 1,000 years

And I saw an angel coming down out of heaven with the key of the abyss and a great chain in his hand.

And he seized the dragon, the original serpent, who is the Devil and Satan, and bound him for 1,000 years.

And he hurled him into the abyss and shut [it] and sealed [it] over him, that he might not mislead the nations anymore until the 1,000 years were ended. After these things he must be let loose for a little while.

And I saw thrones, and there were those who sat down on them, and power of judging was given them. Yes, I saw the souls of those executed with the axe for the witness they bore to Jesus and for speaking about God, and those who had worshiped neither the wild beast nor its image and who had not received the mark upon their forehead and upon their hand. And they came to life and ruled as kings with the Christ for a 1,000 years.

The rest of the dead did not come to life until the 1,000 years were ended. This is the first resurrection.

Happy and holy is anyone having part in the first resurrection; over these the second death has no authority, but they will be priests of God and of the Christ, and will rule as kings with him for the 1,000 years.

Now as soon as the 1,000 years have been ended, Satan will be let loose out of his prison (Revelation 20:1-7).

Here we see the exit of a key member of the old heavens, in that Satan is locked up for 1,000 years, this being the length of the Kingdom of God. We see that the Kingdom of God lasts for 1,000 years. It is a mistake to believe that this 1,000 years is coincident with the 1,000 year abyssing of Satan. Satan is locked up for various 1,000 year long periods before the 1,000 year Kingdom of God begins - see [242]. When the Kingdom of God starts, he is killed, being thrown into the figurative lake of fire and sulphur:

And the Devil who was misleading them was hurled into the lake of fire and sulphur, where both the wild beast and the false prophet [already were] (Revelation 20:10)

And death and Hades were hurled into the lake of fire. This means the second death, the lake of fire. Furthermore, whoever was not found written in the book of life was hurled into the lake of fire (Revelation 20:14,15).

This lake stands for the garbage dump at Gehenna (the Greek word for the Hebrew Geh Hinnom, which means the 'valley of Hinnom'). this valley was outside Jerusalem, and was where the dead bodies of criminals were burnt with fire and sulphur. It was Jerusalem's criminal crematorium. It stands figuratively for the second death, which is the death of the angelic soul. This is the death of Satan as an angel.

The 'dead' who come to life after the 1,000 years have ended is a reference to those who will be physically alive in the 1,000 kingdom but still be under the death sentence that God passed on Adam, and so will still be condemned to death, but not actually dead. Jesus used the same symbolism when he said:

Jesus said to him: Keep following me, and let the dead bury their dead (Matthew 8:22).

Obviously these 'dead' grave diggers were alive physically. They were dead in the sense that they had not been ransomed, so they were still under the death sentence of Adam.

The Bible calls their entrance into the kingdom of God 'the resurrection of the unrighteous'. You will not grasp all of the symbolism of these accounts at this stage but do not worry, we are only using the above to show that the Kingdom of God lasts for 1,000 years.

The Sea is No More

John sees this Kingdom in a vision, in the next chapter of Revelation:

And I saw a new heaven and a new earth; for the former heaven and the former earth had passed away, and <u>the sea is no more</u>.

I saw also the holy city, <u>New Jerusalem, coming down out of heaven</u> from God and prepared as a bride adorned for her husband.

With that I heard a loud voice from the throne say: Look! The tent of God is with mankind, and he will reside with them, and they will be his peoples. And God himself will be with them.

And he will wipe out every tear from their eyes, and death will be no more, neither will mourning nor outcry nor pain be anymore. The former things have passed away (Revelation 21:1-4).

The sea stands for uncoordinated, unruly, structureless mankind. It is those of mankind who do not want to accept authority (which can be from God). The earth stands for those with structure, who do accept administration and authority (which can be from God). But at the end of the day, the earth does set the boundaries for and guides the waters, however fluid they may be.

Ha for the commotion of many peoples, who are boisterous as with the boisterousness of the seas! And for the noise of national groups, who make a din just like the noise of mighty waters! (Isaiah 17:12).

And he says to me: The waters that you saw, where the harlot is sitting, mean peoples and crowds and nations and tongues (Revelation 17:15).

He who is building in the heavens his stairs, and his structure over the earth that he founded; he who is calling for the waters of the sea, that he may pour them out upon the surface of the earth--Jehovah is his name (Amos 9:6).

So boisterous, unruly mankind ends at Armageddon. But the surface of the earth is 75% water and 25% land. This design is living, it is prophetic, it is saying that 25% survive Armageddon and 75% do not. We already know that more are killed than survive at the end of the World from Jesus' words:

Go in through the narrow gate; because broad and spacious is the road leading off into destruction, and many are the ones going in through it. Whereas narrow is the gate and cramped the road leading off into life, and few are the ones finding it (Matthew 7:13,14).

So those saved would have to be considerably less than 50%. The confirmation from the scriptures that 1 in 4 are saved is in Luke 17:

I tell you, In that night two will be in one bed; the one will be taken along, but the other will be abandoned.
There will be two grinding at the same [mill]; the one will be taken along, but the other will be abandoned (Luke 17:34,35 NWT adapted from the Greek Interlinear).

So first of all 50% are abandoned, with two being compared to one in the verse. Then another 50% of the remainder are abandoned. Leaving us with 25% taken along. Because everyone who grinds also sleeps in a bed. So it is the same group that is being divided twice. The scripture is clearly saying this in the symbolic meaning.

We can really learn about the way in which the bible is written by looking at the 'parallel' account of this is Matthew and playing spot the difference, see - The Bible Code:

Then two men will be in the field: one will be taken along and the other be abandoned.
Two women will be grinding at the hand mill: one will be taken along and the other be abandoned (Matthew 24:40,41)

This is saying something entirely different in almost the same set of words. There is a distinction between men and women here absent in Luke. So we are not talking about two divisions of the same group, but rather two divisions of two different groups. Also not everyone who works in the field grinds at the hand mill. In fact, although we have little knowledge of farming we would guess from the sense of the account that you either do one or the other, in a typical working day on a farm. [[The greater meaning of Matthew is that one true religion (FDS) is abandoned in each presence and that one covenant (agreement between God and his people) is abandoned in each presence.]]

So in the kingdom of God, everyone accepts God's authority. One nation under God - No but truly one nation under God.

New Jerusalem

Now Jerusalem was the ruling city of the nation of Israel. So a **New Jerusalem coming down out of heaven** symbolises a heavenly rulership over God's people applying to the earth. So the kings who rule with the Christ are in heaven and are therefore angels, and their subjects are on the earth. The husband is Jesus, and his wife is the kings who rule with Christ for 1,000 years as mentioned in Revelation 20:4, who are the true saints of the New Covenant that Jesus made at the last supper:

And I make a covenant with you, just as my Father has made a covenant with me, for a kingdom, that you may eat and drink at my table in my kingdom, and sit on thrones to judge the twelve tribes of Israel (Luke 22:29,30).

The bible uses marriage agreements, to symbolise agreements or covenants between God and his people. The new covenant saints, being Jesus' wife, live with him in heaven as angels.

The Animals and the Food in the Kingdom of God

In the garden of Eden and until after the flood, the sons of Adam were vegetarians - see [1]. The animals in the garden of Eden were vegetarians as well, existing in an enclosed environment protected from the rest of the carnivores and omnivores see - Millions of year of human fossils reconciled with Genesis at last. This garden was an archetype for the kingdom of God. In this kingdom man is a vegetarian and so is the Lion. In fact the way that animals interact in nature today is a prophetic declaration from God as to how mankind will treat each other. We know of many sharks, mad dogs, hermit crabs, lemmings and even ants, amongst the sons of Adam. Likewise the way that animals interact in the next system, which is the kingdom of God will again declare man's treatment of his brothers. In the this new Kingdom we will not eat each other for breakfast. Isaiah prophetically declares:

**They will not toil for nothing, nor will they bring to birth for disturbance; because they are the offspring made up of the blessed ones of Jehovah, and their descendants with them.
And it will actually occur that before they call out I myself shall answer; while they are yet speaking, I myself shall hear.
The wolf and the lamb themselves will feed as one, and the lion will eat straw just like the bull; and as for the serpent, his food will be dust.
They will do no harm nor cause any ruin in all my holy mountain, Jehovah has said** (Isaiah 65:23-25).
The literal meaning of this is that the Lion will be a vegetarian, and the serpent will be dead. There will be no serpents in the Kingdom of God.

The Great Crowd of Revelation 7:9 and 'You People' of Revelation 19:6

On Sunday Nisan9 33 CE (March 26th 33AD), Jesus came to Jerusalem and a great crowd was there to greet him, many of whom had seen him resurrect Lazarus. In fact the chief priests were so worried by this development they took counsel to kill Lazarus! A man whom Jesus had resurrected ! Blindness in the extreme, or deliberate power politics. The account reads:

Therefore a great crowd of the Jews got to know he was there, and they came, not on account of Jesus only, but also to see Lazarus, whom he raised up from the dead.
The chief priests now took counsel to kill Lazarus also, because on account of him many of the Jews were going there and putting faith in Jesus.

The next day the great crowd that had come to the festival, on hearing that Jesus was coming to Jerusalem, <u>took the branches of palm trees</u> and went out to meet him. And they began to shout: Save, we pray you! Blessed is he that comes in Jehovah's name, even the king of Israel! (John 12:9-12).

This really was Jesus' triumphant entry into Jerusalem on Palm Sunday. This was the recognition by the Jews that Jesus was to be their king. Even the young boys cried out: 'Save we pray son of David' and when the Pharisees, who missed the beauty in everything only having eyes for their status in front of the crowd, complained to him he said:

Did you never read this: Out of the mouths of babes and sucklings you have furnished praise (Matthew 21:16).

Now in Revelation, the apostle John saw in vision the following:

**After these things I saw, and, look! a great crowd, which no man was able to number, out of all nations and tribes and peoples and tongues, standing before the throne and before the Lamb, dressed in white robes; and there were palm branches in their hands.
And they keep on crying with a loud voice, saying: Salvation [we owe] to our God, who is seated on the throne, and to the Lamb** (Revelation 7:9,10).
Obviously this crowd is saved, since they are thanking God for their salvation, so they are in the Kingdom of God. They are the real fulfilment of Palm Sunday. Hence the palm branches in their hands. They are Humans and they are described as:

These are the ones that came out of the Great Tribulation, and they have washed their robes and made them white in the blood of the lamb (Revelation 7:14).

This washing in the blood of the lamb refers to baptism, the robes are priestly garments. So they are priests. The Great Tribulation is that described in the signs of the times in Matthew 24. It is the birth pains of the Kingdom of God, a period just before the Kingdom of God starts (in fact it is the 1,335 days of Daniel 12 - see [153], from 2004Tishri17 to 2008Tammuz1 inclusive). Then we read of this crowd that:

115

That is why they are before the throne of God; and they are rendering him sacred service day and night in his temple; and the <u>One seated on the throne will spread his tent over them</u> (Revelation 7:15).

Again this is the duty of priests. The tent was the first temple of the Jews in the promised land, so it is a fitting symbol for the first earthly temple of Mankind in the Kingdom of God. But not everyone who survives Armageddon as a human will be a priest for we read later in Revelation:

With that I heard a loud voice from the throne say: Look! <u>The tent of God is with mankind</u>, and he will reside with them, and they will be <u>his peoples</u>. And God himself will be with them (Revelation 21:1-3).

So there are those who are with the tent but not under the tent. As was the case with the Jews. These are his peoples. We read further:

And I heard what was as a voice of a great crowd and as a sound of many waters and as a sound of heavy thunders. They said: Praise Jah, <u>you people</u>, because the Lord our God, the Almighty, has begun to rule as king.

Let us rejoice and be overjoyed, and let us give him the glory, because the marriage of the Lamb has arrived and his wife has prepared herself (Revelation 19:6,7).

Jesus is referred to as a lamb because he was the greater passover lamb, dying on the passover day, Nisan14, good Friday, to end all passover lamb sacrifices. We read of John the Baptist:

The next day he beheld Jesus coming toward him, and he said: See, the Lamb of God that takes away the sin of the world! (John 1:29).

'You people' are not the great crowd and not the wife of the lamb, who is Jesus. Jesus' wife is the new covenant saints as a group betrothed to him, through this covenant.

I saw also the holy city, New Jerusalem, coming down out of heaven from God and prepared as a bride adorned for her husband.

This heavenly bride is the new heaven for the new earth. It is all the new covenant saints. The new earth is the 'great crowd' of priests and the 'you people', who are those who are saved through Armageddon without joining the true religion at the time. They are prefigured by those who left Egypt in the Exodus with the Jews, but were not themselves Jews:

And the sons of Israel proceeded to depart from Rameses for Succoth, to the number of 600,000 able-bodied men on foot, besides little ones. And **a vast mixed company** also went up with them, as well as flocks and herds, a very numerous stock of animals (Exodus 12:37,38).

Summary

[1] The Kingdom of God is a 1,000 year kingdom, starting with the destruction of ungodly men (the sea) by fire (which symbolises a permanent destruction, which is Armageddon).

[2] Satan is killed as an angel as it begins.

[3] The heavenly government of this kingdom is the New covenants saints and their King is Jesus, this is the new heavens, the New Jerusalem.

[4] The earthly subjects of this 1,000 year Judgement day do not die of age, and so do not age, and they do not die of disease, and so do not get sick, but they can be killed as a result of sin. These subjects make up the new earth. All of them accept God's authority, and entrance is either by resurrection, or by not being destroyed at Armageddon.

[5] 25% survive Armageddon. The other 75% are not killed because they are not good enough, they are killed because they are not interested. Actually 10% are in the Great Crowd, God's farming tax percentage, the tithe, and the other 15% are 'You people', the citizens, saved by the angels.

[6] God's creatures do not eat each other in the Kingdom of God - This does not mean that we should be vegetarians now however. In fact quite the reverse, Jesus was not a vegetarian, and Christians follow him.

[16] The Date of Armageddon without using the Code

'I can calculate the motion of heavenly bodies but not the madness of people.'
Isaac Newton (1642-1727) English mathematician, philosopher.

This section is designed to be read in conjunction with www.truebiblecode.com.

The first talk public that Gordon gave on the date of Armageddon on March 21st 2000, lasted for 3 hours, and half way through he had to throw away his notes because he was running out of time. Today he can prove the date in a couple of sentences as follows:

In Revelation 13, the beast is the UN. This beast has 10 horns and 7 heads. The 10 horns are 10 years of military power without kingship, and the 7 heads are 7 years of Kingship over the entire world. We all know that the UN got military power during the Gulf War, which ended in March 1991, 10 years after this is 2001 and 7 years after this is 2008. Amen.

A corollary of this is that the UN must gets kingship of the whole world in between 2001Elul and 2002Elul, something that the LWs have been saying since 1992. It finally got this on 2002Tammuz29/30 July 12th 2002, when the US accpeted jurisdiction of the UN ICC after 12 days of negotiation which began on June30/July1 2002 which was 300 BLC days after 911. However, it was not until Thursday 10th October 2002 that the LWs were finally able correctly to calculate the date of the precise Hebrew day when the security council expands to 10 permanent members all of whom agree to reduce or relinquish their veto powers. There now follows a slightly more laborious but nonetheless fundamental scriptural proof of this date of 2008.

Firstly we look at the Maternal genealogy of Jesus painstakingly recorded by Luke:

Furthermore, Jesus himself, when he commenced [his ministry], was as if 30 years old, being the son, as the opinion was, of Joseph, [Mary's Husband].

[son] of Heli, [Mary's Mother's Husband, Mary's Father]
[son] of Matthat, [Mary's Mother's Mother's Husband]
[son] of Levi, [This is the maternal line]
[son] of Melchi,
[son] of Jannai,
[son] of Joseph,
[son] of Mattathias,
[son] of Amos,
[son] of Nahum,
[son] of Esli,
[son] of Naggai,
[son] of Maath,
[son] of Mattathias,
[son] of Semein,
[son] of Josech,
[son] of Joda,
[son] of Joanan,
[son] of Rhesa,

[son] of Zerubbabel,
[son] of Shealtiel,
[son] of Neri,
[son] of Melchi,
[son] of Addi,
[son] of Cosam,
[son] of Elmadam,
[son] of Er,
[son] of Jesus,
[son] of Eliezer,
[son] of Jorim,
[son] of Matthat,
[son] of Levi,
[son] of Symeon,
[son] of Judas,
[son] of Joseph,
[son] of Jonam,
[son] of Eliakim,
[son] of Melea,
[son] of Menna,
[son] of Mattatha,
[son] of Nathan,
[son] of David,
[son] of Jesse,
[son] of Obed,
[son] of Boaz,
[son] of Salmon,
[son] of Nahshon,
[son] of Amminadab,
[son] of Arni,
[son] of Hezron,
[son] of Perez,
[son] of Judah,
[son] of Jacob,
[son] of Isaac,
[son] of Abraham,
[son] of Terah,
[son] of Nahor,
[son] of Serug,
[son] of Reu,
[son] of Peleg,
[son] of Eber,
[son] of Shelah,
[son] of Cainan,
[son] of Arpachshad,

[son] of Shem,
[son] of Noah,
[son] of Lamech,
[son] of Methuselah,
[son] of Enoch,
[son] of Jared,
[son] of Mahalaleel,
[son] of Cainan,
[son] of Enosh,
[son] of Seth,
[son] of Adam,
[son] of God (Luke 3:23-38 NWT adapted from the Greek).

This Maternal line is a list of the husbands of the female ancestors of Mary, in other words Heli was Mary's father, Matthat was Mary's maternal grandfather or Mary's mother's father, Levi was Mary's mother's maternal grandfather or Mary's mother's mother's father etc. etc. The maternal line of Luke and the Paternal line of Matthew chapter 1 merge at King David - see Matthew 1.

Now the question is: Is the genealogy above fact or is it fiction? The fundamental Christian takes it as fact, the scientist has hitherto had to take it as fiction or as 'somewhat symbolic' in order to reconcile it with known archaeology.

Because Luke has Jesus being the 77th in line from God, whereas the fossil record shows that homo sapiens (even in the modern variety) has been around for 100,000 years and Homo habilis, Homo erectus, archaic Homo sapiens, Neanderthal man and Cromagnon man (who is modern Homo sapiens) have between them been around for more than a million years. However we, the Lord's Witnesses, have recently discovered that Adam was the first human to be called 'man' by God, but he was not the first human. In fact Adam means 'man' in Hebrew - see [1] for the full story.

We have discovered that Adam was introduced into the prehistoric world of Homo Sapiens, as more or less an indefinitely long living God. This introduction was the Genesis of civilisation and the origin of all Mythology. In fact all that mankind had achieved prior to the advent of Adam, was the domestication of wheat, the domestication of the dog and the sheep and the manufacture of some primitive stone tools, the decoration of some caves, the making of some skin clothes and settling in small structureless farming cooperatives, living in skin tents.

But then, within 1,000 years of Adam's sin, we had invented writing, built huge cities with temples in them, invented the wheel, domesticating everything, started forging metals (the Bronze age), doubled our population, invented intensive farming, started huge wars to establish kingdoms etc. etc. This is not a coincidence. The point is that the above lineage of Luke, no longer conflicts with Archaeology. Rather, it explains why man became civilised and ceased being prehistoric, because this occurred with Adam, around 6,000 to 5,000 years ago, i.e. between 3000 and 4000 BC. We shall discover that Adam was born in 4027 BC and he lived 930 years and died in 3097 BC, so his extraordinarily long life (to us today) covered almost the entirety of this explosive millennium for mankind.

So now we take the genealogy of Luke as Gospel (in fact as St. Luke's Gospel) and let us discover when some of these characters actually lived!!

Now Genesis says:

And Jehovah God proceeded to form the man out of dust from the ground and to blow into his nostrils the breath of life, and the man came to be a living soul (Genesis 2:7).

And Paul, quoting this scripture, says:

It is even so written: The first man Adam became a living soul. The last Adam became a life-giving spirit.

Nevertheless, the first is, not that which is spiritual, but that which is physical, afterward that which is spiritual.

The first man is out of the earth and made of dust; the second man is out of heaven (1 Corinthians 15:45-47).

From which bible scholars have hitherto deduced that Adam was the first human, and therefore the Archeologists and the Anthropologists must be wrong. But the Archaeologists and the Anthropologists are not wrong. There is overwhelming evidence in support of the existence of modern man for at least 30,000 years. Whereas 77 generations of man from Adam to Jesus obviously cover a far shorter period of time. In fact bible chronology shows that Adam was born in 4027 BC as we shall discover. This scientific evidence has really destroyed the credibility of Genesis as a literally true book to all except the fundamental Christians, who either know or believe that the bible is the infallible word of God and so their faith tells them that Genesis is correct period. The less fundamental Christians have assumed that Genesis is symbolic in some way, or that Adam represents 'all men before a certain time' or the likes. But the Genealogy of Luke is perfectly unambiguous. It is declaring that Adam was a real human, being the great, great, great, great, great, great, great grandfather of Noah, who is more readily acceptable as a real human. As mentioned above we have resolved this apparent contradiction with what could be termed the 2001 theory - [1].

The 2001 Theory

Humans did 'evolve' but by the design process of angels, rather than by random chance. For chance, an unthinking statistical phenomenon, cannot logically create a thinking being. Only intelligence begets intelligence. Descartes said: I think therefore I am. But one could equally well say: I think, therefore I was created by a thinker. In fact the second law of Thermodynamics which states:

Entropy tends to a maximum
Every process increases Chaos

or $dU/dt = PdV/dt - TdS/dt$

(U is energy, P is pressure, V is volume, T is temperature, S is entropy - a measure of Chaos, dU/dt, dV/dt, dS/dt are the rates of change of U, V, S with respect to time)

proves that in the beginning there was more order in the universe than there is now. In some sense there was complete or perfect order and therefore there must have been an orderer, a creator. So the 2nd law of thermodynamics pretty much proves that there is a God. However this 'law' may only be a larger scale statistical phenomenon.

And indeed there was a Homo habilis, created by the angels, then there was a Homo erectus, created by the angels, then there was an Archaic homo sapiens, created by the angels, then there was Neanderthal man, created by the angels and then there was Modern homo sapiens (sometimes called Homo sapiens sapiens or Cromagnon man), created by the angels and then there was Adam, created not by the angels but by God himself by a more direct involvement in the process.

26 And God went on to say: <u>Let us make man</u> in <u>our</u> image, according to our likeness, and let them have in subjection the fish of the sea and the flying creatures of the heavens and the domestic animals and all the earth and every moving animal that is moving upon the earth (Genesis 1:26).

27 And <u>God proceeded to create the man</u> in <u>his</u> image, in God's image he created him; male and female he created them (Genesis 1:27).

Adam's creation had to wait until humans had reached the point in their development when they were ready to become 'spiritual'. The bible describes the difference between the physical man and the spiritual man as follows:

But a physical man does not receive the things of the spirit of God, for they are foolishness to him; and he cannot get to know [them], because they are examined spiritually.

However, the spiritual man examines indeed all things, but he himself is not examined by any man (1 Corinthians 2:14,15).

So the spiritual man is capable of making a wider examination of his environment. He has a higher consciousness of his surroundings, and can rationalise as to what might be the cause of them or what might be behind them. He can deduce the existence of things that he cannot detect physically (such as spiritual things - or gravity!) by applying reason to things which he can detect physically. Animals cannot do this, they only think about things which they can physically detect. Another way of putting this is that man was able to contemplate two stage thinking processes.

Once man had reached this level of perception, then as in the film 2001 a space odyssey, a new stage in our development began. This new stage was the creation directly by God himself of Adam.

Adam was created by God as described in Genesis in the Garden of Eden which is located in the North of Iran around Lake Urmia, in the region where one finds the sources of the Euphrates, the Tigris (Hiddekel), the Gihon (Araxes) and the Pishon (Uizhun) rivers, the 4 rivers of Eden as described in Genesis 2 (Legends - David Rohl) - see [1].

Adam was genetically different from Homo sapiens only in as much as his genes kept him going indefinitely whilst he was within the Garden. He did not age, whereas Homo sapiens, pre adamic man, was ageing and falling apart slowly like we do.

And Jehovah God went on to say: Here the man has become like one of us in knowing good and bad, and now in order that he may not put his hand out and actually take [fruit] also from the tree of life and eat and live to time indefinite.

With that Jehovah God put him out of the garden of Eden to cultivate the ground from which he had been taken (Genesis 3:22,23).

He was created to introduce spirituality to mankind by a God who foreknew that he would sin. Because he said to Adam:

Further, God blessed them and God said to them: Be fruitful and become many and fill the earth and subdue it (Genesis 1:28).

Since the garden of Eden was only one small part of the earth, he would obviously have to leave the garden to obey this command! And as regards Adam's food:

And God went on to say: Here I have given to you all vegetation bearing seed <u>which is on the surface of the whole earth</u> and every tree on which there is the fruit of a tree bearing seed. To you let it serve as food (Genesis 1:29).

This involved food that was outside the garden. All of this was said in the 6th creative day of Genesis, before Adam sinned. His sin marked the beginning of the 7th creative day, the Sabbath, God's 'day' of rest. These 'days' are epochs lasting thousands or millions of years !

As we have stated, historical evidence supports the introduction of a spiritually aware superman at around 4000 BC. But the bible too declares this parallel existence of these two types of men - see [1]:

And God went on to say: Let <u>us</u> make <u>man</u> in <u>our image</u>, according to our likeness, and let <u>them</u> have in subjection the fish of the sea and the flying creatures of the heavens and the domestic animals and all the earth and <u>every moving animal</u> that is moving upon the earth.

And <u>God</u> proceeded to create <u>the man</u> in <u>his image</u>, in God's image he created him; male and female he created them.

Further, God blessed them and God said to them: Be fruitful and become many and fill the earth and subdue it, and have in subjection the fish of the sea and the flying creatures of the heavens and <u>every living being</u> (חיה) **that is moving upon the earth** (Genesis 1:26-28).

So 'man' had in subjection every moving animal, but 'the man' had in subjection every living being (literally every living thing) including Homo sapiens, or 'man'. Also 'the man' was blessed and told to fill the earth, whereas 'man' was not. Man did not fill the earth, there were only around 5-7 million of us at the time of Adam's birth (McEvedy 1978 Atlas of World Population). But 'the man' did fill it, through his descendant Noah! So 'man' was created by a plurality of angels, in the image of all of them, but 'the man' was created by God in his image alone. This is the same distinction as one makes between 'the God' and 'gods'. This distinction is very easy to see using the Repetition Principle of the bible code, and from the The Omission Principle wherein 'the man' is not said to be in God's likeness.

Then again in Genesis 5:

This is the book of Adam's history. In the day of God's creating man he made him in the likeness of God.

Male and female he created them. And he blessed them and called their name Man in the day of their being created (Genesis 5:1,2).

So it was Adam and Eve whom God called 'Man' in the day of their being created. The literal meaning of these two verses relates entirely to Adam and Eve. Homo Sapiens was first called 'Man' at the arrival of Adam. However the 'day' of creation of man is repeated in these two verses. So applying the Repetition Principle of the code, this is a key symbolism with a greater meaning which in this case is a further creation. So there were two days of creation of man (although both of these fall within the 6th creative day). The first day was the creation of Homo Sapiens, the second was the creation of Adam and Eve, at which time we all got the name 'man'.

In the symbolic meaning, verse 1 relates to Homo Sapiens made in God's likeness in his day of creation, and verse 2 relates to Adam and Eve who were blessed and called 'man' in the day of their creation. In the symbolic meaning, 'the man', and 'male and female' who are Adam and Eve are never said to be in God's likeness, but always in God's image. Whereas 'man' is always said to be in God's likeness in Genesis.

So now we can return to Paul's words:

It is even so written: The first man Adam became a living soul. The last Adam became a life-giving spirit.

Nevertheless, the first is, not that which is spiritual, but that which is physical, afterward that which is spiritual.

The first man is out of the earth and made of dust; the second man is out of heaven (1 Corinthians 15:45-47).

Adam was the first to be called 'man' by God. He was not the first human being. For that which is physical, Homo sapiens, came first, then afterward, that which is spiritual, Man. This is classic scripture, the meanings are:

Literal: The first man Adam was out of the earth, being made of dust, the second man Jesus was out of heaven.

Symbolic: The first Homo sapiens was out of the earth, God's heavenly organisation, made by a plurality of angels, and made of dust, the second man Adam was out of heaven being God's own son, not made by God's organisation.

In bible symbolism, the earth stands for an organisation, the sand of the sea stands for adherents to that organisation and the sea itself stands for those who do not support or follow the organisation. This symbolism is revealed in Revelation 17 - see [158]. Remember that the earth was originally covered in seas and then the earth appeared. Symbolically this represents a group of beings forming some sort of organisation.

Spirituality and the bible code

While we keep our eyes, not on the things seen, but on the things unseen. For the things seen are temporary, but the things unseen are everlasting (2 Corinthians 4:18).

This means keeping our mind on the things unseen, the existence of which we have deduced from things that we can see.

As usual Paul has summed this all up beautifully, he grasped the precise meaning of spirituality nearly 2,000 years ago:

Faith is the assured expectation of things hoped for, the evident demonstration of realities though not beheld.

For by means of this the men of old times had witness borne to them.

By faith we perceive that the systems of things were put in order by God's word, so that what is beheld has come to be out of things that do not appear (Hebrews 11:1-3).

It is the ability that Sir Isaac Newton showed in his deducing the existence of the invisible force of Gravity from its effect on visible matter, that makes us capable of having faith in the existence of an invisible God from his effect on our surroundings. And it is this ability which makes us capable of being spiritual.

Be sure! God is as real as Gravity.

In fact God is love, the emotional bond between all humans and gravity is galactic cohesion, or galactic physical love, the physical bond between all matter.

And do not underestimate the place that Isaac Newton has in God's plan. This deductive capability that Newton so clearly demonstrated is what made us ready for God to 'introduce' himself to us. The reason that God waited for us to develop this capability, or should we say for the angels to design this capability into us, before he made himself known to us, was that he did not want to appear to us physically. He did not want to appear physically because he wanted to give us the option of not accepting his existence. He did this because he was not interested in teaching those of his children who did not want to acknowledge the existence of their own father. He only wanted to teach those of us who can find it in our hearts to thank him for creating us. If you do not believe in God and you die at or before Armageddon and you are not resurrected, then as far as you are concerned, what you have missed out on?

So Jehovah wanted to hide from us behind a thin wall of reason. In this way only those of us who wanted there to be true love, real gratitude, true justice, true responsibility for our actions to a perfect and fair and loving God, and only those of us who appreciated these things would actually make the effort required to break through this thin wall with our minds, and use our power of reason to see him, to detect him. Hence Jesus said:

Blessed are the pure in heart, for they shall see God (Matthew 5:8 KJV).

In psychological terms God is playing hard to get, because he wants our love. The concept that God is complete in himself and needs nothing is false. God needs love, he needs our love. For what is the point of being omnipotent omniscient, and the very definition of love, if there is no one for you to teach your wisdom to, no one for you to protect, help and save with your power and no one for you to love? You would be superman with no Lois, you would be Batman with no Gotham City. Now this very same ability to deduce the existence of invisible things from the arrangement of visible things, when used on the bible itself, reveals an unseen code, a hidden bible, a bible born out of faith, in addition to the one written by the prophets. Look! it is just below the surface meaning of the book! Consider this example in Genesis 36:

And this is the history of Esau, that is to say, <u>Edom</u>.
Esau took his wives from the daughters of Canaan: Adah the daughter of Elon the Hittite and Oholibamah the daughter of Anah, the granddaughter of Zibeon the Hivite, and Basemath, Ishmael's daughter, the sister of Nebaioth.
And <u>Adah</u> proceeded to bear <u>Eliphaz</u> to Esau, and Basemath bore Reuel (Genesis 36:1-4).

So Esau took up dwelling in the mountainous region of Seir. Esau is <u>Edom</u>.
And this is the history of Esau the father of Edom in the mountainous region of Seir.
These are the names of the sons of Esau: <u>Eliphaz</u> the son of <u>Adah</u>, Esau's wife; Reuel the son of Basemath, Esau's wife (Genesis 36:8-10).

These are the sheiks of the sons of Esau: The sons of Eliphaz, Esau's firstborn: Sheik Teman, sheik Omar, sheik Zepho, sheik Kenaz, sheik Korah, sheik Gatam, sheik Amalek. These are the sheiks of Eliphaz in the land of Edom. These are the sons by Adah (Genesis 36:15,16).

These are the sons of Esau, and these are their sheiks. He is Edom (Genesis 36:19).

This is a ludicrously repetitive account. Information which is absolutely obvious is just restated again and again. How many times do we need to be told that Esau is in fact Edom, and the his firstborn son by Adah was Eliphaz?? Either God suffers from memory loss or this chapter is written in a code - take your pick!

This sort of thing is why Sir Isaac Newton and many before him, Paul included, knew that the bible was written in a symbolic code. St. Paul said with reference to Abraham and his two wives and Genesis chapter 16:

These things stand as a symbolic drama (Galatians 4:24).

But in truth every account in this book stands inspired by the same God, transmitted by the same son, through whom all things came into existence, and written in the same symbolic code, as the account of Abraham and his wives.

All Scripture is inspired of God and beneficial for teaching, for reproving, for setting things straight, for disciplining in righteousness (2 Timothy 3:16).

All things came into existence through him, and apart from him not even one thing came into existence (John 1:3).

We are saying that the spiritual man, the man who looks behind the visible realities, will see, he will deduce, that the bible is written in a code. If you do not think that humans can do this sort of thing go and see or rent or buy the movie 'The Matrix'. In that film a greater leap of (fictitious) spiritual vision is made for the purposes of entertainment than is required by God for the purposes of salvation! Now it was this very ability, to deduce the existence of the invisible from reason being applied to the visible, that triggered our God to introduce himself to us almost 6,000 years ago, through Adam.

The Chronology Back to Adam, through Abraham and Jesus

We now deduce some dates for these three members of the royal line of 77, from the bible.

Once we have discovered the precise dates of Jesus' birth, his death, Abraham's birth and Adam's birth we will be in a position to deduce the date of Armageddon by two entirely different methods, both of which give the same result.

[16a] The dates of Jesus' birth and death

Jesus was born on Tishri10, 2 BCE (October 9, 2BC)
Jesus died on Good Friday, 33Nisan14 (April 1, 33AD)

The *Quarterly Journal of Royal Astronomical Society* **32,** (Sept. 1991), pp 301-304 says:

http://johnpratt.com/items/docs/newton.html

Newton began by dating the baptism of Christ in AD 29 during the 15th year of Tiberius Caesar (Luke 3:1, 21). He then cited evidence for a total of five (rather than four) passovers during the ministry, implying an AD 34 crucifixion. Then Newton did the calendrical analysis almost exactly as has been done since: determining in which years the crucifixion day, 14 Nisan on the Judean calendar, could have been a Friday (John 19:14, 42) ...

Thus, Newton first narrowed the possible years (for crucifixion) down to AD 33 and AD 34; had he preferred AD 33, his reasoning would probably have been researched sooner because that date now appears to be correct.

In the fifteenth year of the reign of Tiberius Caesar, when Pontius Pilate was governor of Judea, and Herod was district ruler of Galilee, but Philip his brother was district ruler of the country of Ituraea and Trachonitis, and Lysanias was district ruler of Abilene, in the days of chief priest Annas and of Caiaphas, God's declaration came to John the son of Zechariah in the wilderness.

So he came into all the country around the Jordan, preaching baptism of repentance for forgiveness of sins (Luke 3:1-3).

Now when all the people were baptized, Jesus also was baptized (Luke 3:21).

We know that Augustus Caesar died on 19 August 14 CE (Julian calendar). Tiberius became Princeps at that time. So his first regnal year was 15 CE (he became Pontifex Maximus on March 10th 15 CE. So his 15th regnal year was 29 CE (Cambridge Ancient History). So this was the year in which John started baptising.

Now both John and Jesus were under the law of Moses, which stated as regards all priests that:

129

From 30 years old upward to 50 years old, all those going into the service group to do the work in the tent of meeting (Numbers 4:3).

So the Hebrew year starting Nisan 29 CE would have been John's 30th year, since he had to start his priestly duties then. So he would have been born in the year starting Nisan 2 BCE. A Jew was considered one year old for the whole of his first year, which was the first year in which he was alive on Nisan1 - see [How Ages and Reigns are counted - www.truebiblecode.com].

Now we can work out the precise month in which John was born as follows:

In the days of Herod, king of Judea, there happened to be a certain priest named Zechariah of the division of Abijah, and he had a wife from the daughters of Aaron, and her name was Elizabeth (Luke 1:5).

However, the angel said to him: Have no fear, Zechariah, because your supplication has been favourably heard, and your wife Elizabeth will become mother to a son to you, and you are to call his name John (Luke 1:13).

When now the days of his public service were fulfilled, he went off to his home. But after these days Elizabeth, his wife, became pregnant (Luke 1:23,24).

Now we have been told here that Elizabeth conceived after the days of service of Zechariah at the temple. So we should be able to deduce when these days of service were, in order for this scripture to be of any use to us. Well, Zechariah was in the priestly division of Abijah, which was the 8th out of 24 priestly divisions which spanned the 12 months of the Hebrew year:

And David, and Zadok from the sons of Eleazar, and Ahimelech from the sons of Ithamar proceeded to make divisions of them for their office in their service (1 Chronicles 24:3).

And the lot proceeded to come out: the first for Jehoiarib; for Jedaiah the 2nd, for Harim the 3rd, for Seorim the 4th, for Malchijah the 5th, for Mijamin the 6th, for Hakkoz the 7th, for Abijah the 8th (1 Chronicles 24:7-11).

So obviously each service period was half a month long or 15 days long, so that 24 of them spanned the 360 day Biblical Lunar Calendar [BLC] year. So the 8th division would be the last half of the 4th month in the Hebrew year which was Tammuz. So Elizabeth, who conceived 'after these days', must have fallen pregnant early in the 5th Hebrew month of Ab. Next we read:

The time now became due for Elizabeth to give birth, and she became mother to a son (Luke 1:57).

This is really an incredible scripture. The holy spirit is telling us that John the baptist was a full term baby!! Obviously this is because the Holy Spirit wants us to use this information in a chronological calculation for the birth of John. Look! God's spirit wants us to use our heads! To serve him with our whole minds!

He said to him: You must love Jehovah your God with your whole heart and with your whole soul and with your whole mind (Matthew 22:37).

So her pregnancy was of standard duration, i.e. 266 solar days from conception (Babydata.com). Now 3BCE Adar 30 was 9 March 2BCE Gregorian (from the BLC program). And 2BCE Nisan1 was 3 April 2 BCE. So there was a intercalary month at the end of this Hebrew year which is not represented by the BLC. Ab1 in 3BCE started at 6pm on July 13th 3BCE (Gregorian Calendar). So 266 solar days after this was 5th April 2BCE which was Nisan3 2BCE. So Elizabeth would therefore have given birth at the beginning of Nisan in 2BC. But now we read that:

In her sixth month the angel Gabriel was sent forth from God to a city of Galilee named Nazareth (Luke 1:26).

And, look! you will conceive in your womb and give birth to a son, and you are to call his name Jesus (Luke 1:31).

And, look! Elizabeth your relative has also herself conceived a son, in her old age, and this is the sixth month for her, the so-called barren woman; because with God no declaration will be an impossibility (Luke 1:36,37).

She fell pregnant at the beginning of Ab, so her first month by Hebrew counting was Elul. So her sixth month was Shebat 3BCE. So Mary conceived in Shebat, which ran from 9th January to 7th February 2BCE. She therefore gave birth around 266 solar days later, between October 6th and November 4th 2BCE. This was between Tishri7 and Heshvan6 2BCE. But during this period we find Tishri10, the festival of the atonement day. And what better day for Jesus, who was the greater atonement sacrifice to be born on?

However, on the 10th of this 7th month is the day of atonement. A holy convention should take place for you, and you must afflict your souls and present an offering made by fire to Jehovah (Leviticus 23:27).

We have assumed that Jesus too was a full term baby, but he was a sinless son of God, an unblemished lamb, so the concept of his being either late or premature is a non starter. We have only proved that Jesus was born between Tishri 7 and Heshvan 6, but since he certainly was the greater atonement sacrifice, Tishri10 is the only sensible option for his birth. We shall see later that he was actually born on this day, from the Midst

Prophecy. Jesus too, being under law, would then have to start his priestly duties, his ministry, in his 30th year, which ran from 29Nisan to 29Adar as did John's. But how long did his ministry last?

Jesus' ministry contained at least 3 passover festivals, which were annual festivals held on Nisan14 (around easter). They are all mentioned in the Gospel of John:

However, when he was in Jerusalem at the passover, at its festival, many people put their faith in his name, viewing his signs that he was performing (John 2:23).

Now the passover, the festival of the Jews, was near (John 6:4).

This means it is within days because:

Now the passover of the Jews was near, and Jesus went up to Jerusalem (John 2:13).

relates to the passover described in John 2:23 and people went up to Jerusalem to celebrate the Passover just days before the Passover.

Now the passover of the Jews was near, and many people went up out of the country to Jerusalem before the passover in order to cleanse themselves ceremonially (John 11:55).

This is the passover described in John 13:1:

Now, because he knew before the festival of the passover that his hour had come for him to move out of this world to the Father, Jesus, having loved his own that were in the world, loved them to the end (John 13:1).

But there is a further possible passover mentioned, a fourth one:

After these things there was a festival of the Jews, and Jesus went up to Jerusalem (John 5:1).

This festival might have been the passover, or it could have been one of the other two annual festivals which required a presence at the temple. So his ministry included 3 or 4 passovers and so was between 2 and 4 years long.

So this means that Jesus died on good Friday in 31,32,33, at the outside we also consider 30, 34 AD.

Unlike Newton, we have the advantage of computers, so we can calculate with relative ease in which of the 5 cases above the passover day Nisan14 (good Friday) was actually a Friday. The passover on which Jesus died ran from 6pm Thursday to 6pm Friday and Jesus died at the ninth hour on Friday, which was 3pm:

When it became the 6th hour a darkness fell over the whole land until the 9th hour.

And at the 9th hour Jesus called out with a loud voice: Eli, Eli, lama sabachthani? which means, when translated: My God, my God, why have you forsaken me? (Mark 15:33,34).

Then the Jews, since it was Preparation, in order that the bodies might not remain upon the torture stakes on the Sabbath, (for the day of that Sabbath was a great one,) requested Pilate to have their legs broken and the [bodies] taken away (John 19:31).

A great sabbath, was a sabbath as defined by a festival, which was also a sabbath by reason of being the 7th day of a week. In this case, Nisan 15 was the first sabbath of the festival of cakes, and the Jews have Friday 6pm to Saturday 6pm as their weekly Sabbath.

Using the BLC, we find the following:

Hebrew Day	Starts 6pm on
30 Nisan15	Thursday
31 Nisan15	Tuesday
32 Nisan15	Sunday
33 Nisan15	Friday
34 Nisan15	Wednesday

So 33 AD is the only candidate. So Jesus died on 33Nisan14. Now the darkness for 3 hours from 12:00 to 15:00 Jerusalem time cannot have been a solar eclipse because these never last longer than 10 minutes. But there was a partial lunar eclipse on 33Nisan14 lasting 86 minutes with it's maximum effect at 15:01 GMT or 17:01 Friday Jerusalem time. This was April 1 Gregorian, and April 3 Julian:
(http://sunearth.gsfc.nasa.gov/eclipse/LEcat/LE0001-0100.html).

So this eclipse started just after Jesus died, and covered the period when Judas, who was possessed by Satan, committed suicide. Satan is symbolised by the moon, a dead and poor reflection of the Sun which symbolises Jesus: **I am the light of the World** (John 8:12). It has been suggested that a lunar eclipse could result in the moon looking blood red in colour (Joel 2:31).

In conclusion Jesus was born on Tishri 10, 2BCE, and he died on Nisan14, 33CE at 15:00 Jerusalem time. His life was therefore 33 years and 6 months long.

Michaelmas Day

Do not think that we are working out anything that mankind has not known before here. Firstly, Michaelmas is another term for Christmas, and so the birth of Michael and the birth of Christ were related sometime back in the distant past. Secondly Michaelmas day is 29th September in the Catholic calendar. This is Tishri10 if the passover falls on April 6th. So ancient traditions give very strong evidence that Jesus is Michael and that he was born on Tishri10. This means there has been a deliberate obfuscation by the church of the indentity of Jesus as Michael and a deliberate changing of the day of his birth, in order to Christianize the pagan midwinter longest day of the year illumination festival - see [241] for more on the origins of Xmas.

Technical note on Daniel 9

For a more in depth analysis of this great prophecy of Daniel - see [150].

There are 70 'sevens' that have been determined upon your people and upon your holy city, in order to terminate the transgression, and to finish off sin, and to make atonement for error, and to bring in righteousness for times indefinite, and to imprint a seal upon vision and prophet, and to anoint the Holy of Holies (Daniel 9:24).

And you should know and have the insight [that] from the going forth of [the] word to restore and to rebuild Jerusalem until Messiah [the] Leader, there will be 7 'sevens', also 62 'sevens'. She will return and be actually rebuilt, with a public square and moat, but in the straits of the times (Daniel 9:25).

And he must keep [the] covenant in force for the many/the great ones (רב) one 'seven'; and at the half of the 'seven' he will cause sacrifice and gift offering to cease (Daniel 9:27).

From this it is apparent that this one 'seven' of verse 27 occurs after the 69 'sevens' of verse 25 making the total of 70 'sevens' in verse 24. So sacrifice was ended 3½ cycles/units after the Messiah, the leader turned up. But sacrifices under law were ended by Jesus' death:

But this [man] offered one sacrifice for sins perpetually and sat down at the right hand of God (Hebrews 10:12).

And blotted out the handwritten document against us, which consisted of decrees and which was in opposition to us; and He has taken it out of the way by nailing it to the torture stake (Colossians 2:14).

So this death was in the middle of a period of 7 somethings which started with his appearance and during which a covenant was still in force. This covenant was the second Abrahamic covenant, wherein God promised to be God to Abraham's physical seed, who would have Canaan as their land, and he would be their God alone if they became circumcised:

And I will give to you and to your seed after you the land of your alien residences, even the entire land of Canaan, for a possession to time indefinite; and I will prove myself God to them (Genesis 17:8).

This exclusive arrangement for Abraham's physical seed, whereby God promised to be: **God to them,** ended when the first Gentile was admitted to be Abraham's seed at the Conversion of Cornelius in Acts 10. The Ethiopian Eunuch who was baptised by Philip in Acts 8, was baptised in water, and had been worshipping in Jerusalem, so must have been a proselyte. What we are saying is that the poor man must have been circumcised as well as being a Eunuch!!!

So since we know that Jesus' ministry contained 4 passovers it is apparent that the 'sevens' are 7 years, and his ministry was 3½ years long. So he was baptised in 29Tishri and Cornelius was converted in 36Tishri.

The exact length of Jesus' ministry from the code

There is no need to read this section if you are not familiar with the code.

For instance, I tell you in truth, There were many widows in Israel in the days of Elijah, when the heaven was shut up 3 years and 6 months, so that a great famine fell upon all the land, yet Elijah was sent to none of those [women], but only to Zarephath in the land of Sidon to a widow (Luke 4:25,26).

We use the Prophetic Principle of the Code, to deduce that this is a symbolic account. The symbolism of these verses is:

Widow	Covenant with dead mediator
Widows in Israel	2AC, Law covenant, 1AC, 3AC, Isaac's covenant, Jacob's first covenant, Jacob's second covenant, etc.
Widow in Sidon	New covenant
Famine	Food of priesthood of Pharisees is shown by Jesus to have no heavenly backing throughout his ministry
3 years 6 months of heaven shut up	The baptism into Moses failed during Jesus' ministry
Elijah	Jesus

Keep your eyes open and watch out for the leaven of the Pharisees and Sadducees (Matthew 16:6).

Elijah was a man with feelings like ours, and yet in prayer he prayed for it not to rain; and it did not rain upon the land for 3 years and 6 months. And he prayed again, and the heaven gave rain and the land put forth its fruit (James 5:17,18).

The symbolism of these verse is:

Rain	Baptism
Land during 3 years 6 months	Administration of Law by Pharisess
Land when it rained	First Christian administration
Rain	The baptism at Pentecost into the name of the holy spirit, the sealing of the apostles. The reaping of them by Jesus.
3 years 6 months of no rain upon land	The baptism into Moses failed during Jesus' ministry
Elijah	Jesus

This means that no Jew entered the law covenant after Jesus' baptism. In other words Jesus/Michael was the last Jew to enter the law. Being baptised into Moses was also being baptised into the 1AC. This means that the woman caught at adultery by the Pharisees in the account of John 8, may not have been under law if she was young enough. Now John 8 occurred between the 3rd and 4th passovers of Jesus' ministry. So it was in the year 32 AD, whereas the baptism into Moses ended in 29Tishri. So if this girl was 19 in 29, then she would be 22 in 32, and she would not have been under law. This is just guesswork !

Technical note on the date of Jesus' death:

According to http://riemann.usno.navy.mil./AA/data/docs/SpringPhenom.html, the Vernal Equinox in 34 CE was on March 22nd at 9 pm Julian Calendar. So it's 9pm,

March 20th in 34 CE Gregorian Calendar. We assume that the Spring Equinox falls between 6pm March 20th and 6pm March 21st in the BLC program. So that's OK.

There are some theologians that think that Jesus died in 30, but they base their argument on Luke 3:1 being wrong because Herod (who tried to kill Jesus) was thought to have died in 4BC. You cannot use this kind of reasoning on the holy book. Once you decide that Luke 3:1 is wrong, then why not decide that one of the 10 commandments were wrong!

But if they were right then Jesus would be born 4,000 years after 4004 BC, the date that Archbishop Ussher calculated for the birth of Adam (incorrectly), which seemed to be neat and tidy to them. His Chronology was printed in many early King James bibles. John Pratt (The Planetarian, vol. 19, no. 4, Dec. 1990, pp. 8-14) gives good evidence that Herod died in 1 AD. http://johnpratt.com/items/docs/herod/herod.html. In any event, if Luke is wrong we are wasting our time studying the bible.

Barr, James, 1985. "Why the world was created in 4004 B.C.: Archbishop Ussher and Biblical Chronology," *Bulletin of the John Rylands University Library of Manchester* **67**, No. 2, 575-608.

Newton, Sir Isaac, 1733. "Of the Times of the Birth and Passion of Christ", chapter 11 in *Observations upon the Prophecies of Daniel and the Apocalypse of St. John* (London: J. Darby and T. Browne), pp. 144-168.

The First Abrahamic Covenant was inaugurated in 1943Nisan BCE (March/April 1943 BC)

First of all we deduce the date of King Solomon's last regnal year, his 40th regnal year.

Solomon's 40th regnal year was 997 BC

The simplest way one can get to this date (that we are aware of) is by starting with the date of the fall of Jerusalem to Nebuchadnezzar in the 19th year of his reign, which was 586, a date which is relatively undisputed amongst historians - see [99], and counting back to the first year of Jehoiakim the king of Judah, which was 607. We then use Ezekiel's prophetic 390 year siege of Jerusalem in Ezekiel chapter 4 to count back to the last year of Solomon in 997. A more complicated way is to count back from Jehoiakim's first year in 607 through all of the Kings of Judah to Solomon. This is difficult because one cannot just add up all of the reigns of the Kings of Judah, as was done by Archbishop Ussher and many after him, because many of these kings were coregent with their sons following them, and these coregencies were sometimes full, in which case a year was counted to both the King and his son, and they were sometimes inferior in the case of the son so that only the father got the regnal year. Also there were many years where no king at all got the regnal year due to a dispute or no son being old enough etc. However we are the first group to do this accurately (in our opinion) and the precise Chronology is in section [91]. A third way to calculate the last and 40th regnal year of Solomon is to count backwards through the Kings of Israel starting from the historically accepted date of the fall of Samaria to Shalmanezer the King of Assyria, in the year from 723Nisan (March April) to 722Nisan. This was the 9th year of King Hoshea of Israel. This calculation is as difficult as in the case of the Kings of Judah, in fact it is more or less the same calculation. Again we have done it in section [91].

So taking the easier route, we start with the first regnal year of Nebuchadnezzar the king of Babylon being 604 BC - see [99]. We then deduce that Jerusalem fell to Nebuchadnezzar in 586 BC from the following scriptures:

And in the 5th month on the 7th [day] of the month, that is to say, the 19th year of King Nebuchadnezzar the king of Babylon, Nebuzaradan the chief of the bodyguard, the servant of the king of Babylon, came to Jerusalem. And he proceeded to burn the house of Jehovah and the king's house and all the houses of Jerusalem; and the house of every great man he burned with fire (2 Kings 25:8,9).

And in the 5th month, on the 10th day of the month, that is, [in] the 19th year of King Nebuchadrezzar, the king of Babylon, Nebuzaradan the chief of the bodyguard, who was standing before the king of Babylon, came into Jerusalem. And he proceeded to burn the house of Jehovah and the house of the king and all the houses of Jerusalem; and every great house he burned with fire (Jeremiah 52:12,13).

Josephus, the Jewish Historian who was a contemporary of Jesus, describes 586Ab10 as the day when Solomon's temple itself was actually burnt. Nebuchadnezzar's 19th year was 586 BC. Don't worry about the Nebuchadnezzar/Nebuchadrezzar distinction, names got bent somewhat with the many dialects and languages both in Israel and in Babylon, where these accounts were written (see David Rohl - 'Legends' the Book).

Jehoiakim's first regnal year was 607

The word that occurred to Jeremiah concerning all the people of Judah in the 4th year of Jehoiakim the son of Josiah, the king of Judah, that is, the first year of Nebuchadrezzar the king of Babylon (Jeremiah 25:1).

From the 13th year of Josiah the son of Amon, the king of Judah, and down to this day, these 23 years the word of Jehovah has occurred to me, and I kept speaking to you people, rising up early and speaking, but you did not listen (Jeremiah 25:3).

So the 4th year of Jehoiakim was 604 BCE so the first year of Jehoiakim was 607 BCE. 23 years from the 13th year of Josiah, i.e. taking the 13th year as the first of the 23 years of the word occurring to Jeremiah, is the 35th 'year of Josiah' which was 604, so the first year of Josiah was 638. But Josiah only reigned for 31 years:

8 years old was Josiah when he began to reign, and for 31 years he reigned in Jerusalem (2 Chronicles 34:1).

So Josiah's 31st and last regnal year was 608. Rawlinson's 'History of Ancient Egypt' has 608 as the year that Pharaoh Nechoh killed Josiah at Meggido, 'Cambridge Ancient History' has 609. The bible account says:

In his days Pharaoh Nechoh the king of Egypt came up to the king of Assyria by the river Euphrates, and King Josiah proceeded to go to meet him; but he put him to death at Megiddo as soon as he saw him. So his servants conveyed him dead in a chariot from Megiddo and brought him to Jerusalem and buried him in his grave. Then the people of the land took Jehoahaz the son of Josiah and anointed him and made him king in place of his father.

23 years old was Jehoahaz when he began to reign, and for 3 months he reigned in Jerusalem. And his mother's name was Hamutal the daughter of Jeremiah from Libnah. And he began to do what was bad in Jehovah's eyes, according to all that forefathers of his had done.

And Pharaoh Nechoh got to put him in bonds at Riblah in the land of Hamath, to keep him from reigning in Jerusalem, and then imposed a fine upon the land of a hundred silver talents and a gold talent.

Furthermore, Pharaoh Nechoh made Eliakim the son of Josiah king in place of Josiah his father and changed his name to Jehoiakim; and Jehoahaz he took and then brought to Egypt, where he eventually died. And the silver and the gold Jehoiakim gave to Pharaoh. Only he taxed the land, to give the silver at the order of Pharaoh.

According to each one's individual tax rate he exacted the silver and the gold from the people of the land, to give it to Pharaoh Nechoh.

25 years old was Jehoiakim when he began to reign, and for 11 years he reigned in Jerusalem. (2 Kings 23:29-36).

So Josiah was killed in 608, then Jehoahaz was appointed for 3 months by the people of the land, then he was stopped from reigning by Nechoh. So no one was reigning for a period and then Jehoiakim had 11 regnal years starting in 607. So Jehoiakim may have acceded in 608 or in 607. In fact Jehoiakim acceeded on 608Chislev10 (which was Wednesday 13th November 608 BC) - see [97]. He would have got 607 as his first regnal year even if his brother Jehoahaz had been reigning in it, because he was struck from the records by Nechoh who made Jehoiakim king '**in place of Josiah**', not in place of Jehoahaz. Now Jehoiakim was not a vassal king of Jehovah because he was a vassal of Pharaoh Nechoh, being chosen by him and paying him an annual tribute. Nechoh was obviously not a vassal of Jehovah since he was not a son of David. He was not even a son of Abraham. So at this point Pharaoh was 'Caesar' in Jerusalem, since Jesus said:

Pay back Caesar's things to Caesar, but God's things to God (Mark 12:17).

So if Pharaoh was getting the individual's tax, then he was Caesar and not God. So God's protection of Jerusalem ended with Jehoiakim. And the royal line of Davidic Kings representing him also ended then, officially on 607Nisan1.

Ezekiel 4 and the 390 error years of Israel

We can count back from the abandoning of Jerusalem by God to Nechoh as manifested by the Vassal Kingship of Jehoiakim, to the reign of Solomon, without having to do the entire Chronology of the kings of Judah and of Israel, by virtue of the prophecy of Ezekiel 4:

And you, O son of man, take for yourself a brick, and you must put it before you and engrave upon it a city, even Jerusalem.

And you must lay siege against it and build a siege wall against it and throw up a siege rampart against it and set encampments against it and put battering rams all around against it.

And as for you, take to yourself an iron griddle, and you must put it as an iron wall between you and the city, and you must fix your face against it, and it must get to be in a siege, and you must besiege it. It is a sign to the house of Israel.

And as for you, lie upon your left side, and you must lay the error of the house of Israel upon it. For the number of the days that you will lie upon it you will carry their error.

And I myself must give to you the years of their error to the number of 390 days, and you must carry the error of the house of Israel.

And you must complete them. And you must lie upon your right side in the second case, and you must carry the error of the house of Judah 40 days. A day for a year, a day for a year, is what I have given you (Ezekiel 4:1-6).

The iron griddle is protection from God, Ezekiel is representing the enemies of Jerusalem. This protection from God for Jerusalem fails at Pharaoh Necho's victory over Josiah at Meggido, but Jerusalem itself does not fall until Nechoh appoints Jehoiakim.

And to the siege of Jerusalem you will fix your face, with your arm bared, and you must prophesy against it.

And, look! I will put cords upon you that you may not turn yourself from your one side to your other side, until you will have completed the days of your siege (Ezekiel 4:7,8).

So the siege of Jerusalem lasts 390 days, and is completed before Ezekiel turns over for the next 40 days on his other side. So Jerusalem is besieged with iron wall protection from God for 390 years, then this protection goes at the end of this period. This entire 390 year siege period is also an error period for the house of Israel. This error started in Tishri in the year in which Solomon died, his last regnal year:

And Solomon began seeking to put Jeroboam to death. So Jeroboam got up and went running off to Egypt to Shishak the king of Egypt, and he continued in Egypt until Solomon's death (1 Kings 11:40).

And it came about that as soon as Jeroboam the son of Nebat heard of it while he was yet in Egypt (because he had run off on account of King Solomon, that Jeroboam might dwell in Egypt), then they sent and called him (1 Kings 12:2,3).

And it came about that as soon as all Israel heard that Jeroboam had returned, they at once sent and called him to the assembly and made him king over all Israel. None became a follower of the house of David except the tribe of Judah by itself. (1 Kings 12:20).

And Jeroboam began to say in his heart: Now the kingdom will return to the house of David. If this people continues going up to render sacrifices in the house of Jehovah in Jerusalem, the heart of this people will also be bound to return to their lord, Rehoboam the king of Judah; and they will certainly kill me and return to Rehoboam the king of Judah. Consequently the king took counsel and made two golden calves and said to the people: It is too much for you to go up to Jerusalem. Here is your God, O Israel, that brought you up out of the land of Egypt. Then he placed the one in Bethel, and the other he put in

Dan. And this thing came to be a <u>cause for sin</u>, and the people began to go before the one as far as Dan.
And he began to make a house of high places and to make priests from the people in general, who did not happen to be of the sons of Levi. And Jeroboam went on to make a festival in the eighth month on the fifteenth day of the month, like the festival that was in Judah, that he might make offerings upon the altar that he had made in Bethel, to sacrifice to the calves that he had made; and he put in attendance at Bethel the priests of the high places that he had made. (1 Kings 12:26-32).

So Jeroboam returned immediately on Solomon's death. And by the 7th month, Tishri, the sin of the house of Israel had started, since none of the subjects of Jeroboam would have celebrated booths on the 7th month in the face of the wonderful new improved festival arranged so conveniently for the 8th month, with the majestic golden calves. This kind of thing is typical of state run false religions. Now every 7th secular year, which ran from Tishri to Elul, was a land sabbath under the law of Moses:

When you eventually come into the land that I am giving you, then you must observe a sabbath to Jehovah. Six years you should sow your field with seed, and six years you should prune your vineyard, and you must gather the land's produce. But in the seventh year there should be a sabbath of complete rest for the land. Your field you must now sow with seed, and your vineyard you must not prune (Leviticus 25:2-4).

The bible shows that the agricultural year, which was the fiscal year in what was an agricultural economy, started in the seventh month, Tishri:

And you will carry on your festival of weeks with the first ripe fruits of the wheat harvest, and the festival of ingathering, at the turn of the year (Exodus 34:22).

Also the festival of the harvest of the first ripe fruits of your labours, of what you sow in the field, and the festival of ingathering at the outgoing of the year, when you gather your labour from the field (Exodus 23:16).

The festival of booths you should celebrate for yourself seven days when you make an ingathering from your threshing floor and your oil and winepress (Deuteronomy 16:13).

So the turn and outgoing, meaning beginning, of the agricultural year was the seventh month. The ingathering of all the crops is obviously a good end to an agricultural year. The modern Jews celebrate their new year on Tishri1.

The agricultural year is rather like the tax year in the UK, which doesn't run from January1 to January1 but rather from April5 to April5.

Now we know that this 390 year error period contained land sabbath errors, since the house of Israel was evicted from it's land and taken prisoner to Babylon because of these errors.

Furthermore, he carried off those remaining from the sword captive to Babylon, and they came to be servants to him and his sons until the royalty of Persia began to reign; to fulfill Jehovah's word by the mouth of Jeremiah, until the land had paid off its sabbaths. All the days of lying desolated it kept sabbath, to fulfill seventy years (2 Chronicles 36:20,21).

So these 390 error years are agricultural years running from Tishri to Elul, just as the land sabbath years did.

Now we know that the iron griddle had officially failed by Nisan1 in 607, the start of the first regnal year of Jehoiakim. So the agricultural year in which the iron griddle failed was the one from 608Tishri to 607Elul. So this was the 390th year of error for the house of Israel and so 997Tishri to 996Elul BCE was the first agricultural year of error. So Solomon's last regnal year was from 997Nisan to 997Adar BCE - see [BLC].

Counting back from Solomon to Abraham's entrance into Canaan

And the days that Solomon had reigned in Jerusalem over all Israel were 40 years (1 Kings 11:42).

So since his 40th year was 997, his first was 1036.

And it came about in the 480th year after the sons of Israel came out from the land of Egypt, in the 4th year, in the month of Ziv, that is, the second month, after Solomon became king over Israel, that he proceeded to build the house to Jehovah (1 Kings 6:1).

The 4th year of Solomon was 1033. If this was the 480th after the Exodus, then the zeroth after the exodus was 1513. So the Exodus from Egypt was in 1513 during the festival of cakes from Nisan15 to Nisan21. The Jews actually crossed the Red Sea on 1513Nisan21, which is when they stopped having to eat half cooked cakes in a hurry.

And the dwelling of the sons of Israel, who had dwelt in Egypt, was 430 years.

And it came about at the end of the 430 years, it even came about on this very day that all the armies of Jehovah went out of the land of Egypt (Exodus 12:40,41).

Further, I say this: As to the covenant previously validated by God, the Law that has come into being 430 years later does not invalidate it, so as to abolish the promise (Galatians 3:17).

So all the armies of Jehovah entered Egypt 430 years before they left. But we know from Paul, that Abraham crossed over the Euphrates from Haran entering Canaan which was under Egyptian control, inaugurating his covenant with God, 430 years before the first part of the Law of Moses, the passover festival, was held on Nisan14 in 1513:

And Jehovah proceeded to say to Abram: Go your way out of your country and from your relatives and from the house of your father to the country that I shall show you; and I shall make a great nation out of you and I shall bless you and I will make your name great; and prove yourself a blessing. And I will bless those who bless you, and him that calls down evil upon you I shall curse, and all the families of the ground will certainly bless themselves by means of you.

At that Abram went just as Jehovah had spoken to him, and Lot went with him. And Abram was 75 years old when he went out from Haran.

So Abram took Sarai his wife and Lot the son of his brother and all the goods that they had accumulated and the souls whom they had acquired in Haran, and they got on their way out to go to the land of Canaan. Finally they came to the land of Canaan (Genesis 12:1-5).

Now Canaan, the promised land is defined by:

To your seed I will give this land, from the river of Egypt to the great river, the river Euphrates (Genesis 15:17,18).

So when Abraham crossed the Euphrates, then he had finished obeying the commandment of God, and the covenant was inaugurated. This occurred 430 years before 1513Nisan14, the passover day, the day before the sons of Israel started the Exodus from Egypt. So Abraham crossed into the Promised land, which was under Egyptian control in 1943Nisan.

Josephus, the Jewish historian from Jesus' time states:

They left Egypt in the month of Xanthicus (Nisan) on the 15th day of the month, 430 years after our forefather Abraham cane into Canaan, but 215 years only after Jacob removed into Egypt. It was the 80th year of the age of Moses (Book 2 Chapter 15 Antiquities of the Jews).

Stephen the Martyr stated before he was stoned to death:

He said: Men, brothers and fathers, hear. The God of glory appeared to our forefather Abraham while he was in Mesopotamia, before he took up residence in Haran, and he said to him:

'Go out from your land and from your relatives and come on into the land I shall show you.'

Then he went out from the land of the Chaldeans and took up residence in Haran. And from there, after his father died, [God] caused him to change his residence to this land in which you now dwell (Acts 7:2-4).

Joshua informs us:

And Joshua went on to say to all the people: This is what Jehovah the God of Israel has said, It was on the other side of the River that your forefathers dwelt a long time ago, Terah the father of Abraham and the father of Nahor, and they used to serve other gods.
In time I took your forefather Abraham from the other side of the River and had him walk through all the land of Canaan and made his seed many. So I gave him Isaac (Joshua 24:2,3).

So putting this all together: Abraham crossed the Euphrates, coming from Haran (North of that River, in Mesopotamia) and going into Canaan, which was an Egyptian dependency, in 1943Nisan. This action actually inaugurated but did not validate the 1AC - see [9]. We know that he crossed the river after his father died and we know that we was told to cross the river by God before his father died. So it is apparent that he crossed it fairly soon after his father died in Haran, since the family were on the way to Canaan (modulo a mourning period).

31 After that Terah took Abram his son and Lot, the son of Haran, his grandson, and Sarai his daughter-in-law, the wife of Abram his son, and they went with him out of Ur of the Chaldeans to go to the land of Canaan. In time they came to Haran and took up dwelling there.
32 And the days of Terah came to be 205 years. Then Terah died in Haran (Genesis 11:31,32).

So Abram was 75 years old when his dad was 205 years old and in this year in Nisan he crossed over the Euphrates. It is not possible that he crossed the Euphates in the year after his father died (when he would have been 76) because he crossed it in the month of Nisan, the 7th month of the pre-exodus year and Haran was only a few days journey from the Euphrates and he had been instructed by God to cross the river before he reached Haran with his father.

From Abraham's Entrance into Canaan back to Adam's birth

A calendar year is a year starting on the first calendar day of the year. For us this is January 1, for the Jews it was Tishri 1 before they left Egypt and Nisan 1 after they left Egypt. To the Jew a boy became 12 years old on the first day of the 12th whole calendar year of his life. Such a 'boy' could have actually been, in today's terms, anything from 11 years and 1 day old, if he was born on Adar 30, to 12 years old less 1 day, if he was born on Nisan 2. Similarly a king's first regnal year was the first calendar year in which he was reigning on the first day of that year. This gives rise to the accession year, this being the Jewish calendar year preceding the first regnal year, during which the king ruled for a period starting after Nisan 1. In fact the middle east even today thinks of men's ages and king's reigns in terms of actual calendar years, not years from their date of birth or from the date of their investiture. Even in Britain, the Jubilee was the same Gordon thinks. With this method of determining age, a one year old lamb is a lamb in its first whole year, which is apparent from the legal requirements for sacrificing animals. For more on this - see [BLC] and [How Ages and Reigns are counted].

This understanding transforms Genesis into a book of exact Chronology as we shall see:

For simplicity we will define the Hebrew year of Adam's birth as year 0, these years ran from Tishri to Elul. The typical wording of a verse in Genesis 5 is:

And he lived, Kenan 70 year and he fathered namely Mahalalel (Genesis 5:13 NIVHEOT interlinear bible).

This means that Mahalalel was born in the 70th whole calendar year of Kenan's life. Kenan was 70 years old all through this year. Knowing this we can construct the whole chronology of the ancestors of mankind up to the inauguration of the Abrahamic covenant from Genesis 5 & Genesis 11. We have already seen that this covenant was inaugurated in 1943Nisan which was in the Hebrew year starting 1944Tishri, the year in which Abraham was 75 years old. We could, if we were so inclined, count the whole thing backwards and deduce, from the crossing of the Euphrates in the year starting 1944Tishri, that Adam was born in the year starting 4027Tishri. But we prefer to count forwards, because it's easier that way! Doing this, we find that Abraham was 75, 2083 years after the year in which Adam was born.

Son	Father's Age	Creation Year	BLC Year start
Adam born	X	0	4027Tishri
Adam's first whole calendar year	1	1	4026Tishri
Seth born	130	130	3897Tishri
Seth's first whole calendar year	1	131	3896Tishri
Enosh born	105	235	3792Tishri
Enosh's first whole calendar year	1	236	3791Tishri

Kenan born	90	325	3702Tishri
Kenan's first whole calendar year	1	326	3701Tishri
Mahalalel born	70	395	3632Tishri
Mahalalel's first whole calendar year	1	396	3631Tishri
Jared born	65	460	3567Tishri
Jared's first whole calendar year	1	461	3566Tishri
Enoch born	162	622	3405Tishri
Enoch's first whole calendar year	1	623	3404Tishri
Methuselah born	65	687	3340Tishri
Methusaleh's 1st whole calendar year	1	688	3339Tishri
Lamech born	187	874	3153Tishri
Lamech's first whole calendar year	1	875	3152Tishri
Noah born	182	1056	2971Tishri
Noah's first whole calendar year	1	1057	2970Tishri
Noah's 600th whole calendar year	600	1656	2371Tishri

And Noah son of 600 year and the flood he was waters upon the earth (Genesis 7:6 NIVHEOT).

In year of 600 year to life of Noah, in the month the second, in 17th day to the month in the day the that, they burst all of springs of great deep and floodgates of the heavens, they were opened (Genesis 7:11 NIVHEOT).

In other words in the 600th year of Noah's life, when he was 600 years old, the flood occurred, on Heshvan 17. It is an impossible thing to be 600 years old in your 600th year of life by modern day reckoning of age, but the two statements are identical by the Jewish reckoning.

Event	Father's Age	Creation Year	BLC Year start
Flood starts - Noah	600	1656	2371Tishri
Waters had drained off - Noah	601	1657	2370Tishri
Earth had dried off	601	1657	2370Tishri

And he was in 601 year in first [month] in first [day] to the month, they dried up, the waters, from upon the earth, and he removed Noah namely covering of the ark and he looked and Look! they were dry faces of the ground. And in the month the second on 17 day to the month, she was dry the earth (Genesis 8:13,14 NIVHEOT).

So the flood was entirely contained in the Creation year 1656, which ran from 2371T to 2370E, although 1657 was a bit muddy!

These lines of Shem, Shem son of 100 year and he fathered Arpachshad, two after the flood (Genesis 11:10 NIVHEOT).

One year after the flood was the year 1657, so two years after the flood was the year 1658.

Son	Father's Age	Calendar Year	BLC year start
Arpachshad born	100	1658	2369Tishri
Arpachshad's first whole calendar year	1	1659	2368Tishri
Shelah born	35	1693	2334Tishri
Shelah's first whole calendar year	1	1694	2333Tishri
Eber born	30	1723	2304Tishri
Eber's first whole calendar year	1	1724	2303Tishri
Peleg born	34	1757	2270Tishri
Peleg's first whole calendar year	1	1758	2269Tishri
Reu born	30	1787	2240Tishri
Reu's first whole calendar year	1	1788	2239Tishri
Serug born	32	1819	2208Tishri
Serug's first whole calendar year	1	1820	2207Tishri
Nahor born	30	1849	2178Tishri
Nahor's first whole calendar year	1	1850	2177Tishri
Terah born	29	1878	2149Tishri
Terah's first whole calendar year	1	1879	2148Tishri
Terah dies, 205th whole calendar year	205	2083	1944Tishri

We have already deduced that Abraham crossed the Euphrates when he was 75 years old in the same year that his father died aged 205. So now we have identified the year 2083 with the Jewish year from Tishri 1944BCE to Elul 1943BCE, the one containing 1943Nisan, when we know that the crossing occurred. With this as a starting point the above chronology proves that Adam was born in the Jewish year starting 4027Tishri. The flood is therefore put as starting on 2371Heshvan17.

The Chronology we have so far deduced

Jesus died on 33Nisan14 (April 1)

Jesus was born on 2Tishri10 BC (October 9)

The First Abrahamic covenant was inaugurated in 1943Nisan BC

The Flood started on 2371Heshvan17

Adam was born in the year from 4027 Tishri to 4026 Elul

Now we can deduce the date of Armageddon by two different methods both of which give the same answer from these dates.

Armageddon from the corresponding ransom and the 7,000 year 'week'

We shall find out that just as God worked creatively for 6 'days' and then rested from creating anything new on the 7th creative day of Genesis 1,2. So man works for six 1,000 year working 'days' and then rests on his 7th 1,000 year day, his sabbath, the Kingdom of God, this being a rest from our work in this system of trying to combat our intrinsic desire to sin in the face of a giant misleading by Satan. We need to do these works in order to gain entry to the next system. The next system however does not require such works because Satan is dead. So the 7,000 year 'week' of man starts at the beginning of the 7th creative day of God.

And God proceeded to bless the seventh day and make it sacred, because on it he has been resting from all his work that God has created for the purpose of making (Genesis 2:3).

But he answered them: My Father has kept working until now, and I keep working (John 5:17).

So God rested from his creative works only in the 7th creative day of Genesis. This being the day when he did not create anything.

For if Joshua had led them into a place of rest, [God] would not afterward have spoken of another day.

So there remains a sabbath resting for the people of God. (This being the real promised land, the Kingdom of God, which we all pray for in the Lord's prayer, which the greater Joshua leads us into).

For the man that has entered into [God's] rest has also himself rested from his own works, just as God did from his own.

Let us therefore do our utmost to enter into that rest, for fear anyone should fall in the same pattern of disobedience (Hebrews 4:2-11).

So the Kingdom of God is a sabbath. It is a rest from man's work. Hence we read:

For Lord of the sabbath is what the son of man is (Matthew 12:8).

But it is a sabbath that lasts for 1,000 years:

And I saw an angel coming down out of heaven with the key of the abyss and a great chain in his hand.

And he seized the dragon, the original serpent, who is the Devil and Satan, and bound him for 1,000 years.

And he hurled him into the abyss and shut [it] and sealed [it] over him, that he might not mislead the nations anymore until the thousand years were ended. After these things he must be let loose for a little while.

And I saw thrones, and there were those who sat down on them, and power of judging was given them. Yes, I saw the souls of those executed with the axe for the witness they bore to Jesus and for speaking about God, and those who had worshiped neither the wild beast nor its image and who had not received the mark upon their forehead and upon their hand. And they came to life and ruled as kings with the Christ for 1,000 years.

The rest of the dead did not come to life until the 1,000 years were ended. This is the first resurrection.

Happy and holy is anyone having part in the first resurrection; over these the second death has no authority, but they will be priests of God and of the Christ, and will rule as kings with him for the 1,000 years.

Now as soon as the 1,000 years have been ended, Satan will be let loose out of his prison (Revelation 20:1-7).

But it is also a 'day', being the last 'day' and the 'day' of judgmement:

For this is the will of my Father, that everyone that beholds the Son and exercises faith in him should have everlasting life, and I will resurrect him at the last day (John 6:40).

Martha said to him: I know he will rise in the resurrection on the last day (John 11:24).

He that disregards me and does not receive my sayings has one to judge him. The word that I have spoken is what will judge him in the last day (John 12:48).

But by the same word the heavens and the earth that are now are stored up for fire and are being reserved to the day of judgment and of destruction of the ungodly men (2 Peter 3:7).

This is how love has been made perfect with us, that we may have freeness of speech in the day of judgment, because, just as that one is, so are we ourselves in this world (1 John 4:17).

So it is a 1,000 year sabbath day of judgement. But a sabbath is the 7th of 7 equal periods. So there must be a 6,000 year working week preceeding this sabbath. But this is what Peter is referring to when he says in the context of the destruction at Armageddon:

For, according to their wish, this fact escapes their notice, that there were heavens from of old and an earth standing compactly out of water and in the midst of water by the word of God; and by those [means] the world of that time suffered destruction when it was deluged with water.

But by the same word the heavens and the earth that are now are stored up for fire and are being reserved to the <u>day of judgment</u> and of destruction of the ungodly men.

However, let this one fact not be escaping your notice, beloved ones, that <u>one day</u> is with the Lord as 1,000 years and 1,000 years as one day.

The Lord is not slow respecting his promise, as some people consider slowness, but he is patient with you because he does not desire any to be destroyed but desires all to attain to repentance.

Yet the Lord's day will come as a thief, in which the heavens will pass away with a hissing noise, but the elements being intensely hot will be dissolved, and earth and the works in it will be discovered.

Since all these things are thus to be dissolved, what sort of persons ought you to be in holy acts of conduct and deeds of godly devotion, awaiting and keeping close in mind the presence of the day of the God, through which [the] heavens being on fire will be dissolved and [the] elements being intensely hot will melt!

But there are new heavens and a new earth that we are awaiting according to his promise, and in these righteousness is to dwell (2 Peter 3:5-13).

Quite obviously this taking 1,000 years for a day must not escape our notice in respect of a promise of destruction and of a new heavens and a new earth, i.e. a promise of the kingdom of God. A 'day' which we know is 1,000 years long. In fact the **'day of judgement and destruction of the ungodly men'** of verse 7 is one of the 1,000 year days of verse 8. So Peter is saying that one should take 1,000 years for one day in our calculations as regards this promise. So the kingdom of God is a 1,000 year Sabbath day, or judgement day, and being a sabbath it is preceeded by 6 other 1,000 years days making a 6,000 year working week.

What then are man's own works ?

Now the works of the flesh are manifest, and they are fornication, uncleanness, loose conduct, idolatry, practice of spiritism, enmities, strife, jealousy, fits of anger, contentions, divisions, sects, envies, drunken bouts, revelries, and things like these. As to these things I am forewarning you, the same way as I did forewarn you, that those who practice such things will not inherit God's kingdom (Galatians 5:19-21).

In the sweat of your face you will eat bread until you return to the ground, for out of it you were taken. For dust you are and to dust you will return (Genesis 3:19).

So we have to work to eat both physically and spiritually, and we have our fleshly works to try and conquer in the face of opposition and corruption from Satan, this being our spiritual work in this system. So man's working week started when Adam sinned and was evicted from Eden, and started having to work for a living. This was coincident with God starting his rest, since his last creative act was when he made long garments of skin for Adam and Eve:

And Jehovah God proceeded to make long garments of skin for Adam and for his wife and to clothe them (Genesis 3:21).

So much more becoming than fig leaf loin coverings! This is a beautiful cryptic scripture. The long garments of skin were their new bodies, which replaced their indefinitely long garments of skin, which they had before they sinned. In fact the first Adamic body had a maximum lifetime of 960 years - see [235]. YHWH (Jehovah, Yahweh, the true God, Creator) created two new creations, namely an ageing man and an ageing woman. Before this they had just been created as steady state fleshwise perfect creatures, creatures whose flesh does not deteriorate with time. But now these creatures were to become slowly deteriorating fleshly creatures. It is a masterful thing that Jehovah did. To build a car that slowly deteriorates in an uncontrolled way is easy. But, to build one that deteriorates according to plan and maintains all of its faculties during this whole degradation process requires complete understanding of all things mechanical.

In any event, the bible itself describes the new corrupting bodies of Adam and Eve as something that God himself 'proceeded to make'. And the corruption in the bodies is of course a result of and a physical declaration of the corruption in their spirits. But now the very same one, out of his undeserved kindness, as a result of the courage and love of Jesus Christ, is prepared to make a judicial declaration concerning their sons and their daughters and finally concerning both Adam and Eve themselves, that they are righteous in spirit, through the blood of the Christ. And just as the man's and the woman's bodies became corrupt as they left Eden, so we will become incorruptible, though still mortal in many cases, when we enter into the next system, the second Eden at Armageddon.

Scientifically, God would presumably have changed the genes of Adam and Eve, from permanently renewable copies, to slowly degrading copies, and this would have certainly been a divine act of creation, albeit a destructive act of creation. Therefore the seventh creative day began when Adam was thrown out of the Garden after he sinned and after God had remade their bodies, this being God's sabbath from his creative works. But when God stopped working at creation, man started working at cultivation:

God put him out of the garden of Eden, to cultivate the ground from which he had been taken (Genesis 3:23).

In the garden there was no cultivation, God planted the trees himself:

Thus Jehovah God made to grow out of the ground every tree desirable to one's sight and good for food (Genesis 2:9).

So man's working week started at his eviction from Eden. So whilst Adam was resting in the garden, God was working. And as soon as Adam starting working God started resting. So mankind in this world, since the founding of the world, at his sin, has not been able to enter into God's rest (i.e. have a sabbath from our works which is coincident with a sabbath from his works). But in the Kingdom of God we do, at last, for it is the second Eden.

Let the one who has an ear hear what the spirit says to the congregations: To him that conquers I will grant to eat of the tree of life, which is in the paradise of God (Revelation 2:7).

So the Kingdom of God starts 6,000 years after Adam's sin, which was the founding of the world and the start of the 7th creative day. The next question therefore is:

When did Adam sin?

For there is one God, and one mediator between God and men, a man, Christ Jesus, who gave himself a corresponding ransom for all -- [this is] what is to be witnessed to at its own particular times (1 Timothy 2:5,6).

It is even so written: 'The first man Adam became a living soul.' The last Adam became a life-giving spirit (1 Corinthians 15:45).

So Jesus' ransom corresponded to Adam's sin. And Jesus corresponded to Adam. Now Jesus died 33½ years after he was born. So Adam sinned 33½ years after he was born. It is as simple as that.

Because Jesus was perfect for 33½ years. So if Adam was perfect for 32 or for 34 years, would Jesus have been a corresponding ransom? No, because obeying the law (whether it is the law of the tree in the case of Adam or the law of Moses in the case of Jesus) is a test that involves a certain time period. Anyone can obey the law for 10 minutes.

So Adam sinned 33½ years after he was born. But he was born in Tishri, because the ancient bible calendar (before the flood and before the Exodus) started then, and in fact all very ancient calendars started in Tishri because this was when Adam was born see - Ancient Calendars. But we have discovered that Jesus was also born in Tishri in 2 BCE. So this is another reason why Adam was born in Tishri, since he corresponds perfectly with the last Adam, Jesus.

So he was born in 4027Tishri, so he sinned in 3993Nisan, 33½ years later, in the same month that Jesus paid for his sin, Nisan. Now 6,000 years after 3993Nisan, the founding of the World, is 2008 Nisan (there was no 0 BC, it went 1BC then 1AD). So Armageddon starts in 2008Nisan.

One can also deduce that the date of Adam's sin was 3993Nisan (March/April) BC from the Exedenic Times [133], using the Times Principle [code] of the code. In pictorial terms we have:

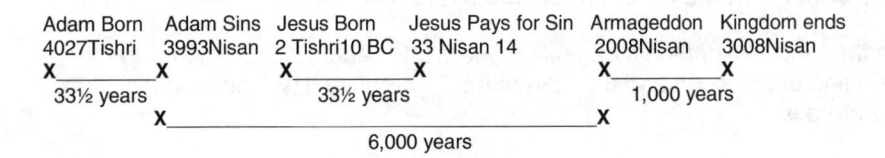

```
Adam Born    Adam Sins   Jesus Born     Jesus Pays for Sin   Armageddon   Kingdom ends
4027Tishri   3993Nisan   2 Tishri10 BC  33 Nisan 14          2008Nisan    3008Nisan
X_____X           X_____X                    X_____X
  33½ years                 33½ years                          1,000 years
             X_____X
                              6,000 years
```

For several other ways of deducing the date of Armageddon, which we worked out in 1993/1994 see - letter to the Elders [F] (It takes a long time to load!).

So now we see why the rock (not the rock mass who is the Christ but the rock - Peter), for that is what his name means, the one with the keys to the kingdom, has asked us to keep this in mind. For what would be the point of keeping in mind that there is this week in which every day is 1,000 years long if we were never to know when this week began?? Truly that would be a waste of time. There is no point in knowing that Armageddon is 6,000 years after 'x'! There is no point in keeping this in mind unless at some stage one is made aware of the value of 'x'!

Well, in fact, x is Nisan 14, 3993BCE, for this was the first ever passover, the original passover. For really the angel should have killed Adam physically, but he did not, in the kindness of God, he passed over him. And the same angel then gave his life as a ransom for him, having spared him at the instruction of his father. But 6,000 years after 3993Nisan is 2008Nisan, where a greater passover still will occur !

In fact Hebrews tells us that: **his works were finished from the founding of the world** (Hebrews 4:3)

So that the blood of all the prophets spilled from the founding of the world may be required from this generation (Luke 11:50).

Father, as to what you have given me, I wish that, where I am, they also may be with me, in order to behold my glory that you have given me, because you loved me before the founding of the world (John 17:24).

Adam was a prophet, because he is quoted in Genesis 2, and all scripture is prophetic, being inspired. The spilling of his blood was the founding of the world.

In fact since Jesus was born on Tishri 10 then so was Adam. Now the BLC program that we have written does not go back before 1999BC, but if we use the metonic cycle (which states that every 19 years the solar and lunar cycles concide) and count back in say 380 year chunks (20 x 19 years) from say 3800 years before Adam was born, i.e. 227Tishri10 BC, then one can see from the pattern of which Gregorian days Tishri10 falls on in the Gregorian calendar that Adam was born on September 20th 4027 plus or minus 1 or 2 days. But this period contained the autumnal equinox when the moon starts to dominate over the sun. So Armageddon which occurs on 2008Nisan14 which is March 21 2008, the vernal equinox when the sun begins to dominate over the moon, is the complete antithesis of Adam's birth on 4027Tishri10 which was more than likely on the autumnal equinox around September 21 4027.

In the sort of irony that this world is full of, we are going to have over 5 billion people on this earth celebrating the Sabbath every week (by not working), right up to and in fact beyond, the very day of Nisan 16, 2008 CE (March 23rd 2008), which is the first day of the greater Sabbath which all of their seventh day celebrations have been symbolising. It being the first day of the Kingdom of God.

And nearly all of these people who celebrate these festivals are not going to accept the existence of the greater festival which their actions have been prophesying 52 times a year for the last 3500 years. It will be just as it was with the Jews. Why are we so blind ??? Why is Satan so successful ??? Men will actually celebrate the Sabbath (or at least have a Saturday/Sunday) ten times in the kingdom of God, before the son of man is revealed! How can they be that stupid ??? Truly spiritual things are more powerful than physical things. And truly men's hearts destroy their minds.

Truly the courage to reason out the existence of the invisible from one's perception of the visible is what is lacking in mankind. A race of beings who took 5,000 years after they had started killing each other in wars (in the city states of Mesopotamia in 3500 BC) to deduce that the reason why their fellow man just fell to the ground when he was chopped to pieces was Gravity.

Say to those who are anxious at heart: Be strong! Do not be afraid. Look! Your own God will come with vengeance itself. God [will come] even with a repayment. He himself will come and save you people. At that time the eyes of the blind ones will be opened, and the very ears of the deaf ones will be unstopped (Isaiah 35:4,5).

Be aware too of Satan. He has the name 'death', being the cause of it. He is the 4th horseman of the apocalypse - the one called 'death' - not a pretty name. He starts riding after famine who start riding in 2002Elul we currently believe - see [151]. He rules and has been ruling as king over most of mankind for 4,000 thousand of the 6,000 years:

Nevertheless, death ruled as king from Adam down to Moses, even over those who had not sinned after the likeness of the transgression by Adam, who bears a resemblance to him that was to come (Romans 5:14).

God became king of the Jews when they agreed to obey his law, for the king is the law maker. At that time, i.e. 1513Nisan14, when they celebrated the passover, God became king of some of mankind (the ones who were descendants of Jacob).

For if by the trespass of the one [man] death ruled as king through that one, much more will those who receive the abundance of the undeserved kindness and of the free gift of righteousness rule as kings in life through the one [person], Jesus Christ (Romans 5:17).

Satan, death, is ruling as king now over the whole world physically. But there have been two 1,000 year periods in the last 6,000 years during which he was locked up - see [242].

Armageddon from the Midst Prophecy

Jesus died in the exact centre of the First Abrahamic Covenant, the mid point between its inauguration and Armageddon.

The Hebrew and Greek words: תוך and קרב and μεσω: all mean: midst, middle, centre, mid-point among or within depending on the context. But תוך normally means: within, among, whereas קרב normally means: in the centre of (according to A. Tennuchi).

And I will tabernacle in the <u>midst</u> (תוך) of the sons of Israel, and I will prove to be their God. And they will certainly know that I am Jehovah their God, who brought them out of the land of Egypt that I may tabernacle in the <u>midst</u> (תוך) of them. I am Jehovah their God (Exodus 29:45,46).

Here, God resides among the sons of Israel in the Tabernacle, the first moveable temple of God.

In the <u>midst</u> (קרב) of the years Oh bring it to life! In the <u>midst</u> (קרב) of the years may you make it known (Habakkuk 3:2).
In the middle of a period of years, something is resurrected, something is made known!

A prophet from your own <u>midst</u> (קרב), from your brothers, like me, is what Jehovah your God will raise up for you .... A prophet I shall raise up for them from the <u>midst</u> (קרב) of their brothers, like you, and I shall indeed put my words in his mouth (Deuteronomy 18:15-18).
This prophet was Jesus, he was raised up in the middle of his brothers!

And he said to the man with the withered hand: Get up and come to the <u>centre</u> (το μεσον) (Mark 3:3).
Jesus positioned himself in 'the centre'.

I am in your <u>midst</u> (μεσω) as the one ministering (Luke 22:27).

John answered them, saying: I baptize in water. In the <u>middle</u> (μεσος) of you one is standing whom you do not know (John 1:26). John baptised into the First Abrahamic Covenant.

John the baptist said:

And do not presume to say to yourselves, 'As a father we have Abraham.' For I say to you that God is able to raise up children to Abraham from these stones (Matthew 3:9).

You are the sons of the prophets and of the covenant which God covenanted with your forefathers, saying to Abraham: And in your seed all the families of the earth will be blessed (Acts 3:25).

So Jesus is in the midst of the sons of Abraham, for they are his brothers, sons by the 1AC, for this is the covenant into which John was baptising people. So Jesus stands in the middle of the 1AC, and 'in the midst of the years' it is brought to life (resurrected) says Habakkuk and it is made known (God's plan for salvation through the ransom of Jesus - his death). So quite plainly Jesus dies and/or is resurrected in the middle of the 1AC.

Now we know that this covenant started in 1943Nisan and that Jesus died and was resurrected in 33 Nisan, precisely Hebrew 1975 years later, so Armageddon is a further 1975 years after Jesus' death, i.e. 2008Nisan.

But we know that Jesus, the 30 year old non adamic human who died at his baptism on 29Tishri10, with the entrance of Michael, was actually the validation sacrifice for the 1AC. So it looks rather likely that Abraham crossed the Euphrates on Nisan14. Not only that but Armageddon is the greatest passover of them all, wherein the firstborn sons of the Kingdom are not killed but the rest of mankind is. So really Nisan14 is going to be the last day of this system, and therefore the last day of possible entrance into the 1AC for any man. So this Midst Prophecy is exact to the day of the BLC.

Now beloved reader, can you see the great symbolism of this prophecy. For God's plan to save man rests entirely on the shoulders of one man, Jesus Christ, and in the case of those born after 1943, all are blessed through the 1AC. The 1AC rests entirely on the validation sacrifice that Jesus made. So given that the whole covenant is supported by one man, where should we place him underneath it to balance it all upon his shoulders? Obviously 'dead' centre by the principle of the see saw. So here it is:

Nisan 14, 1943 BCE	Nisan 14, 33CE	Nisan14, 2008 CE
Covenant inauguarated	Jesus' sacrifice	End of this system
X_____	_____	_____X
1975 BLC Years	X 1975 BLC Years	

As if this was not amazing enough, have another sign:

If we look at the First Abrahamic Covenant from the Solar Calendar (Gregorian) point of view we have 1943Nisan14 being April10 and 33Nisan14 being March31 and 2008Nisan14 being March21. So each half of the covenant is 1975 Solar years less 10 days. So Jesus died in the middle of the Abrahamic covenant to the day, as measured both by the BLC and the Gregorian (True Solar) Calendar!!

Nisan 14, 1943 BCE	Nisan 14, 33CE	Nisan14, 2008 CE
April 10 1943 BCE	March 31 33CE	March 21 2008 CE
Covenant inauguarated	Jesus' sacrifice	End of this system
X		X
1975 Years less 10 days X	1975 Years less 10 days	
721,344 Solar days	721,344 Solar days	

Both half periods of the covenant are 10 days less than 1975 years with 493 Leap years and 20 Century years and 5 Quadracentury years. The Gregorian calendar has an extra day (a leap year) if the year is divisible by 4 and but not if the year is a Century year unless it is a Quadracentury year. So the total number of Solar days in the 1975 Gregorian years in question, in both cases is:

1975x365+494(Leap years 36 to 2008AD) - 20 (Century years) + 5(Quadracentury years) = 721,354 days
1975x365+494(Leap years 32 to 1941BC) - 20 (Century years) + 5(Quadracentury years) = 721,354 days

To get a true Solar calendar BC, since there was no 0BC, we take 1BC as 0, and 101BC as -100 etc. So we just move the leap years one year back BC.

Also, there will be signs in sun and moon and stars, and on the earth anguish of nations, not knowing the way out because of the roaring of the sea and [its] agitation (Luke 21:25).

So Jesus' death is dead centre of the 1AC as measured by the Biblical lunar Calendar and as measured by a true Solar calendar. That is astonishing. Presumably there is some astral centredness going on here too??

So the end of the world is 2008 March 21st. Actually the Kingdom of God starts on the 3rd day counting inclusively, as in the case of all system changes of God, this being 2008 March 23rd. And Armageddon is the first 150 days of the Kingdom of God - see [154], [163]. For the Kingdom of God is the 1,000 year 'day' of destruction of ungodly men and judgement of many of those who enter it.

But by the same word the heavens and the earth that are now are stored up for fire and are being reserved to the day of judgment and of destruction of the ungodly men.
However, let this one fact not be escaping your notice, beloved ones, that one day is with Jehovah as 1,000 years and 1,000 years as one day (2 Peter 3:7,8).

So: Cry out shrilly and shout for joy! Oh you inhabitress of Zion, for great in the MIDST of you is the Holy one of Israel (Isaiah 12:6).

[17] Logical Pathways and One Step Thinking

Logical Pathways
One Step Thinking

Logical pathways are the basis of spirituality

[1] Jesus existed, this is a historical fact, witnessed to by the bible and by Roman (Tacitus) and Jewish (Josephus) historians.
[2] Jesus had a lot of power, this is evident from the number of Christians today and from the calendar.
[3] Jesus never abused his power so as to procure riches status or women for himself.
[4] Every other man that has ever lived after him, who had anything approaching that type of power, abused it to some extent to procure riches, status or women for himself.
[5] Every man that has ever lived after Jesus was a son of Adam.

Therefore all sons of Adam abuse their power to some extent.

Since all sons of Adam abuse their power to some extent, and since Jesus did not abuse his power at all, he cannot have been a son of Adam.

[6] Jesus claimed to be God's son not Adam's son as all other men who lived after him are.

Since we have no further options for Jesus' parenthood other than Adam and God, and since he was not a son of Adam, he must have been a son of God.

The above is a logical pathway. How much confidence do you put in it? If we assume that statements [1] to [5] are true then we have to have complete confidence that Jesus was not a son of Adam. Do you have that confidence (given the assumptions [1] to [5])?

Pathways such as the above are actually the basis of spirituality. God did not introduce himself to pre-adamic man until we had developed the capability to see with our minds what we could not detect with our senses. The mind sees through logic. For example Sir Isaac Newton deduced from the fact that an apple fell towards the earth that an invisible force was attracting the apple to the earth. He could not physically detect that force, he could only deduce its existence form the physically detectable effect that it had on the apple. Newton saw gravity with his mind. That is precisely how one sees God today.

For example, suppose your friend left London at 10:30 am (London Time) and arrived in New York at 9:30 am (Eastern Time) the same day. You would deduce from this that he must have gone on Concorde. There is absolutely no doubt about this at all, as mankind has no other non military was of achieving this. But how much confidence do you have in this deduction?

Your faith, your spirituality and your Christianity are all dependent on your confidence is such deductions because you cannot at this time see God or see Jesus himself. But if you have full confidence in your deductions, and you familiarize yourself with the scriptures then you can see the pair of them.

Have you ever seen your own brain? Most readers will say no. So how do you know that you have got one? Well you deduce it from books and from the fact that you may have seen other people's brains or pictures of other people's brain's and you are the same species as them. But this reasoning is precisely the reasoning we used above to deduce that Jesus was not a son of Adam.

If you can develop confidence in your deductive powers, then you will see God, if you are pure in heart. By this we mean and Jesus meant, if you look without regard for personal consequence. Obviously if there is a God then you are accountable to him. Not everybody likes this idea. So many make a rather limited search for him.

The way to approach this is to first of all forget about consequences and just decide to search for the truth. If you can do this, then you are searching with a pure heart, you are judging without a motive. OK the consequences could theoretically be dire, but you are not considering them. In fact God is a better judge than anyone could possibly imagine and the consequences of discovering him can only ever be good. If he is not going to allow you into the Kingdom of God it is because that is the best thing for you, because you would not benefit from or be able to deal with that particular 'school'.

Here are some examples of deductions that everyone has confidence in:

A Map

A map is not a reality, it is a symbolic representation, an abstraction, of the reality. We all trust maps. Most of us are confident that if we follow a route on a map we will indeed end up at the destination we seek, even though we may have never gone down that road before and may have never been to that destination before. The bible is such a map. It is just rather more symbolic in its representation and rather more abstract in its construction. And no human today has ever been to the destination which it gives the route for. But many people have never been to Stratfield Mortimer, that doesn't mean that the place doesn't exist, or that if you follow the appropriate road map you won't end up there.

Dinosaurs

Most people accept that many years ago Dinosaurs roamed over the earth. But no human has ever seen a Dinosaur. We just have bits of huge skeletons from which we deduce their existence. It is logic and confidence in our deductions that puts the flesh on those bones. We do not actually have any Dinosaur flesh to hand. Likewise we have the skeletal proof of the existence of God from the words of the bible and from nature itself. But logic and confidence in our deductions are required to categorically prove his existence. For logic and deduction are the flesh needed to create the body of God from the bones of nature and the bible. Now if you do not understand logic you may say: Does this mean that God is a Dinosaur? If you ask this question then you have failed to grasp one of the elementary rules of logic which is this:

All Horses are creatures with 4 legs. This does not mean that all creatures with 4 legs are horses. And if you don't get this, then you have just made a horses ass out of logic.

One Step Thinking

Sin is short termism, which is ignoring the consequences of your actions. Sin results from one step thinking. Christianity is basically two step thinking, thinking which takes account of the global consequences of actions when deciding whether or not to go ahead with them.

National Pollution Policy:

One Step Thinking: If we introduce strict anti pollution laws, then our companies will become less profitable so they will sack people and unemployment will rise.

Two Step Thinking: If we cut pollution, we will slow down global warming, so the climate will remain stable. Then the rain will fall evenly and slowly in the right places, rather than falling unevenly and quickly in the wrong places. Since the weather will remain predictable and consistent, we will not get unprecedented floods and droughts and hurricanes, so farming won't fail worldwide, so we won't all starve. (Alright it is a few more than 2 steps! more like 5 steps!)

Self Interest:

One Step Thinking: I want this, I don't care what anyone else feels about it, I am having this because that is what I want.

Two Step Thinking: Everything I want is presently owned by someone else. My welfare is dependent upon others. They also have the same needs and desires as me. If we co-operate as a team we will both reach attain these desires and needs more quickly. So my plan to achieve my goals has to complement other peoples plans to achieve their goals, in other words I'll have to do a deal.

Profit before people:

One Step Thinking: Close down the coal industry in the UK because you can buy cheaper coal from Germany.

Two Step Thinking: The cost of closing down our coal industry to the UK as an economy, in terms of lost jobs, unemployment benefit, lost utility revenues, lost factory rents, lost tax revenue, lost bank profits, lost shop profits, psychological demotivation of people etc. is much greater than the marginal difference between German coal prices and UK coal prices. So we are better off subsidising UK coal. Obviously the Germans understand this and have implemented a policy of subsidy which is based on two stage thinking. In the 1980s the UK was buying German coal which was inferior in quality to ours and which costed more to mine than ours but was subsidised to a greater extent.

The UN:

One Step Thinking: The world is becoming one place, lets have one world wide government to make the world a fairer place.

Two Step thinking: Power corrupts, absolute power corrupts absolutely. After the UN becomes the worldwide government, all of the power being in the hands of one government will be catastrophic. The UN itself will become like an African dictator answerable to no one and so it will inevitably become completely corrupt. We need a worldwide judge yes, for human rights issues, a worldwide social service yes, and worldwide health service yes, but a worldwide king with a worldwide army - NO. That would be the worst and most corrupt from of global police state.

Democracy:

One Step Thinking: Lets ask everyone what they want and give it to them in a political system - Democracy.

Two Step Thinking: Peoples individual desires are not as important as their collective needs. We need a political system which gives people not what they want but what they need. We may all want chocolate pudding, but what we need is protein and greens. To ensure that all people get what they need, which is a job, a house, healthcare, schooling for everyone, moral guidance, security (protein and greens), we need to do things that people don't want us to do, and so would never vote for. So we need to educate people so that they understand how to fulfill collective needs and so that they value these needs as much as they value their own personal wants. This education is Christianity. Christianity is your Brussels Sprouts if you like.

[18] The True Bible Code

'It was revealed to Daniel that the prophecies concerning the last times should be closed up and sealed until the time of the end: But then the wise should understand, and knowledge should be increased (Daniel 12:4,9,10). And therefore the longer they have continued in obscurity, the more hopes there are that the time is at hand in which they are to be made manifest.

If they are never to be understood, to what end did God reveal them?

Certainly he did it for the edification of the church. And if so then it is certain that the church shall at length attain to the understandings thereof. I mean not all that call themselves Christians, but a remnant, a few scattered persons which God hath chosen, such as without being led by interest, education, or human authorities, can set themselves sincerely and earnestly to search after truth. For Daniel hath said that the wise shall understand, so he said also that none of the wicked shall understand' - *Sir Isaac Newton*

[C1] Why would God cause the bible to be written in a code?
[C2] What reason is there to suppose that the bible is in a code?

The 12 Principles of the Code So Far Extracted

[C3] The Consistency Principle
[C4] The Power Principle
[C5] The Prophetic Principle
[C6a] The Designations Principle
[C6b] The Successive Designations Principle
[C6c] The Successive Descriptions Principle
[C7] The Repetitions Principle
[C8] The Immediate Repetition Principle
[C9] The No Coincidences Principle
[C10] The Times Principle
[C11] The Numerical Principle
[C12] The Jigsaw Principle
[C12a] Isaac Newton's exposure of the false doctrine of the Trinity using the Jigsaw Principle

[C12b] The History of the English bible
[C15] The Parallel Account Principle and Spot the Difference
[C16] The Omission Principle

Further Symbolic Meanings

[C17] Yes/No Question Symbolism
[C18] Reader Questions from the holy spirit
[C19] Helpful tips
[C22] The Symbolic meaning of 7

The 2nd 3rd and 4th Dimensions of the code

[C20] Elementary counting and cryptic scriptures
[C21] Equidistant Hebrew Letter Sequences and The 'Bible Code' of Eli Rips and Michael Drosnin
[C23] The Symbolic meaning of literal accounts, and the symbolic meanings of symbolic accounts

These sections are designed to be read in conjunction with
www.truebiblecode.com.

[C1] Why would God cause the bible to be written in a code?

Everything that Jesus said to the crowds was in an illustration:

So with many illustrations of that sort he would speak the word to them, as far as they were able to listen. Indeed, without an illustration he would not speak to them, but privately to his disciples he would explain all things (Mark 4:33,34).

Jesus decoded his symbolic parables for his disciples only, not for the public at large. By speaking symbolically, those who did not want to believe that he was God's son, could write off his speech as meaningless ramblings about farm animals and horticulture. They would therefore never get to know God's plans for men. They would therefore never be in a position to frustrate them. For the ones who do not want to believe in God, are God's and mankind's and their own enemies. They do not want to believe because they do not want God to exist. They do not want him to exist, because if he does exist then they fear that they will have to serve him and obey him, rather than serving and obeying their own desires. They do not know that God is a kinder master to them than their own desires are. Dear reader, do not make this mistake. God gave you your desires to enjoy them whilst controlling them! He did not give you them to replace him!

Even if all of your experience of people who have ever had power over you is bad, even if everyone of them has abused you, and even if everyone you have ever loved has abused you, there is yet in existence a God who behaves just as his son did whilst he was on earth. He does not abuse his power, and does not abuse your love. His name is Jehovah, it is he who is the Father of Jesus. But he does allow Satan to abuse you, your love, his power and anything else he gets his hands on. For Jesus was described by Paul with reference to God as:

He is the reflection of [his] glory and the exact representation of his very being (Hebrews 1:3).

These people who do not believe are, in the great finesse of our God, unwittingly, their own enemies. Because God is their friend and means of life and salvation. Without him they have no future. They are choosing not to believe in their own future.

But they are free to choose such a course if they wish, and most people do so choose. So it is because mankind has one main enemy, a lying murderer, Satan, and it is because this fraud has many unwitting followers, that God's book, the bible is written in a code. Satan has been trying to persuade God to wipe out the whole human race for nearly 6,000 years in order to justify his murderous act on Eve. He is trying to cheat us out of our inheritance, which is to be ageless humans on earth in the Kingdom of God after Armageddon, and to be angels in heaven and eventually to be God's ourselves, just like our Father. Beloved reader, do not be fooled by your physical weakness, the family you come from is a family of Gods, and like begets like. But it is because we are always at war in this system that coded messages are used. We are at war even when the world is at peace:

But I behold in my members another law warring against the law of my mind and leading me captive to sin's law that is in my members (Romans 7:23).

Our mind is at war with our body, as regards sin. God has created us this way to teach us about sin.

In the Second World War, the Germans and the British both used codes. The British cracked the German code using the enigma computer in Bletchley (according to the movies this was as a result of an American submarine crew which stole a German code machine from a U boat). There is a marvelous and tragic story of the great wisdom of Winston Churchill in relation to this. The British decoded a German message that they were going to completely carpet bomb the city of Coventry on a certain day and destroy it. Winston then had to decide whether to save the people of Coventry, by evacuating them or not. The problem with doing this was that the Germans had spies, and would have found out that Coventry was evacuated and then deduced that the British had cracked their code.

Churchill therefore sacrificed the whole town of Coventry, in order to keep this secret undiscovered. Such was the value that he attached to knowing the Enigma Code. He knew that if he confined his actions resulting from the breaking of the Code to ones which would not reveal to the Germans that the British had cracked it, then he could continue to know their entire strategy possibly right to the end of the war! Such knowledge was of greater value to Britain than Coventry. Greater value in terms of saving lives (though not those of the citizens of Coventry) and in terms of shortening and winning the war, which amounted to the same thing.

Likewise God has encoded information in the bible for the purpose of saving our lives, it is for our protection. For God is not going to lose in this battle that he is having with his rebellious son Satan. But we are all caught up in this war. For war is the *inevitable* result of the tolerance of evil or of bad. History shows us this.

God would win this war whether the bible was in a code or not and whether Jesus just blurted out the whole plan for salvation verbatim or not. But God wishes to teach us good from bad with the minimum possible loss of life and damage to our souls. The degree of damage and death that we do experience as a race is the measure of the difficulty he has in teaching us and we have in learning this lesson. We would be the losers if this book was not in a code.

This code needs to be appealing to God's friends and revolting to his enemies. Then his friends will be attracted to it and hopefully spend enough time looking at it to find out that it is in a code and then will be sufficiently motivated to crack the code and then pass on the information only to his friends. Whilst his enemies on the other hand will find the whole thing so revolting and distasteful that they will not study the information hard enough to even realise that it is in a code. Furthermore when they are told that it is in a code, they still will not believe it!

Well, since the distinction between God's friends and enemies is their love or hate for him and his friends, it is obvious that the information that he sends out should be all about him and his friends, because this is the only sort of information which will have a different effect on the two groups. Also this information should look innocuous and intensely boring to his enemies, and be full of praises upon praises of him to drive off the enemies and pull in the friends.

God has done this with the bible. All of the praise in the bible is not because God has a big ego and needs a whole lot of praise. It is to sort the sheep from the goats. He has given to everybody a book about his past dealings with his friends, who lived thousands of years ago, who had many camels and lived in tents and had children and basically did the sort of things that everybody else did back then. This is of no great consequence to the enemies of God. It just looks like an out of date soap opera, written by someone who they do not like. Of what interest to a 20th or 21st century currency speculator is it that Esau lost his birthright to Jacob for a bowl of soup, or that he crossed the Jabbok with 200 female sheep and 20 rams? This sort of information is hardly the sort of thing that would come up on his Reuters screen.

But hidden in amongst all of the banal, mundane and everyday tribulations of these friends of God, is the whole of his military plan for saving mankind from sin and death and retaking the earth from Satan. The plan for men to regain the birthright that Adam lost, namely everlasting human and angelic life.

He is revealing the deep things and the concealed things, knowing what is in the darkness; and with him the light does dwell (Daniel 2:22).

[C2] What reason is there to suppose that the bible is in a code ?

Logically, if we examine God's Modus Operandi with men, we see that he hides from us. We see that he hides what he is doing from us. Nobody has seen him, and who really knows what he is up to? So given that he inspired the bible:

All Scripture is inspired of God (2 Timothy 3:16).

It should be no great surprise to anyone that the bible too contains hidden information. In other words it is written in a code. This is not a new idea. Sir Isaac Newton believed the same to be true, but was unable to discover the code. He could see gravity with his mind, and he knew God well enough to see that the bible was in a code, but he could not himself decode it. He died trying to work out the date of Armageddon. He failed not because he lacked faith and not because he lacked wisdom, for he had them both and in abundance. He failed because it was not God's time in the late 17th and early 18th centuries for this to take place. So instead the true God rewarded one of the most spiritual men of the last millennium with the code of his physical universe. For a spiritual man sees things with his mind, with his power of reason, things that he cannot detect with his senses. It is this capability that separates us from the animals. It is this capability that the reader will need to sharpen as he or she reads this website/book.

Here are two typical sections of the Old Testament:

Polish the arrows. Fill the circular shields, Oh men. Jehovah has aroused the spirit of the kings of the Medes, because it is against Babylon that his idea is, in order to bring her to ruin. For it is the vengeance of Jehovah, the vengeance for his temple. Against the walls of Babylon lift up a signal. Make strong the watch. Post the watchmen. Make ready those lying in Ambush. For Jehovah has both formed the idea and will certainly do what he has spoken against the inhabitants of Babylon. Oh woman residing on abounding waters, abundant in treasures, your end has come, the measure of your profit making (Jeremiah 51:11-13).

For I will tread as my [bow] **Judah. The bow I will fill with Ephraim, and I will awaken your sons, Oh Zion, against your sons, Oh Greece, and I will make you as the sword of a mighty man.
And over them Jehovah himself will be seen, and his arrow will certainly go forth just like lightning. And on the horn the Sovereign Lord Jehovah himself will blow, and he will certainly go with the windstorms of the south** (Zechariah 9:13,14).

These passages are written in colourful, poetic, symbolic language. Here is a typical section of the New Testament:

Therefore we were buried with him through our baptism into his death, in order that, just as Christ was raised up from the dead through the glory of the father, we should likewise walk in a newness of life. For if we have become united with him in the likeness of his death, we shall also be [united with him in the likeness] **of his resurrection** (Romans 6:4,5).

This passage is written in symbolic, logically contorted language. Most people who read the bible, believe that the reason it is hard to understand is that 2,000 years ago people wrote and spoke in this complicated symbolic or logically contorted way. But they did not. Here is a typical passage from Josephus' book on the history of the Jews. He was a Jewish general born ten or twenty years after Jesus:

But as for the richer sort, it proved all one to them whether they stayed in the city or attempted to get out of it, for they were equally destroyed in both cases. For every such person was put to death under this pretense, that they were going to desert - but in reality that the robbers might get what they had. The madness of the seditious did also increase together with their famine, and both those miseries were every day inflamed more and more. For there was no corn which anywhere appeared publicly, but the robbers came running into, and searched men's private houses. And then if they found any, they tormented them, because they had denied they had any. And if they found none, they tormented them worse, because they supposed they had more carefully concealed it. The indication they made use of whether they had any or not, was taken from the bodies of these miserable wretches. Which, if they were in good case, they supposed were in no want at all of food. But if they were wasted away, they walked off without searching any farther.

Likewise if one reads Latin or Greek historical works from the same period (which are mainly about wars) they read just like a history book might read today. The bible is written in a different way to any other book of its time or of this time. Even in the literal meaning of the book, it is hard to deduce precisely what is being said. One needs to think hard, one needs to think logically and think in abstract symbolic terms, just to understand the literal meaning. In other words even the literal meaning is somewhat coded. But there is another reason why this book is written so strangely, and it is that the bible is written in a symbolic, numeric and cryptic code, it is a 4 dimensional book including the literal meaning. This is why sections of it are very strangely written. It is because there is more to this book than the literal meaning. The accounts have to work in the symbolically coded and numerically coded meanings too, which effects the way in which they are written literally. Basically the literal accounts look a bit weird because the words also form symbolic accounts.

Here are 5 further reasons that we can see to suppose that the bible is written in a code:

1. Why would such a clever God write such a stupid book?
2. Spirituality is defined as seeing with the mind things which are undetectable to the senses. The bible is unarguably a spiritual book from God. It is therefore written in a spiritual way. So it's written in such a way that its true meaning is not visible with the eye but is detectable only with the power of reason, the eyes of the mind. The literal meaning is clearly visible with the eye. It therefore has a further meaning which is invisible and is not the literal meaning. So this further meaning is a coded meaning. It is written in a spiritual code, which is a visible vehicle for an invisible meaning.
3. Every word that Jesus spoke publicly was symbolic:

    So with many illustrations of that sort he would speak the word to them, as far as they were able to listen. Indeed, without an illustration he would not speak to them, but privately to his disciples he would explain all things (Mark 4:33,34).

    And Jesus was responsible not only for his own words but for all of the words of every bible writer as we shall see.
4. The bible itself says that it is written in a code!

5. Paul describes one particular account in Genesis 16 as being a symbolic drama.

We now investigate each of these 5 in more detail.

C2.1 Why would such a clever God write such a stupid book?

'God is a comedian playing to an audience too afraid to laugh.' -Voltaire

We are looking at the whole book as being effectively written by one person, because Paul tells us that it was:

All Scripture is inspired of God and beneficial for teaching, for reproving, for setting things straight, for disciplining in righteousness (2 Timothy 3:16).

And Peter tells us:

For prophecy was at no time brought by man's will, but men spoke from God as they were borne along by holy spirit (2 Peter 1:21).

If you truly believe that God, whilst not being the physical author of the book, has inspired every bible writer to express his story in the writer's own literary style, and in his own phraseology, even in the way he wanted to say it but in God's words. Then given this, there is a question that is begging to be asked, and it is this:

How could the creator of the perfect universe, which is a gigantic and inordinately intricate example of hyper intelligence, perfection and complete understanding wisdom and control, write or inspire to be written such a daft book?

Or: Why would such a clever guy write such a stupid book?

How can the true God, the grand creator of the great works that Newton and Einstein could barely scratch into the surface of be an order of magnitude worse than Steven Spielberg when it comes to telling a story?

The reader might think that asking this question is an insult to God, or even a blasphemy. We would argue that not asking this question is the real insult, an insult that all mankind has been repeating for the past 2000 years. Because by not asking this question you are saying that you would expect God to inspire such a badly written book (in the literal meaning). You are saying that you are not surprised that he has written such a book. Which is saying that you do not think he is capable of telling a story properly. Whereas the more logical and more respectful explanation for the peculiar way in which the bible is written, is that just as Newton and Einstein knew that they were only scratching at the surface of the beauty and perfection of God's universe, so the seeker of bible truth knows that he is only scratching at the surface of the beauty and perfection of God's holy book. And this surface is the literal meaning of the book.

For the bible in the literal meaning, the surface itself, is written in an ambiguous, repetitive manner and is full of absolutely crucial omissions, and laden with really unnecessary and trivial detail.

One has to ask rhetorically:

Is God unable to properly focus on the key points in bible stories?

Is he the first person to write a history book with none of the important dates in it?

Why does he keep repeating himself in almost every account?

Does a person who can create hundreds of languages from nothing in one instant of time and simultaneously teach them to every living human in that very instant as described in the account of Babel in Genesis11:

Now all the earth continued to be of one language and of one set of words....
And Jehovah proceeded to go down to see the city and the tower that the sons of men had built. After that Jehovah said: Look! They are one people and there is one language for them all, and this is what they start to do. Why, now there is nothing that they may have in mind to do that will be unattainable for them.
Come now! Let us go down and there confuse their language that they may not listen to one another's language. Accordingly Jehovah scattered them from there over all the surface of the earth, and they gradually left off building the city.
That is why its name was called Babel, because there Jehovah had confused the language of all the earth, and Jehovah had scattered them from there over all the surface of the earth (Genesis 11:1-9).

Does this person have a problem in telling a simple story in just one language when he has all the time in the world to tell it?

Consider please the following masterpieces:

However, they found out of the inhabitants of Jabesh-gilead four hundred girls, virgins, that had not had intercourse with a man by lying with a male (Judges 21:12).

One wonders how else they could lose their virginity?

Now Joshua was old, being advanced in years. So Jehovah said to him: You yourself have grown old and have advanced in years (Joshua 13:1).

What an astute observation!

They stoned them with stones!! (Joshua 7:25)

Abraham's life that he lived!! (Genesis 25:8) Well what else could he have done with it?

Then Abraham expired and died! (Genesis 25:8)

The alien resident who is residing as an Alien?? (Exodus 12:49)

Why in Jeremiah chapter 41 is Ishmael the son of Nethaniah the son of Elishama, described as: **Ishmael the son of Nethaniah** 11 times and as plain old **Ishmael** 6 times in the same account, when there is no other Ishmael in the account? Why does the holy spirit have to tell us the same thing 11 times in one chapter of the bible? Why did mankind have to carry all this unnecessary repetitive information around for 2500 years? How could the God of recycling who wastes absolutely nothing on this planet, waste all those holy words? Something is not right here!

There are four accounts in Matthew 14, Mark 6, Luke 9 & John 6 of the feeding of the 5,000. Why? Why was this particular account repeated 4 times, when the account of the man who had been lame for 38 years at the pool in Bethzatha in John 5 to whom Jesus said:

Get up, pick up your bed and walk (John 5:8).

is only mentioned once in the holy book? How can a perfect God be so inconsistent?

The Rock, perfect is his activity, For all his ways are justice (Deuteronomy 32:4).

How about this one:

In the twenty-seventh year of Jeroboam the king of Israel, Azariah the son of Amaziah the king of Judah became king. Sixteen years old he happened to be when he began to reign, and for fifty-two years he reigned in Jerusalem. And his mother's name was Jecoliah of Jerusalem (2 Kings 15:1,2).

Great, so we get to know his mother's name. But there was not a man alive for a long time until 1999 who knew when the 27th year of Jeroboam II actually was. It is extremely difficult to work this out from the bible. But we have done it (we think) and it's 816 BC - see [91], [101]. It would have been so much more useful if the holy spirit had said: This was 181 years after Solomon died. Or better still: This was 697 years after the Jews left Egypt. Or better still: This being 3177 years after Adam sinned! Instead we get to know his mum's name!

In this vein the bible tells us that a Philistine character called Ishbi-benob had a spear that weighed 300 shekels of copper (2 Samuel 21:16). Well, How fascinating! But it fails to tell us when Jesus was born! or what year he died in! Most people do not know this even today. But all literate mankind knows that Ishbi-benob's spear weighed 300 shekels of copper. What kind of a God could get his priorities so wrong? The dates of Jesus' birth and his death are absolutely crucial to any understanding of God's plan for mankind. The weight of this chap's spear clearly is not (not in the literal meaning at least!)

C2.2 The Bible is a spiritual book

In section [1] which reconciles the millions of years of human fossils with the creation account in Genesis, see - Millions of years of human fossils reconciled with Genesis, we discover that God introduced himself to mankind through Adam and Eve once Homo sapiens had developed, or dare we say evolved? to the point where he had become 'spiritual'. By this we mean that he could deduce with his powers of reason the existence of things which he could not detect with his physical sensory powers. By this we mean that he became able to entertain a logical train of thought, a multi stage thought process. A good example of this is gravity. Isaac Newton 'saw' gravity with his mind, having first 'decoded' God's physical laws of motion. But the ability that modern man has to do what Newton did, was the trigger for God to introduce himself to us.

The reason that God did not introduce himself to us before we had developed spirituality, was that he did not want to introduce himself to us physically. He wanted to introduce himself to us spiritually, because firstly he wanted us all to retain the option of not seeing him if that was our desire, and secondly, he wished only to be seen by those who had a sufficiently great desire to see him that they were prepared to make the effort to use their powers of reason to deduce his existence with their mind from the physical clues which he had prepared for them. Hence Jesus said:

Blessed are the pure in heart for they shall see God (Matthew 5:8).

Those who are pure in heart, want to know the truth about their origins, as a matter of gratitude to a humble God. Their heart will not, out of fear, prevent them from searching with their mind.

In the physical universe one can quite clearly see the character of God, the creator. He is perfect, he wastes nothing but recycles it all, he is incredibly hard working, he is very generous, he is kind, he loves us. But one cannot see God himself physically, one can only deduce what he might be like from what one can see of his works.

Now his book, the bible, is his training manual, his instruction leaflet, his users guide, his online help button for mankind. It was created by the same God who created the universe and therefore is manufactured using the same Modus Operandi. It is therefore a spiritual book. So one will likewise have to use one's powers of reason to see God even through his book. If we really want to know him we will have to look beneath the literal surface meaning of the book. It has a hidden meaning, discernable by the power of reason, a meaning that is not literally stated. So it is written in a code.

C2.3 Every word that Jesus spoke publicly was symbolic

Make no mistake, Jesus only spoke publicly (or to the crowds) in illustrations. His speaking like this was itself an illustration that the truth is not what you see on the surface:

So with many illustrations of that sort he would speak the word to them, as far as they were able to listen. Indeed, without an illustration he would not speak to them, but privately to his disciples he would explain all things (Mark 4:33,34).

But Jesus is called **the word** by John in the famous scripture:

In beginning the Word was, and the Word was with God, and the Word was [a] god (John 1:1).
And John is told by the angel in Revelation that he has the name: **The word of God**.

And he is arrayed with an outer garment sprinkled with blood, and the name he is called is The Word of God (Revelation 19:3).

But the word of God is the bible:

And so you have made the word of God invalid because of your tradition (Matthew 15:6).

Also, accept the helmet of salvation, and the sword of the spirit, that is, God's word (Ephesians 6:17).

But the word of God is Jesus:

On an occasion when the crowd was pressing close upon him and listening to the word of God, he was standing beside the lake of Gennesaret (Luke 5:1).

Jesus wasn't quoting scriptures at them, he was speaking in illustrations as he always did, so here the **word of God** meant Jesus. So Jesus is the word of God which is the bible. So Jesus 'is' the bible. This identification is meant in the sense that God was the author, Jesus was the editor/publisher, and the writers were the journalists. As regards God's son:

All things came into existence through him, and apart from him not even one thing came into existence (John 1:3).

So in particular the bible came into existence through him. Actually no, everything physical before Adam's sin came into existence through Satan, who was the firstborn son of God. But Michael became God's firstborn earning this right from his sacrifice as an angel. But now the reader will see why Michael was called the word. Because Satan lost his firstborn right (for God to act exclusively through him as described in John 1:3) when he killed Adam. The right was then no one's until Jesus died. But Jesus got the firstborn right (of God acting exclusively through him) as regards the bible as a result of his promising to make the sacrifice. So he became 'the word', due to his having this right. So every chapter of the bible, every verse of the bible, every word of the bible came into existence through him. And whether Jesus was speaking to the crowds or writing for the crowds through the prophets, he used the same illustrative modus operandi, he communicated symbolically.

The word of God is an example of a word or phrase in the bible which has two different literal meanings. Another such word is **presence**, which in the bible can mean either the presence of the Christ or the manifestation of the Christ during a presence. The concept of one word or phrase having two literal meanings depending on the context is unusual to English speaking people. We have a language which eliminates such ambiguities by using a larger vocabulary. But the Hebrew language often has one root word with several different meanings dependent on the context.

For more on this see - Appendix 1: Jesus Spoke Symbolically

C2.4 The bible itself says that it is written in a code!

Solomon said:

The Glory of God is the keeping of a matter secret, and the glory of kings is the searching through a matter (Proverbs 25:2).

If you keep seeking for it as for silver, and as for hid treasures you keep searching for it, in that case you will understand the fear of Jehovah, and you will find the very knowledge of God (Proverbs 2:4,5).

So this knowledge is hidden. And it is hidden in the bible, for Paul says of Jesus:

Carefully concealed in him are all the treasures of wisdom and of knowledge (Colossians 2:3).

Well, these treasures are not in his body, they are in the information we have on him. This information is the bible. For as we have seen above, Jesus is the word of God, which is also 'the bible'. Paul describes how it is hidden and revealed:

But we speak God's wisdom in a sacred secret, the hidden wisdom, which God foreordained before the systems of things for our glory (1 Corinthians 2:7).

For it is to us God has revealed them through his spirit, for the spirit searches into all things, even the deep things of God (1 Corinthians 2:10).

So again we see that wisdom is hidden in this book, concealed or coded. For a code is hidden written information. This is why Jesus says:

There is nothing carefully concealed that will not be revealed, and secret that will not become known (Luke 12:2).

Keep on asking, and it will be given you; keep on seeking, and you will find; keep on knocking, and it will be opened to you (Matthew 7:7).

And really you do not have to look that far. But you do have to look, yourself! For God said to Adam:

In the sweat of your face you will eat bread (Genesis 3:19)

And Jesus said to Satan:

177

But in reply he said: It is written, 'Man must live, not on bread alone, but on every utterance coming forth through God's mouth' (Matthew 4:4)
From the two of which it is not hard to deduce that we will digest God's word in the sweat of our faces as well as digesting bread in this way.

Gabriel said to Daniel:

And as for you, O Daniel, make secret the words and seal up the book, until the time of [the] end. Many will rove about, and the [true] knowledge will become abundant (Daniel 12:4).

We are now in this time, this book/website is the proof, see - Daniel 8, Daniel 12. Daniel said to Nebuchadnezzar:

However, there exists a God in the heavens who is a Revealer of secrets, and he has made known to King Nebuchadnezzar what is to occur in the final part of the days (Daniel 2:28).

And not only to him! But also to Jesus, who opened up the minds of his disciples:

Then he opened up their minds fully to grasp the meaning of the Scriptures (Luke 24:45).

It is quite a task.

The woman said to him: I know that Messiah is coming, who is called Christ. Whenever that one arrives, he will declare all things to us openly. Jesus said to her: I who am speaking to you am he (John 4:25,26).

So the scriptures do not declare things openly, but the Christ opened them up. So the scriptures are coded.

Jesus opened up the scriptures to their minds.

There is a holy code for the holy scriptures, and there is a bible within the bible!

C2.5 Paul describes one particular account in Genesis as a symbolic drama

For example, it is written that Abraham acquired two sons, one by the servant girl and one by the free woman; but the one by the servant girl

was actually born in the manner of flesh, the other by the free woman through a promise.

These things stand as a symbolic drama; for these [women] mean two covenants, the one from Mount Sinai, which brings forth children for slavery, and which is Hagar.

Now this Hagar means Sinai, a mountain in Arabia, and she corresponds with the Jerusalem today, for she is in slavery with her children. But the Jerusalem above is free, and she is our mother (Galatians 4:22-26).

Hagar stood for the Law covenant mediated by Moses and Sarah for the new covenant mediated by Jesus, described as Paul's mother. But what is so special about this particular account in Genesis? Is it the only one to be a symbolic drama? And what is so special about Genesis in the old testament. Might there not be some symbolic dramas in Exodus? In fact, we know that the bible is a consistent book having but one ghost writer - if the reader will pardon the metaphor! So any element of the bible code that we find to be true for one account is therefore true in every account. We call this the Consistency Principle of the code. So the whole book stands as one giant symbolic drama.

[C3] The Consistency Principle

Any element of the code that is found to be true for one account, is true for every account in the whole bible

All things came into existence through him, and apart from him not even one thing came into existence (John 1:3).

All scripture is inspired of God (2 Timothy 3:16).

The Bible has one editor, Jesus Christ, and it has one ghost writer, inspirer - God. So it is consistent as a book, it does not contradict itself. This principle follows either from faith that God is the true author of the book, and that it is therefore consistent and therefore all in the same language or code. Or, in the alternative it follows from the academic axiom that 'the bible is perfect'. For if it is perfect then it is consistent, therefore it effectively has only one author and so it is all in the same language or code.

[C4] The Power Principle

Every word in the bible has power in the greater meaning if not in the literal meaning.

For truly I say to you that sooner would heaven and earth pass away than for one smallest letter or one particle of a letter to pass away from the Law by any means and not all things take place (Matthew 5:18).

Indeed, it is easier for heaven and earth to pass away than for one particle of a letter of the Law to go unfulfilled (Luke 16:17).

There are no wasted words in the bible. So repetitions have power, double descriptions have power. Seemingly trivial details have power. Every tense of every verb, every case of every word has power:

For the word of God is alive and exerts power and is sharper than any two-edged sword and pierces even to the dividing of soul and spirit, and of joints and [their] marrow, and [is] able to discern thoughts and intentions of [the] heart (Hebrews 4:12).

But that the dead are raised up even Moses disclosed, in the account about the thornbush, when he calls Jehovah 'the God of Abraham and God of Isaac and God of Jacob. He is a God, not of the dead, but of the living, for they are all living to him (Luke 20:37,38).

So we must look at tense, the angel did not say the he used to be the God of Abraham.

Now the promises were spoken to Abraham and to his seed. It says, not: And to seeds; as in the case of many such, but as in the case of one: And to your seed; who is Christ (Galatians 3:16). So we must look at number, whether a word is singular or plural.

We will use the Power Principle to deduce other principles and symbolic understandings.

First example of the Power Principle

In the midst of years oh bring it to life, in the midst of years may you make it known (Habakkuk 3:2).

This scripture applies to the resurrection of Jesus and to God's means of salvation from death, Jesus' death, being made known in the midst of a period of years. Now in Hebrew the word קרב translated 'midst of' means either 'amongst' or 'middle of'. Obviously if it means 'amongst' then the scripture is telling us very little if anything. But if it means 'middle of' and we know the period of years concerned then we are being told the dates of Jesus' death and his resurrection here. By the Power Principle if we do know the period of years concerned and it is a large period, then the latter meaning of the Hebrew must be correct.

Second example of the Power Principle

There are Irrelevant Details in the bible. The more irrelevant a detail appears to be in the literal meaning, the more relevant it must be in symbolic meaning

This follows from the Power Principle. The bible is full of seemingly irrelevant detail and crucial omissions. We saw in the case of King David's purchasing of the wood and cattle for the first sacrifice on the site of Solomon's temple (that today houses a mosque in Jerusalem) that he paid 50 shekels of silver for them - see [c11.1]. Great, who wants to know this? Are we going to put in a counter offer 3000 years later? But we are not told when Joab handed him the results of the registration, and we are not told how long after this David made this sacrifice, which is what we do want to know, so that we can verify whether our understanding of the 1,100,000 men of Israel drawing sword at one day per man is correct. But actually, the 50 shekels stand for the precise time period that we are looking for between David receiving the results from Joab, completing his registration sin, and him pacifying God with this sacrifice, 50 days, at a day for a shekel. So the price that David paid in shekels, is the period of time for which his sin remained unforgiven in days, a shekel for a day. So this seemingly irrelevant information, actually provides the answer in the symbolic meaning. This is how the bible is written. Here is another classic:

Jesus said: Have the men recline as at meal. Now there was a lot of grass in the place. Therefore the men reclined, about 5,000 in number (John 6:10).
Really, a lot of grass! Were people going to get hay fever? Were there any daisies?

[C5] The Prophetic Principle

The basic principle, which we shall refine later in this section is:

Every word of scripture has a greater meaning, every scripture is prophetic having a further fulfillment

Peter says:

**Consequently we have the prophetic word [made] more sure and you are doing well in paying attention to it as to a lamp shining in a dark place, until day dawns and a daystar rises, in your hearts.
For you know this first, that no prophecy of Scripture springs from any private interpretation.
For prophecy was at no time brought by man's will, but men spoke from God as they were borne along by holy spirit** (2 Peter 1:19-21).

So all of the word of God, the word of life, the bible, is prophetic. They are all prophetic words.

The sovereign Lord Jehovah himself has spoken who will not prophesy? (Amos 3:8).
The bible is the word of God, and is all delivered to us through Jesus, who is also called the word of God - see [C2.3] so it is all prophetic. This is what Paul meant when he said:

For the word of God is alive and exerts power and is sharper than any two-edged sword and pierces even to the dividing of soul and spirit, and of joints and [their] marrow, and [is] able to discern thoughts and intentions of [the] heart (Hebrews 4:12).

The word being alive, means that it has a further life over and above it's literal meaning. This is how it exerts power in the prophetic sense. The bible is not a dead history book of past events. It is also a living history book of future events symbolically encoded in the stories of the past events. This works because history is fractal. Was it Churchill who said: The further back you look into history, the further forward you see? The same is true of the bible, but actually because each account has more than one life. They all have greater meanings. These meanings are normally the further fulfillments of the scriptures.

One can use the Consistency Principle to deduce that the whole bible is prophetic just from the fact that certain scriptures are prophetic. Likewise since certain scriptures are laws, we can deduce that the whole bible is the 'Law of God', using the same principle. And since certain scriptures are Psalms, we can deduce that the whole bible is a giant praise to God, it is one huge Psalm, by the Consistency Principle.

Even when we are being told that Jacob crossed a river with 200 she goats, 20 he goats, 200 female sheep, 20 rams, 30 camels giving suck and their young ones, 40 cows, 10 bulls, 20 she asses and 10 full grown asses (Genesis 32:14,15) this is prophetic. It is symbolic, it stands for something greater.

So either the word of God is alive and is exerting power today, through further fulfillments of words written thousands of years ago or it is dead and powerless. Either the flaming blade of the sword guarding the way back to the tree of life in the Garden of Eden (Genesis 3:24), the two edged sword (Hebrews 4:12) that pierces even to the dividing of soul and spirit, is continuously turning, or it has broken down and has come to a standstill. Either the word of God has a height and a breadth and a length and a depth, which we are able to grasp mentally (Ephesians 3:18), or it is flat. Either this book has further meaning upon further meaning upon further meaning, or it has one meaning and we should all become Hasidic Jews and start declaring Sabbath-free zones everywhere.

Example 1

1 When Israel was a boy, then I loved him, and out of Egypt I called my son. (Hosea 11).

These words from the prophet Hosea are a historical statement about the calling of the nation of Israel out of Egypt at the time of Moses. But Matthew knew that they had a further fulfilment involving a further son:

15 and he stayed there until the decease of Herod, for that to be fulfilled which was spoken by Jehovah through his prophet, saying: Out of Egypt I called my son (Matthew 2).

This time the son was Jesus who was taken to Egypt by his parents to avoid persecution by Herod.

Example 2

Consider now the words of Jesus in Matthew 24:

21 For then there will be great tribulation such as has not occurred since the world's beginning until now, no, nor will occur again.
22 In fact, unless those days were cut short, no flesh would be saved; but on account of the chosen ones those days will be cut short (Matthew 24).

This looks like it applies to a great tribulation leading into Armageddon, since the 'world', which is biblical terms is the system of things post Adam's fall and pre Armageddon, is still ongoing, and we haven't all died yet (neither do we all die at the end). But in the same chapter we read:

15 Therefore, when you catch sight of the disgusting thing that causes desolation, as spoken of through Daniel the prophet, standing in a holy place, (let the reader use discernment,) 16 then let those in Judea begin fleeing to the mountains (Matthew 24).

This looks like it applies to the end of the Jewish system of things, and the great tribulation on the inhabitants of Jerusalem from 66Tishri when the Roman General Cestius entered the temple in Jerusalem until to 70Ab when the Roman General Titus burned the temple in Jerusalem. Obviously fleeing to the mountains of Judea is not a viable option for people in Colorado. For these reasons and other reasons many Christian churches understand that Matthew 24 applies both to the end of the Jewish system of things 66-70 AD and the end of this system of things (The great tribulation and Armageddon).

However what they have hitherto failed to understand is that rather than some verses applying to one end and other verses applying to the other end, the whole account has a first symbolism applying to the end of the Jewish system of things and a symbolism applying to this whole system of things, 'the world'. So actually every verse applies to the end of Jerusalem by the Romans and the end of the World by the final corruption of the UN. For the UN started as a great humanitarian organisation but ends as a corrupt worldwide dictatorship. If you do not believe that this sort of thing happens read animal farm by George Orwell, or go see Star Wars, the attack of the clones. The bad guys always begin by posing as saviours.

Here are another couple of famous examples from Matthew 24

2 Truly I say to you: By no means will a stone be left here upon a stone and not be thrown down (Matthew 24).

In the literal meaning, the temple was destroyed by the Roman General Titus in 70 CE, and the temple was knocked down, and no stone was left standing upon a stone. In the greater meaning the temple stones are the living stones of the Christian temple of the body of the Christ, which is all of the new covenant saints. And this is a prophecy that this temple will be knocked down, whilst the stones are still around. In other words what happened to the Jews, their rejection by God, will also happen to the first administration of the Christian church, under the New covenant Saints, these stones.

Jesus when describing the signs of the times to his disciples said:

34 Truly I say to you that this generation will by no means pass away until all these things occur (Matthew 24).

In other words one generation will see all of the signs of the time and the end. Now we know that this was true in the case of the disciples and Jewish system of things. They saw the signs of the times and they saw General Titus destroy Jerusalem and burn the temple in 70CE. But there is a further meaning that applies to the generation that sees the signs of the times today during Jesus' second presence. He is present right now, see - The 2 Presences and 6 related comings of the Christ. In the current meaning the generation that saw the first world war will see Armageddon.

Example 3

The apostle Paul in Galatians 4 informs us that 3 chapters of Genesis are written in a Symbolic Code. He says:

22 For example, it is written that Abraham acquired two sons, one by the servant girl and one by the free woman;
23 but the one by the servant girl was actually born in the manner of flesh, the other by the free woman through a promise.
24 These things stand as a symbolic drama; for these [women] mean two covenants, the one from Mount Sinai, which brings forth children for slavery, and which is Hagar.
25 Now this Hagar means Sinai, a mountain in Arabia, and she corresponds with the Jerusalem today, for she is in slavery with her children.
26 But the Jerusalem above is free, and she is our mother (Galatians 4).

Now we read about Hagar giving birth to Ishmael in Genesis 16, and we read about Sarah conceiving Isaac in Genesis 17 and her giving birth to Isaac in Genesis 21. So Paul is saying to us that these three chapters at the least, are a 'Symbolic Drama'. They have a greater meaning which is encoded symbolically. So these three chapters are not just dead history they are also living prophecy written in terms of dead history. They have a greater meaning relating to covenants (Which is outside the scope of this book). But for the full story see www.truebiblecode.com/understanding210.html

So come now dear reader, son or daughter of the greatest mind in the universe. Can you think of a question that is being begged of you by the holy spirit at this time?

What is so special about Genesis 16, Genesis 17, Genesis 21, Matthew 24 and Hosea 11?

Example 4

Here are the words of David before he became King of Israel. David was speaking about his own persecution as he hid in the wilderness for 7 years from the jealousy of King Saul.

1 My God, my God, why have you left me? (Psalm 22)

16 For dogs have surrounded me;
The assembly of evildoers themselves have enclosed me.
Like a lion [they are at] my hands and my feet.
17 I can count all my bones.
They themselves look, they gaze upon me.
18 They apportion my garments among themselves
And upon my clothing they cast lots.

These words were uttered by David about his own personal situation. But they are inspired prophetic words, and they have a second fulfilment in the impalement/Crucifixion of Jesus Christ. For he said just before he died:

46 Eli, Eli, lama sabachthani? that is, My God, my God, why have you forsaken me? (Matthew 27).

Not only this but the soldiers guarding him cast lots over his garments, none of his bones were broken on the stake (the legs of crucifixion victims were routinely broken to speed up their death if necessary). The robbers on either side of him had their legs broken. Jesus was of course fastened by his hands and his feet to the stake. So here again is history which is also living prophecy.

So now we can ask what is so special about Genesis 16, Genesis 17, Genesis 21, Matthew 24, Hosea 11 and Psalm 22?

Example 5

17 But as for the tree of the knowledge of good and bad you must not eat from it, for in the day you eat from it dying you will die (Genesis 2).

The literal meaning was that Adam died, not physically but judicially on the literal day that he ate. By Judicial death we mean that Adam was under a death sentence, and 'as good as dead' from then on. He was living merely by means of a stay of execution of that sentence. Jesus meant the same thing when he said:

22 Let the dead bury their dead (Matthew 8).

He meant: Let those who are still under Adam's death sentence bury their physically dead ones. The greater meaning of God's command in Genesis is that all of Adam's sons die physically during the period or 'day', wherein they continue to eat from this tree of knowledge of good and bad. So today, for example, even though we are no longer in the garden of Eden, we are still eating and we are still dying. The 'Day' of Genesis 2:17, is therefore the 'day' of this system of things, it is still ongoing! But not for much longer. When God threw Adam out of the garden he stopped him gaining access not to the tree of knowledge of Good and Bad, but to the tree of life:

24 And so he drove the man out and posted at the east of the garden of Eden the cherubs and the flaming blade of a sword that was turning itself continually to guard the way to the tree of life (Genesis 3).

Example 6

Jesus regarded the whole bible as the prophetic law of God, he said:

44 He now said to them: These are my words which I spoke to you while I was yet with you, that all the things written in the law of Moses and in the Prophets and Psalms about me must be fulfilled.
45 Then he opened up their minds fully to grasp the meaning of the Scriptures (Luke 24).

How can the law of Moses be fulfilled? A law is supposed to be obeyed not fulfilled! But he says again:

17 Indeed, it is easier for heaven and earth to pass away than for one particle of a letter of the Law to go unfulfilled (Luke 16).
So the law is all prophetic having a fulfillment. For Paul says further:

1 For since the Law has a shadow of the good things to come, but not the very substance of the things... (Hebrews 10).

But both Jesus and Paul show us that the 'Law' does not merely refer to the Law of Moses, in the Exodus, Leviticus and Numbers. It is the whole bible. The whole book is the law of God for mankind.

Paul says:

21 Tell me, you who want to be under law, Do you not hear the Law?
22 For example, it is written that Abraham acquired two sons, one by the servant girl and one by the free woman (Galatians 4).

But the account of Abraham and his sons and wives is not in the Law of Moses, it is in Genesis, which must therefore be a part of the 'law' of God. Jesus says:

34 Jesus answered them: Is it not written in your Law, I said: You are gods? (John 10).

But this wasn't written in the law of Moses, it was written in Psalm 82:6

6 I myself have said, You are gods, And all of you are sons of the Most High (Psalm 82).

And again Jesus says:

25 But it is that the word written in their Law may be fulfilled, 'They hated me without cause.' (John 15:25).

But this wasn't written in the law of Moses, no, it was written in Psalm 69:4

4 They that hate me without a cause are more than the hairs of my head (69 - Septuagint bible LXX)

So Psalms must be a part of the 'law' of God.

But Isaiah said, over 700 years after Moses was given the law:

3 Out of Zion law will go forth and the word of Jehovah out of Jerusalem (Isaiah 2).

In one meaning this law out of Zion is the word of God out of heavenly Jerusalem, which is the whole bible. What we have just done is extend an element of the bible code, namely, that every scripture has a further fulfillment, from the Law of Moses to the whole bible, by considering other scriptures to define precisely what Jesus meant. But we could equally well have done this using the Consistency Principle above.

This then, was how Jesus opened up the minds of his disciples fully to grasp the meaning of the scriptures (Luke 24). He explained to them how every verse of the bible had a further fulfilment

Opening up your mind fully to grasp the meaning of the scriptures

Every verse of the Law of Moses, every verse of Genesis, every verse of the Psalms, is to be fulfilled again. In fact the whole bible was the law of mankind and all of it, every letter of it, has to be fulfilled a second time. And for the majority of scriptures, we are now living in that time, which is why the same one, Jesus Christ, is opening up our minds yet again. For if every scripture has a further fulfilment then so does Luke 24 when it says:

45 Then he opened up their minds fully to grasp the meaning of the Scriptures.
46 and he said to them: In this way it is written that the Christ would suffer and rise from among the dead on the third day (Luke 24).

So how can our minds be opened up? In what way is the suffering and resurrection timing of Jesus written in the scriptures? Well Jesus has already explained...

40 For just as Jonah was in the belly of the huge fish three days and three nights, so the Son of man will be in the heart of the earth three days and three nights (Matthew 12).
30 For just as Jonah became a sign to the Ninevites, in the same way will the Son of man be also to this generation.

It is encoded symbolically in a historical account about a prophet who was eaten by a big fish! Yes, it is another symbolic drama. Jesus opened up the minds of his disciples by making them aware that the book was written in this symbolic way and that every account stood symbolically for something else. This indeed is one reason why Jesus spoke to the crowds entirely in illustrations. He was teaching them and teaching us, that the whole bible was written in this way. Even his famous parables have a greater meaning in addition to the obvious moral message!

34 All these things Jesus spoke to the crowds by illustrations. Indeed, without an illustration he would not speak to them (Matthew 13).

Here is the Prophetic Principle of the Bible Code in its full glory as we currently understand it:

The Prophetic Principle

Every literal account in the bible has a first literal meaning (which can contain some symbolism) and a second coded set of one or more word symbolic meanings.

Every symbolic account in the bible, such as a dream or vision or parable has a first event symbolic meaning and a second coded set of one or more word symbolic meanings.

Definition: The Event symbolic meaning is the symbolic interpretation of the events in an account

Definition: The Word symbolic meaning is the symbolic interpretation of the words of the account.

So the Word symbolic meaning is the symbolic interpretation of the words used to describe the events in the account, rather than the symbolic interpretation of the events themselves. Perhaps this is another reason why Jesus is called: The Word.

If the reader is puzzling over what precise distinction we are making, then please consider the following non scriptural example:

King Nebuchadnezzar went fishing. The king caught a fish. Nebuchadnezzar put the fish back. His servants said: My Lord, why did you not eat the fish. Nebuchadnezzar the King of Babylon said: Because I didn't have any chips to eat it with my servants!

In the literal meaning of this little (made up) story the character referred to variously as:

King Nebuchadnezzar
The King
Nebuchadnezzar
My Lord
Nebuchadnezzar the king of Babylon

... is just one character. He is Nebuchadezzar, the King of Babylon, the Lord over his servants. But in the Word symbolism, we are talking about 5 different but related characters. 'My Lord', 'the King' and 'Nebuchadnezzar' may be totally unrelated, but King Nebuchadnezzar will be related to 'The King' and to 'Nebuchadnezzar' and to 'Nebuchadnezzar the king of Babylon', since it shares common words with these other designations.

Event symbolism is referred to variously in this book and in the website www.truebiblecode.com as the first symbolism, the straight symbolism, or the easy symbolism.

Word symbolism is referred to as the second symbolism, the coded symbolism, the account symbolism or the hard symbolism.

First Proof of the Prophetic Principle

The first 2 verses of the book of Revelation read:

1 A revelation by Jesus Christ, which God gave him, to show his slaves the things that must shortly take place. And he sent forth his angel and presented [it] in signs through him to his slave John,
2 who bore witness to:

the word God gave
and to the witness Jesus Christ gave,
even to all the things he saw (Revelation 1:1,2).

Obviously 'all the things he saw' is the literal account of the vision. But John is also bearing witness to 'The word God gave'. This therefore is a witness to God's words themselves which is the word symbolic meaning. John is also bearing witness to the (symbolically expressed) witness that Jesus gave him in the form of the vision, this then is the event symbolic account, the symbolic meaning of the events of the vision.

All the things he saw	Literal account of the vision
The Word God gave	Coded word symbolic meaning of the vision
The Witness Jesus Christ gave	Straight event symbolic meaning of the vision

But then the reader must consider the following question. Did God, like we men do in many of our great projects, only work out how to write the bible properly when he had almost finished the job? Did he only work out how to inspire a symbolic bible account when he reached Revelation, having not thought of it at the time Moses wrote Genesis?

Obviously not for he is:

10 The one telling from the beginning the finale, and from long ago the things that have not been done (Isaiah 46).

He is the one who knew that Man would walk on the moon before he said: Let there be light. So we deduce that every symbolic account in the whole bible is written in this same way as Revelation. So all symbolic accounts have an event symbolic meaning and a word symbolic meaning.

It is not hard to see that literal accounts, such as the history of Abraham or David etc. have the same set of meanings as symbolic accounts except that the literal account is the event symbolic meaning. For a literal account is a symbolic account with no symbolism if you see what we mean. In mathematical terms this would be the identity symbolism. A symbolism in which an apple is always an apple and an orange is always an orange etc.

Accounts which contain both literal and symbolic portions, such as dreams, explanations and fulfilments, obey the two rules above for their respective portions.

Second Proof of the Prophetic Principle

Do you remember the famous words of Jesus:

16 In this way the last ones will be first, and the first ones last (Matthew 20).

There are many meanings of this scripture and other scriptures which repeated this last being first concept. But one interesting one is that the last words of the bible tell the reader how to decoded it. Hebrew books are read from the back to the front, they are read backwards. And this is a living prophecy from God, the creator of both English and Hebrew, that the decoding of the bible works backwards from the end. Much of our Chronology works backwards from the date of Armageddon. And as regards the bible code, well the answer is in the back of the book.

18 I am bearing witness to everyone that hears the words of the prophecy of this scroll: If anyone makes an addition to these things, God will add to him the plagues that are written in this scroll;

19 and if anyone takes anything away from the words of the scroll of this prophecy, God will take his portion away from the trees of life and out of the holy city, things which are written about in this scroll (Revelation 22).

The literal meaning of these two verses is that one should not remove any holy words from or add any non holy words to the literal holy words of the book of Revelation.

The symbolic meaning is actually an account symbolism, and is further the very definition of how all the symbolic meanings of the bible work! It defines the event symbolic and account symbolic meanings as follows:

Words	Symbolic meaning
Scroll	Account
Prophecy	Events
Scroll of this prophecy	Account of the events
Prophecy of this scroll	Events of the account
Words of the scroll of this prophecy	Symbolic meaning of the account of the events
Words of the prophecy of this scroll	Symbolic meaning of the events of the account

So the bible has two symbolic grammars, if you like. There is a symbolic meaning of the prophecy of the scroll, which is the straight forward symbolism of the events in the account. Then there is the symbolic meaning of the scroll of the prophecy, which is the symbolic meaning of the account of the events, the words that describe the events, hence the name 'Word Symbolism' for this symbolic meaning. This may be another reason why Jesus is called the 'Word' of God.

This is an implicit definition. Revelation describes Event Symbolism and Account Symbolism using Account symbolism. But nonetheless, the definition is there. Furthermore the two verses actually say that:

On should not add any further symbolic meanings to the event symbolism, and one should not remove any symbolic meanings from the account symbolism.

This is saying that every account has an account symbolic meaning, that cannot be removed, and event symbolic meaning cannot have extra symbolic threads. Then we apply the Omission Principle of the code.

If an account contains an obvious and glaring omission, then the word symbolic fulfillment of the account involves this omission.

Form this principle we deduce that one can add further symbolic threads in the account symbolic meaning and the event symbolic meaning might not exist.

So we are being told that there is always on and possibly more than one account symbolic meaning. And there is at most one and sometimes no event symbolic meaning. But this, of course, is how we defined these two symbolisms above. So Revelation 22:18,19 confirms out definition of these two symbolisms (implicitly).

For those who do not understand the meaning of explicit, consider the two equations below:

$x=2+1$ (explicit)
$x+3=2x$ (is implicit)

Both equations have the same solution, namely $x=3$, the latter equation defines x in terms of itself, this is the meaning of 'implicit'. Likewise Revelation 22:18,19 define event and account symbolisms through account symbolism.

So now we can finally understand the meaning of verse 10:

10 He also tells me: Do not seal up the words of the prophecy of this scroll, for the appointed time is near (Revelation 22).

The words of the prophecy of the scroll is the event symbolic meaning. This meaning is the straight symbolism, it is not sealed. In fact mankind saw that the wild beast of Revelation 13 and 17 was the League of Nations in 1920. This is the event symbolic meaning. But the account symbolic meaning, the word symbolism, was sealed up until the time of the end, which began in 1992Shebat21 - see [157].

Not only this but the plagues of Revelation are referred to by event symbolism and the trees of life and the holy city are referred to by account symbolism.

So the same account that tells us not to mess around physically with the physical holy words of Revelation, also tells us how precisely to mess around symbolically with these words in order to get their symbolic meanings. And by the Consistency Principle, this symbolic methodology, the two symbolisms, applies not just to the book of Revelation, but to the whole bible.

Finally we have the shortest parable in the bible which is:

33 Another illustration he spoke to them: The kingdom of the heavens is like leaven, which a woman took and hid in three large measures of flour, until the whole mass was fermented/leavened (Matthew 13).

Ok you young paduan learners! If it is the most insignificant and smallest of the parables in the whole bible, then what does this tell you about its spiritual meaning in this upside down world in which we live?

Yes, it is the greatest of them all in meaning. Well, the event symbolic meaning is as follows:

The woman is the holy spirit, the leaven is the bible code, and the three lumps of flour are the literal, the event symbolic and the account symbolic meanings of the bible. When the whole mass is fermented/leavened (decoded), then we can truly eat the whole book and see both the code and the truth and God and the true religion and his plan and his love and his humour and his righteouness, and our total and utter pretentiousness and stupidity. As regards the account symbolic meaning of Matthew 13:33 and the parallel account in Luke 13:20 please see section [69].

[6a] The Designations Principle

If one character in an account is referred to by several different designations, then each designation can stand for a different character in the word symbolic meaning.

For example in the account of the Rich Man and Lazarus - see [61], Abraham is referred to as:

Abraham
Father Abraham
My Father

In our understanding, in the word symbolic meaning, which is the interesting meaning of the parable, the symbolism is as follows:

Abraham	Abraham as a father physically
Father Abraham	Abraham as a father through the 1AC
My Father	Physical fatherhood.

[6b] The Successive Designations Principle

If a character or item in an account is referred to by two or more successive designations, then the account splits into two or more accounts respectively in the Word symbolic meaning. Each split account has a key designation or descriptor. Each split account is the same as the original account except that any phrase containing successive designations or descriptors and containing the key designation or descriptor is reduced to contain only the key designation or descriptor for that split account.

The first designation occurs first in Time. If several items or characters have successive designations then all the first designations form the first word symbolic account, and all the second designations from the second word symbolic account etc.

Some examples:

Sarah, Abraham's wife
Hagar, Sarah's maidservant

Splits into name and position as designation types.

Nebuchadnezzar the King
My Lord the King

Splits into king, and anything else as designation types.

Let us apply the Successive Designations Principle to the following made up and non scriptural example:

Sarah, Abraham's wife went shopping with Hagar her maidservant.
Hagar picked up a nice cooking pot
Abraham's wife picked up a bag of rice
Sarah, Abraham's wife, paid for them
She then took her maidservant home
Hagar, her maidservant boiled the rice in the pot
Her mistress gave the rice to Abraham
Abraham said: What a great meal Sarah, my wife
Sarah said: Hagar, my maidservant cooked it.
Abraham said: Thank you Hagar.

This splits into first and second designations as follows:

The Word symbolic account with the first designations

Sarah, went shopping with Hagar
Hagar picked up a nice cooking pot
Abraham's wife picked up a bag of rice
Sarah, paid for them
She then took her maidservant home
Hagar, boiled the rice in the pot
Her mistress gave the rice to Abraham

Abraham said: What a great meal Sarah
Sarah said: Hagar cooked it.
Abraham said: Thank you Hagar.

The Word symbolic account with the second designations

Abraham's wife went shopping with her maidservant.
Hagar picked up a nice cooking pot
Abraham's wife picked up a bag of rice
Abraham's wife, paid for them
She then took her maidservant home
Her maidservant boiled the rice in the pot
Her mistress gave the rice to Abraham
Abraham said: What a great meal my wife
Sarah said: My maidservant cooked it.
Abraham said: Thank you Hagar.

For the whole story on Genesis 16 the first part of the symbolic drama referred to by Paul in Galatians 4, please read www.truebiblecode.com/understanding210.html

The two great interpreters of dreams in the holy book are Joseph and Daniel. They are the two archetypical bible decoders. Get to know them and you get to know about this amazing code.

Forasmuch as an extraordinary spirit and knowledge and insight to interpret dreams and the explanation of riddles and the <u>untying of knots</u> had been found in him, in Daniel, whom the king himself named Belteshazzar. Now let Daniel himself be called, that he may show the very interpretation (Daniel 5:12).

Daniel chapter 5 has three designations for Belshazzar the king of Babylon. These are: The King, Belshazzar, and Belshazzar the king / King Belshazzar. In the symbolic meaning Belshazzar stands for someone, the king stands for someone else, and Belshazzar the king stands for both of them. If you do not realise this then the account is all tied up in a knot and you get nowhere. Once you realise this you can untangle the account into its two different strands. For the whole symbolism of Daniel 5, which you are unlikely to follow as yet! - see [164].

But this multiple designation untangling does not only apply to Daniel 5, it applies to the whole bible, by the Consistency Principle.

A classic example of Multiple Designation Symbolism is Revelation 12. Here we read:

So down the great dragon was hurled, the original serpent, the one called Devil and Satan, who is misleading the entire inhabited earth; he was hurled down to the earth, and his angels were hurled down with him (Revelations 12:9).
There are 4 designations for Satan in this one verse: The great Dragon, the original serpent, the Devil and Satan. Four different names for the same angel. In the rest of the account we read of the exploits of: The dragon, the devil and the serpent:

And war broke out in heaven: Michael and his angels battled with the dragon, and the dragon and its angels battled (Revelation 12:7).

On this account be glad, you heavens and you who reside in them! Woe for the earth and for the sea, because the Devil has come down to you, having great anger, knowing he has a short period of time (Revelation 12:12).

And the serpent disgorged water like a river from its mouth after the woman, to cause her to be drowned by the river (Revelation 12:15).
We are not going into the symbolism of this chapter at this point, save but to point out that the dragon represents Satan's secular kingdom over men, the serpent represents his corrupt members of God's true people (as in the original case of Eden) and the Devil is plain old Satan. Bearing this symbolism in mind please read this:

**And the <u>serpent disgorged water like a river from its mouth</u> after the woman, to cause her to be drowned by the river.
But the earth came to the woman's help, and the earth opened its mouth and swallowed up the <u>river that the dragon disgorged from its mouth</u>** (Revelation 12:15,16).
Now you are beginning to pull this book apart, to untangle its knots, to decode it. There is a reason that the designation 'serpent' in verse 15 is changed to the designation 'dragon' in verse 16. For a fuller explanation of Revelation 12 - see [165]

Example 1

And God proceeded to create the man in his image, in God's image he created him; male and female he created them (Genesis 1:27).
We have the creation of man by God mentioned three times in this verse. Applying the Repetition Principle, we know from the symbolic meaning that God has created men twice. In the section: Millions of years of human fossils reconciled with Genesis, we saw that he created Homo Sapiens, actually through the angels with a step by step design process that took millions of years (if our dating techniques are correct). Then once Homo sapiens had

developed spiritually sufficiently, God created Adam. Two creations of men. Now in verses 26 to 28 we have 2 designations for Adam, 'man' and 'the man'. This might not seem like two designations but remember the 'the God' and 'a god' can be two different characters. The former is the Father, the creator, who is Jehovah. The latter can be any angel:

I myself have said: You are Gods, and all of you are sons of the most high (Psalm 82:6)

Now as regards 'man' we read:

And God went on to say: Let us make man in our image, according to our likeness, and let them have in subjection the fish of the sea and the flying creatures of the heavens and the domestic animals and all the earth and every moving animal that is moving upon the earth (Genesis 1:26).
Whereas as regards 'the man' and his wife, we read:

Further, God blessed them and God said to them: Be fruitful and become many and fill the earth and subdue it, and have in subjection the fish of the sea and the flying creatures of the heavens and every living creature that is moving upon the earth (Genesis 1:28).
Now in the literal meaning Adam is 'man' and 'the man'. But in the Word symbolic meaning. Homo sapiens is 'man' and Adam is 'the man'. So 'man', Homo sapiens, pre-adamic man, is not blessed and has in subjection all animals. But Adam is blessed and has in subjection every living creature, which would include Homo sapiens. Not only that but Adam is told to fill the earth, and he has done this. Homo sapiens had only managed around 5 - 7million when Adam appeared in 4027 BC (McEvedy, Atlas of World Population). So the two designations split the account, in the Word symbolic meaning.

Example 2

1 For the kingdom of the heavens is like a man, a householder, who went out early in the morning to hire workers for his vineyard (Matthew 20).

So we have a man and a householder. Now the rest of the account refers variously to 'the man', 'the householder', and 'him'. So by the Account Splitting Principle we have two word symbolic meanings to Matthew 20 - see [192].

Example 3

1 Now Sarai, Abram's wife, had borne him no children; but she had an Egyptian maidservant and her name was Hagar (Genesis 16).

Two designations for Sarah, split the account into two Word Symbolic meanings - see [210]

[6c] The Successive Descriptions Principle

If a character or item in an account is referred to by two or more successive descriptors then that character or item has two or more word symbolic meanings, in each word symbolic account.

This principle gives us a test as to whether an account is scriptural or not! We expect soon, God willing, to be able to determine whether an account is scriptural or not by applying some of the principles of the code.

Some examples:

The famous example is 'The faithful and discreet slave' of Matthew 24:45. The Word symbolic account refers to two slaves, a faithful slave and a the discreet slave. The two descriptors 'faithful' and 'discreet' define two separate slaves in the word symbolic meaning - see [34].

Example 1

8 Now come, write it upon a tablet with them, and inscribe it even in a book, that it may serve for a future day, for a witness to time indefinite (Isaiah 30).

Two successive descriptions for writing on something, two future times of witness - this is the successive descriptions principle telling us that there are two fulfilments to the account, which we already know from the successive designations principle - see [270].

But having split up the literal account into several word symbolic accounts, how do we know whether or not a word takes the same meaning in the literal\event symbolic account as it does in the various Word symbolic accounts? Well this question is answered by the Repetition Principle of the code.

Example 2 (the successive descriptions principle and the successive designations principle)

And the Lord said: Who really is the faithful steward, the discreet one, whom his master will appoint over his body of attendants to keep giving them their measure of food supplies at the proper time? (Luke 12:42)

Who really is the faithful and discreet slave whom his master appointed over his domestics, to give them their food at the proper time? (Matthew 24:45).

In Luke we have two successive designations for the appointed one: 'the faithful steward' and 'the discreet one', so we know from the Successive Designations Principle that there are two greater Faithful Stewards in two word symbolic fulfilments

In Matthew we have one designation: 'the faithful and discreet slave'. But this designation describes the slave in two ways: faithful & discreet. So we have two successive descriptions of one slave in Matthew and two successive designations for one slave in Luke. The question we asked before we formulated the Successive Descriptions Principle was: Should we treat them in the same way in the word symbolic meaning? Should we treat two descriptions joined by a conjunction in the same way as two designations. Well the Greek in the two cases is:

ο πιστος δουλοσ και φρονιμος (Matthew) ο πιστος οικονομος ο φρονιμος€ (Luke)
The faithful slave and discreet (Matthew). The faithful steward the discreet [one] (Luke).

We know from the Immediate Repetition Principle to the concept of a description of a slave, that there are two successive repetitions of descriptions of the slave so there are two greater slaves in the symbolic meaning. But the account does not split, into two accounts as it does with a successive designation, because the parable of the Talents in Matthew 25 would be a nonsense if it did - see [35].

Therefore the faithful and discreet slave is in the greater meaning a faithful slave and a different discreet slave. The noun is distributing over the adjectives in mathematical terms. So these two accounts refer to 4 stewards/slaves, who are appointed over all of Jesus' belongings:

Truly I say to you, He will appoint him over all his belongings (Matthew 24:47).
I tell you truthfully, He will appoint him over all his belongings (Luke 12:44).

And here we have described the 4 true Christian administrations of Abraham's seed from Jesus' death to Armageddon. The 4 true Christian Religions. We call them FDS1, FDS2, FDS3, FDS4 in this book/website, standing for the first to the fourth Faithful and Discreet Slave. There were two slaves, two true religions in each of the two presences. Matthew refers to FDS1 and FDS3 and Luke refers to FDS2 and FDS4. The apostle Peter was the first head of FDS1, the apostle Paul was the first head of FDS2, these were both in the first presence. Charles Russell, who founded the Watchtower, was the first head of FDS3 (although he was never appointed over all of Jesus' belongings, but the second president of the Watchtower Joseph Rutherford was), and Gordon is the first head of FDS4, the Lord's Witnesses. For more on this - see [34]

Example 3

So now let Pharaoh look for a man discreet and wise and set him over the land of Egypt (Genesis 41:33).
This was Joseph in the literal meaning, who is described successively as being discreet and wise. In the word symbolic meaning the greater land of Egypt has two rulers, a discreet one and a wise one. The greater Egypt is this world just before the Kingdom of God, the greater promised land. The two greater Joseph's, the administrators of the true people of God in the Lord's day, the day of the second presence, are FDS3 and FDS4. FDS3 (Watchtower) was discreet and FDS4 (Lord's Witnesses) is wise.

Example 4

And here ascending out of the river Nile were seven cows beautiful in appearance and fat-fleshed, and they went feeding among the Nile grass.
And here there were seven other cows ascending after them out of the river Nile, ugly in appearance and thin-fleshed, and they took their stand alongside the cows by the bank of the river Nile (Genesis 41:2,3).
Joseph gave us the meaning of the literal dream in the same chapter. He revealed that we should take a cow for a year in that case. But both sets of 7 cows are described successively in two ways: beautiful and fat, ugly and thin. So there are two greater meanings of the cows in this dream, two further fulfillments for cows. We now have a reasonable understanding this account - see [304].

[C7] The Repetition Principle

If a non trivial word or phrase is recited three times in an account, and if the account has 3 different fulfilments in the literal meaning, the event symbolism and the word symbolism, then that word or phrase takes a different meaning in each of the 3 fulfilments.

This applies for 2 recitals or 4 recitals or any other number of recitals. The total number of recitals of a word or phrase is the total number of different meanings you have to play with in all the different fulfilments of the account.

If the total number of recitals (say 2) of a non trivial word or phrase is less than the total number of fulfilments of the account, then each there will be 2 different meanings of the word of phrase in the various fulfilments of the account.

If the total number of recitals of a non trivial word or phrase is equal to the total number of fulfilments of the account, then the word or phrase will take a different meaning in each fulfilment.

If there are more recitals of a non trivial word or phrase than there are fulfilments to the account then the word or phrase may take different meaning in each fulfilment or may not.

For God speaks once and twice - though one does not regard it (Job 33:14).
But one should regard it!!

Phrases do not have to be repeated word for word to qualify, but must be conceptually the same in the second recital. Because Amos has said:

Will two walk together unless they have met by appointment?

Will a lion roar in a forest when it has no prey?
Will a young maned lion give forth its voice from its hiding place if it has caught nothing at all?

Will a bird fall into a trap on the earth when there is no snare for it?
Does a trap go up from the ground when it has absolutely caught nothing?

If a horn is blown in a city, do not also the people themselves tremble?
If a calamity occurs in the city is it not also Jehovah who has acted/caused [it]**?**

For the sovereign Lord Jehovah will not do a thing unless he has revealed his confidential matter/secret to his servants, the prophets

There is a lion that has roared! Who will not be afraid?
The sovereign Lord Jehovah himself has spoken who will not prophesy? (Amos 3:3-8)

The forest is the hiding place of the lion, the roar is the giving forth of its voice, if it has caught nothing then it has no prey. These repeated concepts in slightly different words are how the sovereign Lord Jehovah reveals his confidential matters, his secrets to his servants the prophets today. A repeated recital does not need to use exactly the same words! Incidentally

God causes every calamity and every good thing, being behind it all. But he does not directly cause every calamity or every good thing.

Even though all scripture has a greater Word symbolic meaning some words and phrases (the ones that are not repeated) are invariant in this larger meaning. By this we mean that these particular words and phrases mean exactly the same in both the literal meaning/event symbolism and the word symbolic meaning.

Joseph says referring to the two similar dreams of Pharaoh:

And the fact that the dream was repeated to Pharaoh twice means that the thing is firmly established on the part of the [true] God, and the [true] God is speeding to do it (Genesis 41:32).

And so to repeat the dream to Pharaoh two times, because being decided upon by the God and being soon to do him (Genesis 41:32 - NIVHEOT Hebrew Interlinear Bible)

But the whole bible is a dream, in the sense that bible writers spoke under inspiration not from their subconscious mind but from God. So what Joseph is saying is:

If any inspired scripture is repeated twice then, the thing is decided upon by God and God will do it soon.

Our Historical mistakes in trying to understand Joseph's words

Our first interpretation of this verse, which is quite obviously explaining the meaning of a repeated scripture in an account, was that a repetition meant a further fulfillment. This was a correct interpretation, but it became meaningless when we realised that every scripture had a further fulfillment whether it was repeated or not. Our second interpretation of Joseph's definition of the meaning of a repeated scripture was that two recitals meant two fulfillments or two greater meanings. This interpretation relied on the argument that a future fulfillment of a future fulfillment is a second future fulfillment. But this argument is false. A future fulfillment of a future fulfillment can be the first future fulfillment. A second fulfillment is not required. So our logic was false. Another problem with this interpretation was that 11 recitals would have to mean 11 fulfillments and that does not work.

The Wheat and the Weeds

Jesus actually confirms our current understanding of the Repetition Principle and the correct interpretation of Joseph's explanation of a repetition in Matthew 13:24-30, in the account of the wheat and the weeds:

24 Another illustration he set before them, saying: The kingdom of the heavens has become like a man that <u>sowed fine seed</u> in his <u>field</u>.
25 While men were sleeping, his <u>enemy</u> came and oversowed zizania/darnel/<u>weeds</u> through [the] midst of the <u>wheat</u>, and left.
26 When the blade sprouted and produced fruit, then the <u>weeds</u> appeared also.
27 So the slaves of the householder came up and said to him: Master, did you not <u>sow fine seed</u> in your <u>field</u>? How, then, does it come to have <u>weeds</u>?
28 He said to them: An <u>enemy</u>, a man, did this.
They said to him: Do you want us, then, to go out and <u>collect</u> them?
29 He said: No, that by no chance, while collecting the <u>weeds</u>, you uproot the <u>wheat</u> with them.
30 Let both grow together until <u>the harvest</u>; and in the appointed time/season of <u>the harvest</u> I will tell the reapers, First <u>collect</u> the <u>weeds</u> and bind them in bundles to burn them up, then go to gathering the wheat into my storehouse (Matthew 13:24-30).

9 For we are God's fellow workers. You people are God's field under cultivation, God's building (1 Corinthians 3).

The repeated non trivial words are underlined.

Non repeated: sleeping, oversowed, left, blade sprouted and produced fruit, slaves of the householder, Master, reapers, bind them in bundles to burn them up, then go gathering, storehouse

Here is the straight symbolism, the event symbolism, the first symbolism of the account

The weeds are judged to be burned and so must be rotten saints. So the seed, both the wheat and the weeds must be sanctified Christians. The event symbolism is one group and the account symbolism is another. We only have two groups, the first new covenant saints and the second new covenant saints. Jesus sowed the first new covenant saints when he baptised and called his 12 apostles (although he baptised and personally called no one else). So in the event symbolism where Jesus is the man who sowed, the householder and the master, the seed must be first new covenant saints. So in the account symbolism it is second new covenant saints.

Man that sowed fine seed	The original Son of Man, Jesus (he baptised the apostles only - whom he chose and called). He only sowed this seed in the first presence obviously
Fine Seed	First new covenant saints
His Field (under cultivation)	Those baptised into the 1AC through John (Elijah1) and Paul (Elijah2)
Oversowed	Corrupted true seed into false seed, destroying their faith
Men were sleeping	Sanctified Christians not paying attention to the scriptures.
His enemy	Man of lawlessness, The son of destruction, the greater Judas of the first new covenant. The Evil slave of the fallen FDS1. 3 Let no one seduce you in any manner, because it will not come unless the apostasy comes first and the man of lawlessness gets revealed, the son of destruction (2 Thessalonians).
Enemy left	When FDS1 was disfellowshipped, then the man of lawlessness, the head of the GNS left the field of cultivation, which consists of water baptised brothers, i.e. non disfellowshipped sons of the 1AC.
Wheat	Those who finish their spirit baptism faithful, and are declared righteous in the spirit
Weeds	Those who don't and aren't
Blade sprouts	FDS2 Appointed to feed and later appointed over all Jesus' belongings
Blade produces fruit	FDS2 begins to grow, at this time, good and bad clearly visible. Only when the wheat and the darnel are fully grown can they be visibly distinguished
Householder, Master	Jesus
Slaves of the householder	FDS1, FDS2
Do you want us to collect the weeds	Should FDS1 and FDS2 collect the weeds within and deal with them?
No, lest you uproot the wheat	Man cannot judge this. The angels do it by moving the wheat into the next True Christian Congregation FDS2 and leaving the weeds behind in bundles to be burned the fallen congregations of FDS1 and other false religions at the time.
Bundles	All false churches during the period of administration of FDS2 during the presence
The Harvest	The Manifestation of the presence
The Harvest Season	The period of administration of FDS2 during which the manifestations of each presence occur.
Storehouse	God's true temple in the harvest season, the Congregation of FDS2
Gathering wheat into my storehouse	The angels direct faithful sanctified Christians out of FDS1 and into FDS2.

Here is the Word Symbolism

The Fine seed is sown in the World according to Jesus. There are two word symbolic fulfilments (man and enemy) by the Successive Designations Principle of the code, these are the first and second presence fulfilments. New covenant saints and sons of the 1AC are only sown in the true Christian congregation. It is second new covenant saints that are sown in the world. So these are the fine seed in the two word symbolic meanings.

Man that sowed fine seed	Paul and Gordon are both sons of man as was Jesus. A 'son of man' (literally a 'son of the man') is someone with a subcovenant of the 3AC. He provides angelic children to Adam. (Paul baptises the Nethinim from heaven?) 34 Who is this 'Son of the man' ? (John 12).
Fine Seed	Second new covenant saints
His Field (under cultivation)	The World - we were sowed everywhere
Oversowed	Corrupted true seed into false seed, destroying their faith
Men were sleeping	Sanctified Christians not paying attention to the scriptures.
His enemy (the enemy that sowed them)	the Devil
A man, an enemy	Man of lawlessness, the son of destruction, the greater Judas of the second new covenant. The presidents of the Good for Nothing Slave (GNS) and the Sluggish Slave (SS). Internal counterfeits to Paul and Gordon within the congregations of the fallen FDS1 and FDS3 3 Let no one seduce you in any manner, because it will not come unless the apostasy comes first and the man of lawlessness gets revealed, the son of destruction (2 Thessalonians).
His enemy left	Satan left the world after the fall of FDS2 (in 634 AD 1260 years before the second presence started, and 2 years after the Muslim prophet Mohammed died). He was imprisoned for 1000 years during the 1260 year period. Then he leaves the world again after Armageddon when he dies the second death.
Wheat	Those who finish their spirit baptism faithful, and are declared righteous in the spirit
Weeds	Those who don't and aren't
Blade sprouts	FDS2 and FDS4 Appointed to feed and later appointed over all Jesus' belongings
Blade produces fruit	FDS2 and FDS4 mature with full congregations, at this time, good and bad clearly visible. Only when the wheat and the darnel are fully grown can they be visibly distinguished
Householder, Master	Jesus (Jesus is not referred to as 'the householder', the slaves are referred to as 'slaves of the householder'). Jesus does not sow the second new covenant seed, as required by the Yes/No Question: Master did you not sow fine seed in your field?
Slaves of the householder	FDS2, FDS4
Do you want us to collect the weeds	Should FDS2 and FDS4 collect the weeds from the World? This is a Yes/No question again but it is answered as No. So this is the only answer. We wouldn't be able to do this anyway.
No, lest you uproot the wheat	No, Man cannot judge this. The angels make sure that only the wheat moves into the next True Christian Congregation FDS2, FDS4 and leaving the weeds behind in bundles to be burned the fallen congregations of FDS1 and FDS3. In this way neither FDS2 nor FDS4 collect them.
Bundles	False churches during the periods of administration of FDS2 and FDS4
The Harvest	The Manifestation of the presence
The Harvest Season	The periods of administration of FDS2 and FDS4 during which the manifestations of each presence occur.
Storehouse	God's true temple in the harvest season, the Congregations of FDS2, FDS4
Gathering wheat into my storehouse	The angels direct faithful sanctified Christians out of FDS1 and FDS3 and into FDS2 and FDS4.

Normally, when Jesus explains his parables, he gives the straight symbolic meaning, the event symbolism. This is true for example in the case of the Sower of Matthew 13 and Mark 4 - see [63]. But the explanation that Jesus gives for the parable of the Wheat and the Weeds is very ingenious. Jesus provides symbolic meanings only for the repeated words in the account with the exception of the word 'reapers' which appears only once. Now we know that the repeated words take a different meaning in the coded account symbolism to the meaning they take in the straight event symbolism in a symbolic account. So he is giving us the word symbolism here. Also in the event symbolism, 'an enemy, a man' is a man who is an enemy, and so he cannot be the Devil, who is not a man but is a fallen angel. The enemy can only be the Devil in the word symbolic meaning.

Here is his symbolic Jesus' look up table. We used this to get the word symbolic meaning above

The sower of the fine seed	is the Son of man
The field (under cultivation)	The 'cosmos' the World. (Those baptised in water Jesus purchased with his human soul and those baptised in spirit he purchased with his angelic soul.)
As for the fine seed	these are the sons of the Kingdom
but the weeds	are the sons of the wicked one
and the enemy that sowed them	is the Devil
The harvest	is a conclusion of a system of things
and the reapers	are the angels

Therefore, just as the weeds are collected and burned with fire, so it will be in the conclusion of the system of things (Matthew 13:36-40).

Since Jesus describes 'the harvest' as 'a conclusion of a system of things (an age)' there are two harvests, one during FDS2, the end of which was the end of the first Christian system in 455Tishri, and the other during FDS4 the end of which is Armageddon. The Greek language has no indefinite article, no word for 'a', but it does have a word for 'the' and this word was used in the case of 'harvest' and not in the case of 'conclusion of system of things'. Neither of these conclusions is the end of the Jewish System of things in 66-70CE. The wheat and the weeds both are spirit begotten Christians, not physical Jews.

Since the bundles in the second presence are the fallen FDS3 (now the evil slave of Matthew 24 and the wicked and sluggish slave of Matthew 25) and other false religions containing ex Jehovah's witnesses and ex International bible students (their original name) who are first or second new covenant saints. And since these bundles are collected by angels in order to keep the final FDS of the second presence, FDS4, clean, and since these bundles are burnt with fire, we must say to all faithful men in other churches: Get out of her my people! (Revelation 18:4). The JWs have been a harlot church riding on the back of the wild beast having become an NGO affiliate of the UN applying in 1991, being granted affiliate status on 1992January28 and once they were found out and people started putting it on the net and in the Guardian Newspaper on October 8th 2001, the Watchtower left the UN on 9 October 2001 - see [246].

But just because the lady has jumped down from the beast for a while does not mean that she is no longer a harlot.

So to decode an account first look for repeated phrases, and then for repeated words, and ponder over what their symbolic meaning could be. Once the key symbolism is realised the rest falls into place - eventually!

Example 1

The last creative act of God, on the day that Adam sinned was:

And Jehovah God proceeded to make long garments of skin for Adam and for his wife and to clothe them (Genesis 3:21).
The literal meaning is that God was their tailor. One consequence of this is that it is not a sin for women to wear fur coats. Because Adam and Eve were vegetarians when God killed the animal for it's skin. But the concept of clothing them is repeated, being recited first in terms of making long garments. So there is a greater way in which God clothed them. This greater way was that he created new bodies for them which instead of being indefinitely long lasting bodies which did not age, as were their previous bodies in the garden, were just long lasting, and were ageing. Adam lived for 930 years (Genesis 5:5). So these new ageing bodies, shorter versions of which we all inhabit today, were their long garments of skin as it were.

Example 2

However, let this one fact not be escaping your notice, beloved ones, that one day is with Jehovah as a thousand years and a thousand years as one day (2 Peter 3:8).
In the literal meaning, God lives forever, and so to him one day is just like 1,000 years. But this phrase is repeated, and so by the Repetition Principle, there is a greater way in which one day is as 1,000 years to God. This greater way is that one day represents 1,000 years in some scriptures.

And you must lie upon your right side in the second case, and you must carry the error of the house of Judah forty days. A day for a year, a day for a year, is what I have given you (Ezekiel 4:6).

In the literal meaning, the 40 days of Ezekiels laying on his right side represents 40 years or error of the house of Judah. But in the greater meaning, we know that the phrase: 'A day for a year' has a greater meaning. This meaning is that God has given 'a day for a year' to all would be Ezekiel's, 'prophets' who want to interpret the bible. A day for a year is an acceptable substitution and may give you the correct interpretation of any scripture in the symbolic meaning. It is a symbolism that God uses, we are being told.

Example 3

In the midst of the years oh bring it to life, in the midst of the years may you make it known (Habakkuk 3:2).

Bringing it to life refers to the resurrection of Jesus, and making it known likewise refers to his death which is the salvation plan of God, which Jesus made known - by dying. Now in the literal meaning we have his resurrection and his death in the midst of 'the years'. In the symbolic meaning, since the phrase 'in the midst of the years' is repeated, it has a different meaning to that which it has in the literal meaning.

Now the Hebrew word for 'midst' is קרב which can mean either amongst or middle. So in the literal meaning it must mean one and in the symbolic meaning the other. So however you look at it, Jesus died and was resurrected in the middle of 'the years'. For the full story see - The Midst Prophecy.

Example 4

**Consequently the Egyptians made the sons of Israel <u>slave</u> under tyranny.
And they kept making their life bitter with hard <u>slavery</u> at clay mortar and bricks
and with every form of <u>slavery</u> in the field.
Yes, every form of <u>slavery</u> of theirs in which they used them as <u>slaves</u> under tyranny** (Exodus 1:13,14).
This is just included to show the reader how repetitive a bible account can be!

Example 5 - Deep !

Now the earth proved to be formless and waste, and there was darkness on the surface of the deep, and God's spirit was moving to and fro over the surface of the waters (Genesis 1:2).

The surface of the deep is a repeated concept. The literal meaning is the surface of the seas on the earth, the symbolic meaning is the faces or the characters of the angels in the heavens (the Hebrew word translated surface, means face). For Genesis 1 is not just the story of the creation of the earth and of men, it is also the story of the creation of the heavens and of the angels, like it says in the first line of the bible: even the first 7 Hebrew words:

In the beginning God created the heavens and the earth (Genesis 1:1).

Then we read:

Now the earth proved to be formless and waste and there was darkness upon the surface of [the] watery deep. And God's active force was moving to and fro over the surface of the waters (Genesis 1:2).

Then God said:

Let there be light. Then there was light (Genesis 1:3).

This is a big scripture, and it is the second example of a repeated phrase in the bible, the existence of light being repeated.

Firstly it was said after the earth had been created, since we have already read how there was darkness on the surface of the oceans in verse 2. The literal meaning of this statement is therefore a second physical creation of physical light. Because we know that light was around before the earth was created.

But the symbolic meaning, the greater meaning, is actually the creation of a spiritual form of illumination which is time. This creation of time, was the means by which God could hold his angels to account. For without time, angels could misbehave and then 'undo' their works in some sense. But time is what condemns bad works and praises good works. This big bang therefore illuminated the faces of the angels (not that they have physical faces), but their characters were exposed. Hence we read:

After that God saw that the light was good, and God brought about a division between the light and the darkness. And God began calling the light Day and the darkness he called Night. And there came to be evening and there came to be morning, a first day (Genesis 1:5).

The light shows up good and bad. Light representing good and darkness representing bad. The symbolism of the account of the first 'day' of creation of Genesis 1 is:

Waters	Angels
Earth	God's heavenly administration
Surface of Waters	Characters of angels
Formless	Invariant adjective
Waste	Invariant adjective
Light	Time

So our two repeated phrases: the surface of the waters, and the existence of light, are the two key symbolisms of the account. The former means the characters of the angels and the latter means the creation of Time, which from our knowledge of Physics was the creation of space time, i.e. it was the Big Bang.

God has reset the speed of light !

Now we are in a position to try and solve the problems of modern physics and the dilemma of the Big Bang not producing enough background radiation and the universe being unstable with only one constant speed of light from the Big Bang until today. And we are in a position to discredit the erroneous belief that the universe has been around for billions of years. There have been at least two forms of light in the history of the universe. The universe was created with one form of light and then before man came along another form of light was created. Putting this in simple terms, the universe was created in warp drive and then light slowed down to 300 million metres per second just before man appeared (actually to trap man in his playpen, the solar system, until he grew up). Yes the speed of light is a constant. But it is a constant set by God. A constant that was reset by the command:

Let there be light.

It might have been 300 billion or 300 trillion or 300 billion trillion metres per second before this command. Amen. For a fuller account of this, see section [234]. God will reset the speed of light again in the future to enable us to reach every star in the universe, like Anakin Skywalker said. But he will not do this until we have grown up. It is not man who will invent warp drive in order to beat God. It is God who invented it in order to create the universe and in order to teach us. It is God who took the universe out of warp drive, for us, and for the angels, since they learn through us, and we through them, for they are our brothers. For we are moral minors and technological teenagers. It is no coincidence that one cannot explain this fundamental feature of the universe without admitting the existence of God.

This sort of realisation is the power of the Repetition Principle.

The Repetition Principle can be deduced to some extent from the Power Principle. Because if a phrase is repeated in an account, then it has no power in the literal meaning, because it is saying nothing new. The only way for it to have power is for it to mean something different in the greater meaning. So by the Power Principle, this must be the case. It must indeed have a greater meaning in the greater meaning.

[C8] The Immediate Repetition Principle

If a word or phrase or concept is recited two or three or any number of times successively in an account, then it has two or three or that number of distinct greater word symbolic meanings.

Abraham, Abraham (Genesis 22:11)
Jacob, Jacob (Genesis 46:2)
Impale him, impale him (John 19:6)
Conspiracy, conspiracy! (2 Chronicles 23:13)
And he said: Moses, Moses (Exodus 3:4)
Lord, Lord, did we not prophesy in your name, and expel demons in your name, and perform many powerful works in your name (Matthew 7:22)

By the Power Principle, the second recital must have a greater meaning, otherwise it is saying nothing at all. By the Repetition Principle the second recital has a greater meaning. But when the repetition is immediate then both recitals have a greater meaning. So there are two further Abrahams, two further Jacobs, fathers of 12 tribes, two further impalements, two further conspiracies, two further Moses' etc.

In the case of the impalement, the further two are represented by the two robbers impaled one on each side of Jesus. In the case of Moses, Jesus was one greater Moses, and there is another. The two further Abraham's, in the sense of Genesis 22:11, which is fathers who sacrifice firstborn sons validating covenants are beyond the scope of this book/website today. The principle works with phrases too:

And you must lay siege against it
and build a siege wall against it
and throw up a siege rampart against it
and set encampments against it
and put battering rams all around against it (Ezekiel 4:2).

The literal meaning referred to the 390 year siege of Jerusalem by its enemies from Rehoboam to Jehoiakim. The 5 greater sieges on the next five administrations of God's people were on Jerusalem with Zerubbabel's temple, and on the 4 true Christian religions.

A day for a year, a day for a year is what I have given you (Ezekiel 4:6).

However, let this one fact not be escaping your notice, beloved ones, that one day is with Jehovah as a thousand years and a thousand years as one day (2 Peter 3:8).

We already know that the symbolisms of a day for a year or a thousand years can apply to any bible account.

[C9] The No Coincidences Principle

There are no coincidences in the bible. Every apparent coincidence is appointed by God

As regards whatever our hearts may condemn us in, because God is greater than our hearts and knows all things (1 John 3:20).

Since God knows all things he is aware in particular of all of the coincidences in the bible. Since he is not given to deliberately misleading us (unless it is in our interest), we must assume that such scriptural similarities are a matter of design, rather than coincidence. The prophet Amos is saying:

Will two walk together unless they have met by appointment?
i.e. are there any coincidences in God's actions, and therefore in the bible?

Will a lion roar in a forest when it has no prey?
Will a young maned lion give forth its voice from its hiding place if it has caught nothing at all?
These two lines are saying the same thing, and it is not a coincidence

Will a bird fall into a trap on the earth when there is no snare for it?
Does a trap go up from the ground when it has absolutely caught nothing?
These two lines are saying the same thing, and it is not a coincidence

If a horn is blown in a city, do not also the people themselves tremble?
If a calamity occurs in the city is it not also Jehovah who has acted/caused [it]?
The horn was blown when a calamity was about to occur as a warning. God is indirectly behind everything.

For the sovereign Lord Jehovah will not do a thing unless he has revealed his confidential matter/secret to his servants, the prophets (Amos 3:3-7).

This applies to calamities on cities of his people. So he warns us all through his prophets, in a secret way, using apparent coincidences. But at the end of the day in the bible if two walk together then it is not a coincidence it is by appointment.

[C9a] Example 1

And Jehovah God went on to say: It is not good for the man to continue by himself. I am going to make a <u>helper</u> for him, as a complement of him (Genesis 2:18).

But the <u>helper</u>, the holy spirit, which the Father will send in my name, that one will teach you all things and bring back to your minds all the things I told you (John 14:26).

We know that it is not a coincidence that God himself called Adam's wife his helper, and that John called the holy spirit a helper. It means that the holy spirit is someone's wife. Well if God is our father then we must also have a mother. Paul identifies his mother as the Jerusalem above:

But the Jerusalem above is free, and she is our mother (Galatians 4:26). So the Jerusalem above is God's wife obviously, and so it is the Holy spirit. But the Jerusalem above is just God's administration of all of his loyal heavenly people. Just as the Jerusalem below was his administration of all of his loyal earthly people at one time. So the Holy spirit is all of God's holy angels, it is all of the holy spirits. So there it is, the precise identity of the Holy Spirit, from the No Coincidence Principle.

The Holy Spirit is a living thing it is not a force as some religions (such as the Jehovah's Witnesses) believe, because it pleads for us:

In like manner the spirit also joins in with help for our weakness; for the [problem of] what we should pray for as we need to we do not know, but the spirit itself pleads for us with groanings unuttered (Romans 8:26).

Who ever heard of a force that pleads? No, it is our mother who pleads with our father, God, for her children! It is so beautiful. It is not a mysterious trinity as most of Christendom would have us believe. It is all of the holy angels who are sealed.

Example 2

For example, the sect of Nicolaus is mentioned in the counsel to Ephesus and to Pergamum in Revelation 3. The only other mention of his name is as one of the 7 ministerial servants in Acts 6:

And the thing spoken was pleasing to the whole multitude, and they selected Stephen, a man full of faith and holy spirit, and Philip and Prochorus and Nicanor and Timon and Parmenas and Nicolaus, a proselyte of Antioch (Acts 6:5).

Still, you do have this, that you hate the deeds of the sect of Nicolaus, which I also hate (Revelation 2:6).

This is not a coincidence. God is fully aware of this situation. It may not of necessity be the case that the Nicolaus of Acts 6 develops for himself a sect, but it is the case that we can learn about the sect by reading Acts 6, it is of help to us. If it is not literally of help, then it is symbolically or cryptically of help.

[C10] The Times Principle, the Generalisation of Daniel 4

The phrase 'n times' can mean 'n years' or 'n years of years' which is '360n years'

We read in Revelation 12:

But the two wings of the great eagle were given the woman, that she might fly into the wilderness to her place; there is where she is fed for a time and times and half a time away from the face of the serpent (Revelation 12:14).

Where 'times' is obviously in the plural (since Greek has no dual number as Hebrew does). But earlier in the same chapter we read:

And the woman fled into the wilderness, where she has a place prepared by God, that they should feed her there a thousand two hundred and sixty days (Revelation 12:6).

In the actual vision, (but not in it's symbolic meaning) the two periods are the same period and so we are being told by holy spirit that the phrase 'a time, times and half a time' is 1260 days of the BLC (Biblical Lunar Calendar), which is 3.5 lunar years of 360 days. But a year is a time, a cycle, of the earth around the sun. So 3.5 years is 3.5 times. So 3.5 times is 1260 days. So 7 times is 2520 days. So n times is 360n days.

The first example of the Times Principle - Daniel 4

In Daniel chapter 4, Nebuchadnezzar, who is the King of Babylon and the King of God's people the Jews, who are prisoners in Babylon, is removed from his throne for a period of 'seven times' and then he is re instated as King. The phrase 'seven times' appears several times in the account:

Let its heart be changed from that of mankind, and let the heart of a beast be given to it, and let <u>seven times</u> pass over it (Daniel 4:16).

And from mankind they are driving even you away, and with the beasts of the field your dwelling will be. Vegetation they will give even to you to eat just like bulls, and <u>seven times</u> themselves will pass over you, until you know that the Most High is Ruler in the kingdom of mankind, and that to the one whom he wants to he gives it (Daniel 4:32).

This period of 7 times is 2520 days in the literal meaning, 7 Biblical Lunar years. So Nebuchadnezzar was a foreign king over God's people who lost his kingship over them and over his own people and then regained it after 2520 days.

Now God ceased having a vassal king that represented him over his people sometime before Nebuchadnezzar besieged Jerusalem and burnt the temple in 586Ab10 BC (13th August). In fact the first king over the Jews who did not represent God was Jehoiakim who acceded sometime between 608 Tishri BC (September/October) and 607 Elul (August/September), in fact it was on 608Chislev10 (13th November) - see [97]. So the last agricultural year of God's Kingship started in 608Tishri, and the first agricultural year without God as king over the seed of Abraham started on 607Tishri1 (23rd September). Jehoiakim was appointed by Pharaoh Nechoh of Egypt and was a vassal of his, see - The Chronology from Solomon to Zedekiah.

So the big question for God's people as prisoners in the foreign land of Babylon, having been deported there by Nebuchadnezzar after he burnt Jerusalem and Solomon's temple, is not how long will it be until we get Nebuchadnezzar back as our king? But, how long will it be after God ceased being our king, before he again becomes our king through a vassal King who actually represents him?

It is this period that has been taken as the greater meaning of Daniel chapter 4 by many Second Adventists, who realised of course that the vassal King that the Most High God wants to give the kingdom of mankind to at the end of this period is Jesus. This appointment is then possibly the 'second coming' or the 'second presence' of the Christ. The Watchtower originally thought that the end of this period would be Armageddon (not unreasonably on the basis of Daniel 4 alone).

Historically, what 'second adventists' have done is to take Nebuchadnezzar to represent: God's vassal king over his people. They then say that the 2520 day period, which represents the time during which God does not have a vassal king over his people, is obviously way too short and so should be taken at 'a day for a year', using the acceptable symbolism we deduced in [c2.3]. Therefore, the period during which God's people do not have a vassal king representing God over them is 2520 years long.

This would mean that Jesus becomes God's vassal king over his people in 1914Tishri, 2520 years after 607Tishri1 (there was no 0 BC, it went 1BC then 1AD). Incidentally, no religion on this earth until the Lord's witnesses has had the correct Chronology for the kings or the correct understanding of whom the last vassal king of Judah representing God was.

In fact Jesus did become God's vassal king in heaven over God's true people, who were no longer physical Jews, but by now had become Christians, but were all Abraham's true seed, sons of the First Abrahamic Covenant, baptised by an Elijah into the 1AC, who came first, before Jesus came again in 1914Tishri15 (7th October), as we shall see. This Elijah was actually Charles Russell, the founder of the Watchtower (see later).

And they began to question him, saying: Why do the scribes say that first Elijah must come?
He said to them: Elijah does come first and restore all things; but how is it that it is written respecting the Son of man that he must undergo many sufferings and be treated as of no account? (Mark 9:11,12).

The problem with the naive interpretation of the symbolic Nebuchadnezzar as being God's vassal king over Abraham's true seed, who is Jesus at the end of the 2520 year period, is that Daniel says to him:

Therefore, O king, may my counsel seem good to you, and remove your own sins by righteousness, and your iniquity by showing mercy to the poor ones. Maybe there will occur a lengthening of your prosperity (Daniel 4:27).
Jesus had no sin, but was unblemished, and he had no iniquity, so this counsel cannot apply to him.

The solution to this problem is to realise that the 7 Prophetic Times fulfilment is a Word symbolism and so we have the latitude to assign a different symbolic meaning to each designation for King Nebuchadnezzar.

'Lord of me', and 'My Lord the king' do not suffer any passages in the account which cannot apply to Jesus. Daniel 4 is the account of the loss and regaining of several kingships over God's people. We are not going into them here however. The purpose of the above was to show how the Designations Principle is necessary to find the true interpretation of Daniel 4. However there is a scripture in Ezekiel which shows us that God's kingship over his people is ruined three times. It is:

**And as for you, Oh profane, wicked chieftain/prince of Israel, whose day has come in the time of the error of [the] end, this is what the Sovereign Lord Jehovah has said: Remove the turban, and lift off the crown. This will not be the same. Put on high even what is low, and bring low even the high one.
A ruin, a ruin, a ruin I shall make it. As for this also, it will certainly become no [one's] until he comes who has the legal right, and I must give [it] to him** (Ezekiel 21:25-27 NWT adapted by NIVHEOT).

So the crown comes off, when the head one is not a king (from God's standpoint). Three greater ruins, are made of the kingship: a ruin, a ruin, a ruin, using the Immediate Repetition Principle. The one with the legal right is Jesus in the literal meaning.

Verifying that the Kingship malediction period is 2520 years from Leviticus 26

There is an independent confirmation that 2520 years is the correct symbolic interpretation of Daniel 4 to be found in Leviticus 26 - see [121]. This is a contract under the law of Moses between God and the whole Nation of Israel collectively. One of the penalties for breaking this contract was a 2520 year Kingship Malediction on God's people, wherein God did not act as King over the sons of Abraham, who are enlarged to mean under through either of his first two covenants - see [9]. The 2520 year penalty is a sevenfold retribution for a 360 year combined idolatry error of both the houses of Israel and Judah added together, which is deduced from Ezekiel 4. In this chapter the Holy Spirit tells us to interpret the actions of the prophet taking a day for a year. So it is not unreasonable to interpret the actions of King Nebuchadnezzar, which being in the bible are prophetic, in the same way. So that his 2520 day loss of kingship stands for a 2520 year loss of kingship, as we have seen above.

The History of the First Bible Key

The phrase 'n times' can be 360n years in a bible account.

The phrase 'x times' in the bible can mean 360x years. When it does, these 360 year periods are called Prophetic Times. Amazingly this is where mankind in general and the Jehovah's Witnesses in particular have been blind.

The JWs know that 'x times' means 'x periods of 360 years' in Daniel chapter 4, and so do many other Christian and Jewish religions and theologians. But no one ever thought of applying this key to any other incidence of the phrase 'x times' in the bible. This is because no one had grasped the Consistency Principle.

This is of course the same mistake that bible scholars and the Watchtower have made in the case of greater meanings. They believe that Daniel 4 has a greater meaning, they know from Paul's words in Galatians 4:24 that Genesis 16 has a greater meaning, but they have failed to realise that perhaps Daniel 5 or perhaps Genesis 17 and just maybe every other chapter in the bible has a greater meaning too! This is because no one had grasped the Prophetic Principle. Why did not one ask the question:

If Daniel 4 has a greater symbolic meaning, then does Daniel 5 have one too? Would this have been a giant leap of inordinate intellectual perspicacity?? Look what the good book has to say on this matter:

For upon you men Jehovah has poured a spirit of deep sleep, and he closes your eyes, the prophets, and he has covered even your heads, the visionaries. And for you men the vision of everything becomes like the words of a book, that has been sealed up, which they give to someone knowing writing saying: Read this out loud, please. And he has to say: I am unable for it is sealed up. And the book must be given to someone that does not know writing, saying: Read this out loud please. And he has to say: I do not know writing at all (Isaiah 29:10-12).

Those who do know writing today are the modern day Pharisees, the elders of the third true congregation (now a false congregation). They cannot see the meaning of the book, which is the bible, because they are asleep with a bag over their heads. But the one who does not know writing, who has not been taught in the pharisaical schools for leaders in the Watchtower, this one does not say that he is unable. So we deduce that he is able. He stands for the 4th true congregation. The first members of this congregation were Gordon, Tony and later Massoud.

Gordon and Tony, two Lord's Witnesses, when there were only two of us (although Gordon does not think that Tony and Massoud were baptised until 1994Elul), grasped this bible key in February/March 1992. They then charged through the bible substituting '360 years' for 'times' everywhere, and deduced the following:

The Great Prophetic Times Periods

Name	x times	Start	Finish	Chapter	Section
Exedenic Times	7 times	3993Nisan16	1473Nisan15	Genesis 4:15	[133]
Alienation Times	7 times	2488Sivan	33Sivan6	Leviticus 4:6,17	[129]
Gentile Times	7 times	607Tishri	1914Tishri15	Daniel 4:25	[121], [123]
Intermission Times	5 times	95Tishri	1895Tishri	John 5:2 (5 Collonades)	[191]
Temple Times	3 times	1048Nisan16	33Nisan16	1 Chronicles 21:12 (3 days, months, years)	[40]
Joseph's Times	2 times	2488Sivan	1768Sivan	Genesis 45:6,7 Not proved	Not proved
Pharaoh's Times	10 times	1593Nisan	2008Nisan14	Genesis 31:7	[31]
Lamech's Times	11 times	3928Nisan	33Nisan14	Genesis 4:24, Matthew 18:22 (77 times compared to 7 times)	Vaguely covered in [133]
Separating Times	¼ time	1918Nisan16	2008Nisan16	Luke 12:54,55	Not covered in website

The rest of our early understandings, many of which were wrong, are in 'Letter to the Society'.

The Blindness of the Watchtower

The reason that the Watchtower never worked this out in scriptural terms is that God blinded them because they lost their love for him. For their founder Charles Russell was not the Laodicean Messenger, as is inscribed on his gravestone, but was in fact the Ephesian messenger (see [15,16]), the angel of the first congregation of the second presence (which he believed would be the last). And the counsel to him from Jesus was:

Nevertheless I hold this against you, that you lost the love you had at first (Revelation 2:4).

Isaiah prophesies that the JWs will become blind and deaf:

You are my witnesses, is the utterance of Jehovah: <u>Even my servant</u> whom I have chosen, in order that you may know and have faith in me, and that you may understand that I am the same One. Before me there was no God formed, and after me there continued to be none.

I--I am Jehovah, and besides me there is no savior.

I myself have told forth and have saved and have caused [it] to be heard, when there was among you no strange [god]. So you are my witnesses, is the utterance of Jehovah, and I am God (Isaiah 43:10-12)

Hear, you deaf ones; and look forth to see, you blind ones.

Who is blind, if not my servant, and who is deaf as my messenger whom I send? Who is blind as the one rewarded, or <u>blind as the servant of Jehovah</u>?

It was a case of seeing many things, but you did not <u>keep watching</u>. It was a case of opening the ears, but you did not keep listening (Isaiah 42:18-20).

This is why Jesus said to Peter:

And he came and found them sleeping, and he said to Peter: Simon, are you sleeping? Did you not have strength to <u>keep on the watch</u> one hour? (Mark 14:37).

The reason that the Watchtower did not see these in psychological terms was because Russell set the goals of the Society as follows:

The work in which the Lord has been pleased to use our humble talents has been less a work of origination than of reconstruction, adjustment, harmonisation (Kingdom Proclaimers).

An honest and humble appraisal (although saying that you're humble in circumstances where humility is considered to be a virtue is more immodest than it is humble!!) But why should the past restrict the future? Why should he cut short the hand of God in that way. Is there anything that is too extraordinary for him? Jesus thought not:

And he went on to say: Abba, Father, all things are possible to you; remove this cup from me. Yet not what I want, but what you want (Mark 14:36).

This is rather like a motivational speech very well given by Will Carling about the British Lions at an Amway conference. The Lions set as their goal, a place in the Final of the World Cup in South Africa. And they got there. And then they lost the final because they had not set the winning of that match as their goal.

Russell was not the first Adventist to realise that Daniel 4 related to a period of 2520 years. Neither was he the first to get the start date of 607 correct. But he was the first and only Adventist to get the end date of this period absolutely correct to the Hebrew month 1914Tishri and to set up a religion which had the guts to declare it, guts which they have now lost, along with their faith and their love. The incredible thing is that he did this believing that Jerusalem fell to Nebuchadnezzar in 606 BC, when it fell in 586. He worked things backwards from 536Tishri, a false date for the end of either of the two 70 year land Sabbath exiles. He did not even know there were two of them! Basically he made a series of mistakes and yet got the right answer. Now there is the activity of the holy spirit and the love of our God ! For the history of the main second adventist prophecy - see [120].

But what Russell did absolutely marvellously was to adopt the following crucial philosophy for bible research, although it is a matter of faith and logic as well. He proposed that:

The way to test your interpretation, is not against doctrines of churches but against all other scriptures relating to the subject matter of your interpretation. When you have harmonised them all then you have God's interpretation.

He was not the first to have this idea either (Isaac Newton had it for example). God very rarely gives us the whole picture in one piece. He prefers to give us jigsaws. This we have made a principle of the code called the Jigsaw Principle!

[C11] The Numerical Principle

A given number of living or inanimate items in a bible account can stand symbolically for that number of 'Times'.
A 'Time' can stand literally or symbolically for a day, a month or a year.

And God went on to say: Let luminaries come to be in the expanse of the heavens to make a division between the day and the night; and they must serve as signs and for seasons and for days and years (Genesis 1:14).

The planetary luminaries of the Sun and the moon define years and months. The earth itself defines days although it is the rotation with respect to the Sun that we actually see. So a day is one time of the earth around itself. A month is one time of the moon around the earth. A year is one time of the earth around the Sun. All three are 'times' of revolution. These are God's celestial time pieces. In scientific terms a 'time' is a 'cycle'.

So in the bible a 'time' can mean a day a month or a year.

The penalty that God prescribed through Gad, to David, for his part in the registration sin was:

Accordingly Gad went in to David and said to him: This is what Jehovah has said: Take your pick, whether for three years there is to be a famine, or for three months there is to be a sweeping away from before your adversaries and for the sword of your enemies to overtake [you], or for three days there is to be the sword of Jehovah, even pestilence, in the land, with Jehovah's angel bringing ruin in all the territory of Israel.

And now see what I should reply to the One sending me (1 Chronicles 21:11,12).

All three penalties were '3 times' in duration, and they prefigure the three times of the temple times - see [40]. These times were, days, months and years.

Joseph, the 11th son of Jacob whose name was changed to Israel, was sold into slavery by his brothers and ended up in prison in Egypt with the chief of the bakers and the chief of the cupbearers of Pharaoh. The chief of the cupbearers dreamed about three twigs, and the chief of the bakers dreamed about three baskets. Joseph interpreted these parts of their dreams as follows:

As regards the cupbearer:
Then Joseph said to him: This is its interpretation: The 3 twigs are 3 days (Genesis 40:12).

As regards the baker:
Then Joseph answered and said: This is its interpretation: The 3 baskets are 3 days (Genesis 40:18).

So Joseph, the first bible decoder recorded in the holy book, is telling us that a given number of twigs or baskets can stand for a given number of days or times or cycles. Then Pharaoh himself had one dream about 7 fat cows and 7 thin cows (this was not a dream about women), and then a second dream about 7 fat ears of grain and 7 thin ears of grain. Guess how Joseph interpreted these parts of these dreams:

223

The 7 good cows are 7 years. Likewise the 7 good ears of grain are 7 years. The dream is but one (Genesis 41:26).

So the 7 cows and the 7 ears of grain were 7 years or 7 times or 7 cycles. So a cow or an ear of grain or a twig or a basket can be a time which can be a day or a year. Now we apply the all powerful Consistency Principle, and it is not hard to generalise this to:

A given number of living or inanimate things in a bible account can stand for that number of times, i.e. days or months or years

C11.1 First example of the Numerical Principle

This is the account of the registration sin of David, mainly taken from 1 Chronicles 21, but also using the parallel account in 2 Samuel 24. Please do not be put off by the apparent contradictions in these two accounts. Read them very carefully in an accurately translated bible (we suggest the New World Translation of the Watchtower or our own translation when it comes out, or any Hebrew Interlinear Translation), and you will see that these are not actually contradictions. For example there were 800,000 valiant men drawing sword in Israel according to 2 Samuel 24, but there were 1,100,000 men drawing sword according to 1 Chronicles 21. The distinction being made is that 300,000 of them were not 'valiant'.

Now Joab, the head of the army, who conducted the registration, would have made such a distinction, knowing which ones would make good soldiers and which ones would not. This was his business. Likewise the 7 year famine 'in your land' proposed by Jehovah in 2 Samuel 24 is reckoned including the 3 year famine that had just ended in 2 Samuel 21, which is referred to in the first verse:

And <u>again</u>, the anger of Jehovah came to be hot against Israel (2 Samuel 24:1).

In the case of the previous famine, God was pacified and the famine therefore halted by a sacrifice. The 3 year famine of 1 Chronicles 21, is reckoned excluding the earlier 3 year famine. One presumes that the period between these two famines was one year, and food was not exactly plentiful during that year between two famines.

And Satan proceeded to stand up against Israel and to incite David to number Israel.
So David said to Joab and the chiefs of the people: Go, count Israel from Beer-sheba to Dan and bring it to me that I may know their number.
But Joab said: May Jehovah add to his people a hundred times as

many as they are. Do they not, O my lord the king, all of them belong to my lord as servants? Why does my lord seek this? Why should he become a cause of guilt to Israel?
The king's word, however, prevailed over Joab, so that Joab went out and walked through all Israel, after which he came to Jerusalem. Joab now gave the number of the registration of the people to David; and all Israel amounted to a million one hundred thousand men drawing sword, and Judah four hundred and seventy thousand men drawing sword (1 Chronicles 21:1-5).

There is a lot of drawing of swords that goes on in this account, so by the Repetition Principle, this is the key symbolism in the greater meaning:

When David raised his eyes, he got to see Jehovah's angel standing between the earth and the heavens with his drawn sword in his hand extended toward Jerusalem (1 Chronicles 21:16).

Moreover, YHWH said the word to the angel, who accordingly returned his sword to its sheath (1 Chronicles 21:27).

We now apply the Numerical Principle to these 1.1 million men of Israel drawing sword, and deduce that they represent 1.1 million days or 3055 years 200 days in the greater meaning of this account. They end when the passover angel himself, Michael, puts his sword back in his sheath at the end of Armageddon, on 2008Elul16 - see [163]. They start 1.1 million days earlier which is 1049Shebat26 BC. But this is 50 days before 1048Nisan16 when the 3 day plague ended and David purchased the threshing floor of Ornan. This was 22.5 years before Solomon's temple was inaugurated because all temples are commissioned 22.5 years before they are inaugurated. And Solomon's was inaugurated in 1026Tishri - see [The 3 Times of the Temple Times - section 40]. So Solomon was commissioned to build his temple and the foundation was purchased on 1048Nisan16.

50 days is a reasonable period within which David could start feeling bad, and eventually pray to God for forgiveness, then Gad could come and tell him about his penalty choices, then the 3 day plague could occur. But we can actually confirm this 50 day period using the Numerical Principle again in the parallel account of this registration, plague and temple site purchase in 2 Samuel 24:

But Araunah said to David: Let my lord the king take it and offer up what is good in his eyes. See the cattle for the burnt offering and the threshing sledge and the implements of the cattle for the wood. Everything Araunah, Oh king, does give to the king. And Araunah went on to say to the king: May Jehovah your God show pleasure in you. However, the king said to Araunah (Ornan): No, but without fail I shall

buy it from you <u>for a price</u>; and I shall not offer up to Jehovah my God burnt sacrifices without cost. Accordingly David bought the <u>threshing floor and the cattle</u> for 50 silver shekels (2 Samuel 24:22-24).

Whereas in the 1 Chronicles 21 account we read:

**However, King David said to Ornan: No, but without fail I shall make the purchase <u>for the money in full</u>, because I shall not carry what is yours to Jehovah to offer up burnt sacrifices without cost.
So David gave Ornan for <u>the place gold</u> shekels to the weight of 600** (1 Chronicles 21:24,25).

These two accounts again look contradictory at first sight. But they aren't. The 600 gold shekels represents the price for the real estate, 'the place'. The 50 silver shekels represents the price for the threshing floor equipment (all wood) and the cattle, all of which was used for the first sacrifice of cattle burnt over wood, by David which halted the plague:

**Then David built there an altar to Jehovah and offered up burnt sacrifices and communion sacrifices, and he proceeded to call upon Jehovah, who now answered him with fire from the heavens upon the altar of burnt offering.
Moreover, Jehovah said the word to the angel, who accordingly returned his sword to its sheath** (1 Chronicles 21:26,27).

If you go into a florists shop and say: How much for the whole shop? They will take it that you wish to purchase all of their stock, not the shop. This is the distinction being made between the 50 shekels of silver and the 600 shekels of Gold.

Now 50 shekels of silver was the cost of pacifying the true God by this sacrifice. But the period during which God was upset, started the moment that Joab handed the result of the registration to David (this being when he had actually completed the registration - he could have stopped it before then) and ended with the fire from the heavens burning up and accepting the offering. Now we apply the Numerical Principle to the 50 shekels, and take them as a day for a shekel, i.e. God was upset for 50 days. So he started to be upset on 1049Shebat26, 50 days before 1048Nisan16.

But this date 1049Shebat26 is precisely the day we got by subtracting 1,100,000 days from 2008Elul16, the last day of Armageddon. So since we already know that the Numerical principle is true, we have just confirmed the end date of Armageddon to the very day by simply employing one rather huge calculation!!

That is what we call symbolism! The 470,000 men of Judah, are 470,000 days or 1305 years 200 days. They count backwards to 2354Ab6 BC when the first separation between good and bad occurred, 16 years after the flood. It was incited of course by Satan as was the registration. The bible describes how this first recorded sin after the flood occurred in Genesis 9. Ham looked upon his father Noah's nakedness and told his brothers about it, dishonouring his dad, who had just discovered alcohol. Whereas Shem and Japheth covered their father's nakedness by walking in backwards with a mantle into the tent where the naked intoxicated Noah lay. They did this without looking. So Ham did not honour his father, whereas the other two sons did. It is all a question of gratitude to the ones to whom you owe your existence. These actions identify the good sons and the bad son. Remember that honouring one's parents was one of the 10 commandments.

The final separation between good and bad sons of Noah, (for that is what we all are) is 470,000 plus 1,1000,000 days later. So in the symbolic meaning, the greater registration is of the time period of God's people after the flood, from when the first distinction is made in Noah's tent, and the fight begins between the good seed and the evil seed, and the swords are unsheathed, until the last distinction at Armageddon in the greater Noah's ark when the fight ends and the sword of the passover angel is sheathed.

So here it is, the history book with no dates. There is of course no such thing, so the dates must be coded. Many can be decoded using the Numerical Principle.

[C12] The Jigsaw Principle of the Code

An interpretation is true if and only if it satisfies every scripture in the bible relating to the subject of the interpretation

God very rarely gives us the whole picture in one account. Normally one has to piece together information from different accounts to get the full picture. But when one has logically harmonised one's interpretations of every scripture on a given subject then one has the true interpretation and the true understanding of that subject. This is the best way to work out congregational doctrine etc. This principle follows from the Consistency Principle, because if the bible was inconsistent in the literal meaning, then it would be of no use. But it is consistent as far as we are aware. There may be some errors in the best manuscripts we have today, but God is aware of them and they will be corrected if this is necessary, possibly by the bible code itself!

Many false religions have been founded on one or two scriptures and have ignored this principle. By a false religion we mean one which claims that their baptised members have their sins forgiven by God, but actually they do not. We mean a religion incapable of baptising its members into the First Abrahamic Covenant.

Charles Russell's Extinguishing of the Fires of Hell using the Jigsaw Principle

Charles Russell, who founded the Watchtower said:

A God that would use his power to create human beings whom he foreknew and predestinated should be eternally tormented, could be neither wise, just nor loving. His standard would be lower than that of many men (Kingdom Proclaimers).

He was credited by many as the man who put out the fire in hell! He did this by comparing all of the scriptures relating to:

Gehenna (The Greek word properly translated as 'Hell')
Sheol (The Hebrew word properly translated as 'The Grave')
Hades (The Greek word properly translated as 'The Grave')
Death

Hell, Gehenna:

The Greek word for Hell is Gehenna (γεεννα). Gehenna is the Greek for the Hebrew: Geh Hinnom, which means the valley of Hinnom, which was a valley directly over the south wall of Jerusalem. This valley was the burial place for the dead of the city.

'To avoid pestilence...constant fires were kept burning there' (William D Mounce, Analytical Lexicon to Greek NT).

And he himself made his own sons pass through the fire in the valley of the son of Hinnom, and practiced magic and used divination and practiced sorcery and made spiritistic mediums and professional foretellers of events. He did on a grand scale what was bad in the eyes of Jehovah, to offend him (2 Chronicles 33:6).

**And they have built the high places of Topheth, which is in the valley of the son of Hinnom, in order to burn their sons and their daughters in the fire, a thing that I had not commanded and that had not come up into my heart.
Therefore, look! days are coming, is the utterance of Jehovah, when it will no more be said [to be] Topheth and the valley of the son of**

Hinnom, but the valley of the killing; and they will have to bury in Topheth without there being enough place (Jeremiah 7:31,32).

So it is a burning burial ground. This prophecy was fulfilled in destruction of Jerusalem by Titus as described by Josephus. They ran out of space in Gehenna, and piled up the corpses in large houses in the city, around 600,000 were thrown out of the gates of the city by 70Tammuz1, during the last siege of Jerusalem according to the Jewish Historian Josephus - who was at the siege (The complete works of Josephus can be downloaded from this site (www.bibledecoded.com) or purchased from bookshops).

Scriptures which indicate that we roast in Hell:

And if ever your hand makes you stumble, cut it off; it is finer for you to enter into life maimed than with two hands to go off into Gehenna, into the fire that cannot be put out (Mark 9:43).

And the Devil who was misleading them was hurled into the lake of fire and sulphur, where both the wild beast and the false prophet [already were]; and they will be tormented day and night forever and ever (Revelation 20:10).

Scriptures which show that we definitely do not roast in Hell:

For the living are conscious that they will die; but as for the dead, they are conscious of nothing at all, neither do they anymore have wages, because the remembrance of them has been forgotten (Ecclesiastes 9:5).

For he who has died has been acquitted from [his] sin (Romans 6:7).

Scriptures which reveal the precise condition of the dead:

And do not become fearful of those who kill the body but cannot kill the soul; but rather be in fear of him that can destroy both soul and body in Gehenna (Matthew 10:28).
The Soul is standing for your angelic body here, the mechanism for your resurrection. So Gehenna is a destruction, not a torment. A destruction of your escape pod, your potential for everlasting life.

And death and Hades were hurled into the lake of fire. This means the second death, the lake of fire. Furthermore, whoever was not found written in the book of life was hurled into the lake of fire (Revelation 20:14,15).
The lake of fire cannot be a torment because one cannot torment death itself!! Gehenna, is the second death, which is everlasting death. The first

death is physical death, which may only be a temporary death by virtue of the mercy of God.

For the wages sin pays is death, but the gift God gives is everlasting life by Christ Jesus our Lord (Romans 6:23).
Not death plus torment in fire, death plus more death plus more death ad infinitum.

So nobody gets roasted either in Hell, which is the part of Hades from which there is no resurrection, or from the memorial tombs, which is the part of Hades wherefrom this is a resurrection. The latter is the recycle bin and the former is the permanent deletion of your character from the universe, in computer terminology. Go with the latter, it's like a certain sister once said: Everlasting life is worth any effort. Make that effort. Use every piece of the jigsaw. Build as many jigsaws as you need. Keep studying until you get it, keep asking in prayer until it is given, keep knocking until the door is opened, keep seeking until you find, keep conquering the evil with the good.

For the Scripture says: None that rests his faith on him will be disappointed (Romans 10:11).

[C12a] Isaac Newton's exposure of the false doctrine of the Trinity using the Jigsaw Principle

The History of the Trinity: (The Life of Isaac Newton - Westfall, Isaac Newton - Michael White)

Newton returned to the works of the men who had formulated Trinitarianism: Athanasius (Anaesthesius might have been a better name for him), Gregory Nazienzen, Jerome, Augustine.... The conviction possessed him that a massive fraud, which began in the 4th and 5th centuries, had perverted the legacy of the early church (Life of Isaac Newton).

The Trinity doctrine was debated and adopted by the early church at the church council of Nicaea in 325 AD. The debate was between Arius who opposed it and Athanasius who proposed it. Arius lost the debate and the corruption started. Newton discovered that this fraud extended to deliberate corruptions of the bible itself. So that the King James version of 1 John 5:7 even today is:

For there are three that bear record in heaven, the Father, the Word, and the Holy Ghost, and these three are one (! John 5:7 - King James Version).

Newton observed that: It is not read thus in the Syrian bible. Not by Ignatius, Justin, Irenaeus, Tertullian, Origen, Athanas, Nazanianzen...Augustine, Beda and others.

The Greek Interlinear version is:

Because there are three giving testimony (1 John 5:7 UBS 3rd edition, Nestle Aland 26th edition)

The underlined part in the King James Version of 1 John 5:7 above is therefore a fraudulent addition to the Holy Scriptures by, well, Satan basically.

Newton found a second corrupted text at 1 Timothy 3:16. The KJV has:

And without controversy, great is the mystery of godliness: <u>God</u> was manifest in the flesh, justified in the Spirit, seen of angels, preached unto the Gentiles, believed on in the world, received up into glory (1 Timothy 3:16 - KJV).

The word 'God' is not in the original Greek, rather it is 'Who'. The Greek Interlinear version is:

And confessedly great is the mystery of godliness: Who was manifested in the flesh, vindicated in spirit, was seen by angels, was proclaimed among Gentiles, was believed in [the] world, was taken up in glory (1 Timothy 3:16 UBS 3rd Edition, Nestle Aland 26th Edition).

The Definition of the Trinity:

The Catholic Encyclopedia, the trinity section of which can be found at: http://www.newadvent.org/cathen/15047a.htm defines the trinity as follows:

The Trinity is the term employed to signify the central doctrine of the Christian religion -- the truth that in the unity of the Godhead there are Three Persons, the Father, the Son, and the Holy Spirit, these Three Persons being truly distinct one from another. Thus, in the words of the Athanasian Creed:

"The Father is God, the Son is God, and the Holy Spirit is God, and yet there are not three Gods but one God."

In this Trinity of Persons the Son is begotten of the Father by an eternal generation, and the Holy Spirit proceeds by an eternal procession from the Father and the Son. Yet, notwithstanding this difference as to origin, the Persons are co-eternal and co-equal: all alike are uncreated and omnipotent. This, the Church teaches, is the revelation regarding God's nature which Jesus Christ, the Son of God, came upon earth to deliver to the world: and which she proposes to man as the foundation of her whole dogmatic system.

This is illogically defined and therefore not defined and therefore non existent. There are 3 inconsistencies in the definition:

1. That God is three independent beings who are one being
2. Jesus is God and the father is God. So the Father is the Son
3. The Son is uncreated

1	It is not possible for three oranges to be one orange.
2	It is not possible for a Father to be a Son, this contradicts the definitions of both father and son. The son is defined as an offspring of a father not an 'onspring' as it were.
3	Sons are by definition created by their fathers, a son cannot be uncreated.

Basically the Trinity is defined as a number that is both less than two and more than two. Obviously there is no such number. The Trinity is like a hotel in North London which is situated South of the Thames. Obviously there is no such hotel. But when the poor uneducated, logically uninitiated, spiritually naive, churchgoer complains, saying: How can this be? He is told by his priest: Aha! that is the mystery of God. God can put a hotel which is in North London in a South London postcode. God can make a number that is larger than 2 actually be less than 2. At which point the poor naive churchgoer gives up and says to himself. Wow! I will never understand God, I had better leave the understanding of him to my priest. This of course is the precise effect that the priest wants. Now he can continue to play God to his congregation.

[C12b]The History of the English Bible

The first man to translate the bible from Latin into English was John Wycliffe, whose translation came out in 1382 (www.wycliffe.org/history/jwycliff.htm). John Wycliffe was an Oxford Professor, he also invented bifocal eye glasses! He therefore improved not only our spiritual vision but also our physical vision!! (www.greatsite.com/engbibhis/main.html). Wycliffe's belief was that:

[i] The sacred Scriptures be the property of the people, and one which no party should be allowed to wrest from them.

[ii] The authority of the Scriptures is independent on any other authority, and is preferable to every other writing, but especially to the books of the church of Rome.

[iii] It is impossible for any part of the Holy Scriptures to be wrong. In Holy Scripture is all the truth, one part of Scripture explains another.

The subsequent persecution of him and of those who possessed his bible was extraordinary. Many were burnt at the stake with copies of his translation around their necks. During the reign of Henry V (1413-1422) an Act was confirmed by which:

English Sheriffs were forced to take an oath to persecute the Lollards, and the Justices must deliver a relapsed heretic to be burned within 10 days of his accusation (Armitage a History of the Baptists, 1890, I, p323).

The Lollards were those who valued the teachings of the bible over the doctrines of the Church of Rome. They read and preached in English from Wycliffe's Bible. In 1414 a law was passed as follows:

All who read the scriptures in their mother tongue should: Forfeit land, cattle, life and goods from the heirs for ever !! (Eadie: History of the English Bible).

In 1416 Archbishop Chichele at Oxford declared that the clergy should make:

A thorough search in the parish twice a year, for all persons that: Hold any either heresies or errors, or have any suspected books in the English tongue (Blackburn, History of the Christian Church 1880 p346).

However Wycliffe himself had the support of Queen Joan (1328-1385), of Queen Ann (the wife of Richard II), and ultimately of God himself:

In May 1382, Wycliffe was called before yet another synod of ecclesiastical authorities. This is called the Blackfriars Synod, because it was held in the monastery of Blackfriars in London. When the 47 Bishops and monks and religious doctors took their seats, a powerful earthquake shook the city. Huge stones fell out of the castle walls and pinnacles toppled (John Wycliffe and the Lollards - Fundamental Baptist Information Service).

Wycliffe's argument to the Catholic authorities for translating the bible into English was as follows:

You say it is heresy to speak of the Holy Scriptures in English. You call me a heretic because I have translated the Bible into the common tongue of the people. Do you know whom you blaspheme? Did not the Holy Ghost give the Word of God at first in the mother tongue of the nations to whom it was addressed ? (Fountain, John Wycliffe)

In 1506 William Tylsworth was burned for his faith in the Word of God and his own daughter was forced to ignite the fire. In 1519 six men and a woman were burned for:

Teaching their children the Lord's Prayer and the ten commandments in English (Eadie: History of the English Bible).

The Lollard's Tower, where people possessing an English bible were tortured and killed, still exists today in Lambeth Palace, the London home of the Archbishop of Cantebury. But despite all of this persecution, Wycliffe's bible was still being read at the time of the next great bible translator William Tyndale (1484 - 1536), the Father of what eventually became the King James Bible. Tyndale's first translation had to be finished abroad, but 3,000 copies reached England in December 1526.

The persecution then continued. John Tewkesbury had been reading Wycliffe's bible since 1512, and had obtained a copy of the Tyndale New Testament in 1526. He was first arrested in April 1529 and tortured and crippled. He was finally burned on December 20th 1530 for: Distributing copies of the word of God and believing in salvation by faith in Christ alone (www.whidbey.net/~dcloud/articles/williamtyndale.htm).

Tyndale was imprisoned in May 1535. Whilst he was in prison, three editions of his new testament were printed. He was strangled and the burnt at the stake on October 6th 1536. At his death he prayed out loud:

Lord open the King of England's Eyes !

On October 4, 1535 John Rogers and Miles Coverdale who were loyal disciples of Tyndale, finished Tyndale's translation of the Old Testament into English and printed abroad the first complete English Bible, known as the Coverdale Bible. John Rogers then changed his name to Thomas Matthew (an interesting name for a bible translator!) and printed the Coverdale Bible again, under this nom de plume, since Tyndale's work was banned. This edition is called the Matthews Bible

In 1539, 3 years after Tyndale was executed, his spoken prayer was answered. Thomas Cranmer, the Archbishop of Cantebury, hired Miles Coverdale, at the bequest of King Henry VIII to publish what was called the Great Bible.

These were Tyndale's words as a prologue for his translation of Jonah:

As the envious Philistines stopped the wells of Abraham, and filled them up with earth, to put the memorial out of mind, to the intent that they might challenge the ground; even so the fleshly minded hypocrites stop up the veins of life, which are the scripture, with the earth of their traditions, false similitudes and lying allegories. And that, of like zeal, to make the scripture their own possession and merchandise. And so shut up the kingdom which is in God's word, neither entering in themselves, nor suffering them that would. (Willam Tyndale)

However bequest from King Henry did not end the persecution of bible translators! Because the persecution originated not with the crown but with the Church. When Bloody Mary (Queen Mary) came to the throne, being possessed to return England to the Roman church, she burned both John Rogers (Thomas Matthew) and Thomas Cranmer at the stake.

Meanwhile Miles Coverdale had taken refuge in Geneva in Switzerland. There, in exile, he and John Foxe with the protection of John Calvin and John Knox produced the Geneva Bible, which was first published in 1560. It was Queen Elizabeth I whose reign brought this persecution to an end. The English Bible History site (www.greatsite.com/engbibhis/main.html) says this about the Geneva bible and William Tyndale:

The Geneva Bible was the first Bible to add verses to the chapters, so that referencing specific passages would be easier. Every chapter was also accompanied by extensive marginal notes and references so thorough and complete that the Geneva Bible is also considered the first English "Study Bible". William Shakespeare quotes thousands of times in his plays from the Geneva translation of the Bible. The Geneva Bible became the Bible of choice for over 100 years of English speaking Christians. Between 1560 and 1644 at least 144 editions of this Bible were published. Examination of the 1611 King James Bible shows clearly that its translators were influenced much more by the Geneva Bible, than by any other source. The Geneva Bible itself retains over 90% of William Tyndale's original English translation. The Geneva in fact, remained more popular than the King James Version until decades after its original release in 1611! The Geneva holds the honor of being the first Bible taken to America, and the Bible of the Puritans and Pilgrims.

The King James Bible, although the work of 50 scholars, is very close to Tyndale's original Translation:

In the Gospel of St. Mark and the Epistle to the Hebrew there are not more than 80 words (in Tyndale's translation) ... which are not found in our Authorised Version of the Bible (Moulton - History of the English Bible).

The Authorised version is the King James Version. The English Bible changed the World in the early 17th century. Multitudes of commoners were driven to learn to read by their desire to study the bible. The 16th century historian John Foxe, who had supported Miles Coverdale whilst he was producing the Geneva Bible observed:

Everybody that could bought the book or busily read it or got others to read it to them if they could not themselves, and divers more elderly people learned to read on purpose. And even little boys flocked among the rest to hear portions of the holy Scripture read.

It is important that the story above is told and the antics of the church are exposed. We are fortunate today that a greater freedom of religious belief and worship exists in many countries than was enjoyed in the 14th, 15th and 16th centuries. The Church of that time did not want the common man to be able to understand the bible, they wanted it to remain a mystery to them written in a foreign language. In that way the church could play God to its flock, which is what they wanted to do, what they did back then and what they are doing today. The 'Trinity' turns a logical book into an incomprehensible marvel. It renders it as meaningless as if it was written in Latin. Arius, Wycliffe, Tyndale, Newton, are the enlighteners from God. The church has become a daughter of the darkness.

Both John Wycliffe and William Tyndale wanted the ploughboy to know as much about the bible as the priest. So does God and so do we. Hence this book/website. For there is a bible within the bible and there is a holy code within the holy scriptures. Therefore we have written out this hidden bible today for the same ploughboy and for the same stable girl whose heart and mind and soul John Wycliffe and William Tyndale valued more highly than their own.

Newton's observations and conclusions:

Sir Isaac would have benefited from a modern Mathematics degree course at his university. He of course is the father of half of it, the Calculus/Analysis half. Although algebra and abstract symbolism (the other half of Pure Maths) are of more use in interpreting the bible (as far as we are aware). He would then have known instantly that the Trinity, being illogically defined, is simply not defined and therefore non existent.

Newton, being a fellow at Trinity College Cambridge, was required to attest to his acceptance of the 39 articles of the Anglican Church, one of which was the doctrine of the Trinity. He was bothered about signing something which contained the Trinity that he had no evidence as to the truth of. So he applied his standard scientific and logical method to the issue of whether the Trinity was a true or false doctrine. This method is to read all of the available relevant literature on the subject, then assimilate it, think about it, kick it about, digest it and see if it makes sense, or if there is an underlying pattern or flaw in it. See if there is an underlying truth or an underlying lie. This method when applied to the bible is what we call the Jigsaw Principle.

Newton produced two knock out blows to the Trinity:

[1] The Father is God of the son
[2] It is defined illogically

We have covered the latter on these two. As regards the former. Newton used:

The Christ, who is the image of God (2 Corinthians 4:4).

You loved righteousness, and you hated lawlessness. That is why God, your God, anointed you with [the] oil of exultation more than your partners (Hebrews 1:9).

From this he reasoned that the Father was God of the Son. He could just as well have used Jesus' famous last words:

Eli, Eli, Lama Sabachthani, which means when translated: My God, my God, why have you forsaken me (Mark 15:34).

Newton's observations and deductions from reading most of the works of the early church fathers, (Irenaeus, Tertullan, Cyprian, Euasebius, Eutychius, Sulpitius Severus, Clement, Origen, Basil, John Chrysostom, Alexander of Alexandria, Epiphanius, Hilary, Theodoret, Gregory of Nyssa, Cyril of Alexandria, Leo I, Victorinus Afer, Rufinus, Manentius, Prudentius, Ignatius, Justin, Augustine, Jerome etc), and from reading many manuscripts of the bible, and applying the Jigsaw Principle to them (finding an interpretation which logically harmonised them) were recorded in one of his early theological manuscripts (1672-1675):

1	The [word] God, is no where in the scriptures used to signify more than one of the three persons at once.
2	The word 'God', put absolutely without particular reference to the Son or Holy Ghost, does always signify the Father from one end of the scriptures to the other.
3	When ever it is said in the scriptures that there is but one God, it is meant of the Father.
4	It is a proper epithet of the Father to be called almighty. For by God almighty we always understand the Father.
5	The son in all things submits his will to the will of the Father, which would be unreasonable if he were equal to the Father.
6	The son confesses the Father greater than him, calls him his God etc.
7	The son acknowledges the original pre-science of all future things to be in the Father alone.
8	The union between him and the Father he interprets to be like that of the saints one with another. That is, in agreement of will and counsel.

Then Newton, who was by now the Lucasian professor of Mathematics at Trinity College, decided to go to King Charles II to seek a dispensation allowing him to remain as professor but withdraw his attestation. He prepared his arguments as above to present to the King of England to save his career. The King agreed and stipulated that all future holders of his chair were to be exempt from holy orders.

Newton believed that God's works, his creation and God's word, his book, the bible, were twinned. And that both were a riddle, a code to be cracked. Newton believed that cracking this code was a duty owed to God by man, in both cases (*Isaac Newton, the last sorcerer* - Michael White - But Newton was not a sorcerer, he was a true worshipper).

What Gordon finds so wonderful and yet so tragic, is that Newton succeeded in the case of God's Universe in cracking the code. But he failed (notwithstanding a very valiant attempt) in the case of God's word (he did believe that the bible was God's word), he died trying to decode the bible and find out when Armageddon was. His failure was not his fault. It was not God's time from 1642-1727 to release that information. So what the true God did, who must have dearly desired to show Sir Isaac the whole of the holy code of the bible, was to let him see the entirety of the mechanical code behind his physical creation of the universe instead. It was all that his own justice would allow. And here God was, holding back his love for the sake of his justice.

The date upon which mankind was first allowed to see the date of Armageddon was 1992February1, 1991Shebat21, 4600 solar days before 1290 biblical lunar days before it is to begin (Daniel 8 and Daniel 12 - see [157], [152]). This was the day upon which Gordon worked out the Exedenic Times, and it began the 'Time of the end'. Which is the time of the knowledge of the true date of the end. And Gordon will say here this. It was his appreciation of the perfection of the works of God as exhibited by Newton which convinced him that the bible, since it shared that perfection, must be in a code.

So we have the dynamic code of the universe, as discovered by Newton. We have the genetic code of the human body, as discovered by Crick and Watson. And here at last is the grammatical code of the bible, as discovered by Gordon Ritchie, Tony Moore and Massoud Vakili as a result of the leadings of the true God, and on the realisation by Gordon that this God whom Newton showed was perfect must have written a book every bit as perfect as his universe. A realisation which unknown to Gordon at the time he had it, had hit Newton some 300 years earlier. So here we are, the three wonder decoders, Cambridge men the three of us. Let us all therefore, with God's help through Jesus, finish the work that Newton, the Father of all three Cambridge divine code breakers began (Please do not ask if we are the real trinity!)

For the precise nature of God, Jesus and the Holy Spirit - see [14]. Here is some of Sir Isaac Newton's Chronology, deduced in the late 17th and early 18th century, mainly from Daniel 9 and Daniel 12.

1948	Second Coming of Christ
1944	End of the great tribulation of the Jews
1899	Call to return to Jerusalem
1638-9	Church of Rome's spiritual domination ends
609-800	Period during which the Roman Catholic Church (Whore of Babylon) was at its peak
70	Transgression of desolation of Jerusalem
34 AD	Death of Christ
2 BC	Birth of Christ
456 BC	The Jews return to Jerusalem

Although begun during the 1670's Newton continued his work of interpretation until the month of his death in 1727 (Isaac Newton - Michael White, the table above is from his book).

The table above is a quite amazing prophetic achievement for a man living around 1700 AD.

[C15] The Parallel Account Principle - Spot the Difference

If there are 2 or 3 or 4 parallel accounts of an event, in the bible, then the 2 or 3 or 4 word symbolic meanings all share the same symbolism and all refer to distinct separate non overlapping fulfillments all of which relate to each other to from one global word symbolic picture for all the parallel accounts.

In the 4 Gospels, in Kings & Chronicles, in Ezra and Nehemiah, there are parallel accounts of the same events. For example the feeding of the 5,000 is mentioned 4 times, once in each Gospel! Each account has a greater symbolic meaning by the Prophetic Principle, so there are 4 greater meanings to the feeding of the 5,000. These actually relate to the feeding campaigns of the 4 true Christian religions - see [67]. The thing to do with these accounts, using the Power Principle, is to play 'spot the difference'. Because any differences are not mistakes, or omissions wherein God overlooked something, and thought he better put an account in Mark just in case Matthew made a bit of a mess of it. They are deliberate.

Then we take the repeated accounts as simultaneous equations for the further fulfillments to which they relate. They may be simple and not implicit with each account relating to just one further fulfillment. Or they may be implicit with each account relating to things common to a number of the fulfillments. For an example of how this works see - [67] 'The feedings of the 5,000 and the 4,000' or [34] 'The Faithful Slaves'.

[C16] The Omission Principle

If an account contains an obvious and glaring omission, then the word symbolic fulfillment of the account involves this omission.

Samson now called to Jehovah and said: Sovereign Lord Jehovah, remember me, please, and strengthen me, please, just this once, Oh you the [true] God, and let me avenge myself upon the Philistines with vengeance for one of my two eyes (Judges 16:28).

What about the other eye!

So David said: Anyone striking the Jebusites first, he will become head and prince. And Joab the son of Zeruiah got to go up first, and he came to be head (1 Chronicles 11:6).

Why didn't he become the prince?

Next he commanded the crowd to recline on the grass and took the 5 loaves and 2 fishes, and, looking up to heaven, he said a blessing, and, after breaking the loaves, he distributed them to the disciples, the disciples in turn to the crowds. So all ate and were satisfied, and they took up the surplus of fragments 12 baskets full (Matthew 14:19,20).

Great, wonderful, miraculous, but what did he do with the 2 fishes??

Sometimes, as in the case of Yes/No Questions - see below, the omitted thing is fulfilled in the symbolic meaning. In the case of Matthew 14, which is a multiple account scripture, the omission helps us to know which feeding miracle or miracles this chapter is defining - see [67].

[C17] Yes/No Question symbolism

Any question asked in the scriptures with two possible answers (normally yes and no), has the answer in the word symbolic meaning, the account symbolism, being the opposite of the answer in the literal or straight symbolic meaning, the event symbolism.

In other words both answers are true in either the literal or the symbolic meaning (or both). Take for example the great words of Nicodemus, a man whose love exceeded his pride:

Nicodemus said to him: How can a man be born when he is old? He cannot enter into the womb of his mother a second time and be born, can he? (John 3:4)

Well literally, no, of course he cannot. But symbolically, yes, that is precisely how one is born again. Born from the womb of his heavenly mother, God's wife, the holy spirit. Born as an angel.

What has been born from the flesh is flesh, and what has been born from the spirit is spirit (John 3:6).

What has been born from fleshly women is men and what has been born from the spirit woman, the holy spirit, is angels. When you are born again, God creates an angel in heaven through his wife, the holy spirit for you, Amen. See - How is one born again, and see - The Trinity is just God's family.

That is the level of beauty that you will see if you are pure in heart and if your love exceeds your pride. Look how Nicodemus was repaid for one act of faith. It was enough. But his works did not stop there:

Nicodemus also, the man that came to him in the night the first time, came bringing a roll of myrrh and aloes, about a hundred pounds [of it]. So they took the body of Jesus and bound it up with bandages with the spices, just the way the Jews have the custom of preparing for burial (John 19:39,40)

Why it was 100 (Roman) pounds we do not know, but we do know that this is a numerical symbolism by the Numerical Principle. If the reader has any good ideas here please contact us. We know that Nicodemus was born again, because we know something about God's love, we would be blind if we could not see the love of Nicodemus. Which brings us nicely to another Yes/No question:

Nicodemus, who had come to him previously, and who was one of them, said to them:
Our law does not judge a man unless first it has heard from him and come to know what he is doing, does it?
In answer they said to him: You are not also out of Galilee, are you? Search and see that no prophet is to be raised up out of Galilee (John 7:50-52).

No Nicodemus was not out of Galilee (precious few Pharisees were). But the antetypical Nicodemus is out of the antetypical Galilee.

But John, having heard in jail about the works of the Christ, sent by means of his own disciples and said to him: Are you the Coming one, or are we to expect a different one? (Matthew 11:2,3)

So John summoned a certain two of his disciples and sent them to the Lord to say: Are you the Coming one or are we to expect a different one? (Luke 7:19).

In the literal meaning, yes Jesus was the 'coming one', in the sense that he was the one prophesied as coming to restore Israel. But in the greater meaning, there will be several different ones.

For instance, which is easier, to say: Your sins are forgiven, or to say: Get up and walk? (Matthew 9:5)

Which is easier, to say to the paralytic: Your sins are forgiven, or to say: Get up and pick up your bed and walk? (Mark 2:9)

Obviously the former. But in the greater meaning they are both the same thing because:

'Get up' is the baptism into the name of the father Abraham, the bath of the flesh, the water baptism, the forgiveness of sins in the past, giving one a clean standing before God.

'Pick up your bed' is: Have a resurrection into the kingdom of God. This is the finishing of the water baptism, the righteous decree in the flesh, the free gift of citizenship of the Kingdom of God, the forgiveness of all sins up to Armageddon, the granting of the entrance Visa through the ambassador Abraham.

'Walk' is the baptism into the name of Jesus, or Paul or Gordon etc, the sanctification in holy spirit, being born again, the forgiveness of all sins until time indefinite, the walking before God with a clean conscience, the creation of an angelic son of God, the entrance into the holy family of God, through a covenant mediated by a mediator.

Who will file accusation against God's chosen ones? God is the One who declares [them] righteous (Romans 8:33).

In the literal meaning no one. In the greater meaning Gordon! See [The Faithful and Discreet Slave cut in two]

Pilate said to Jesus: **Are you the king of the Jews?** (Mark 15:2).

Literally, no, he wasn't at that time. Symbolically, yes, in 1914Tishri, - see [121], [123], he became vassal king of God over the true human seed of Abraham, the Jews of that time, who were the New Covenant Saints, all of them also baptised into the First Abrahamic Covenant. He alluded to this in his answer:

Jesus answered: My kingdom is no part of this world. If my kingdom were part of this world, my attendants would have fought that I should not be delivered up to the Jews. But, as it is, my kingdom is not from this source (John 18:36).

So Pharaoh said to his servants: Can another man be found like this one in whom the spirit of God is? (Genesis 41:38)

Literally no, Joseph was unique. But in the greater meaning, yes, it's the antetypical Joseph.

[C18] Reader Questions from the holy spirit

These are questions that are asked of various characters in the bible, but that are really meant for the various readers of the bible. These are questions asked by the holy spirit of the bible reader:

You with little faith. Do you not yet see the point, or do you not remember the five loaves in the case of the five thousand and how many baskets you took up?
Or the seven loaves in the case of the four thousand and how many provision baskets you took up? (Matthew 18:8-10)

Who is Jesus really speaking to here? Not just his disciples in the boat who forgot to bring along the loaves, the bible wasn't written for them. So tell us please oh ye reader with much faith, much more than the disciples: Do you know what the significance of the 12 baskets in the case of the 5,000 and the 7 baskets in the case of the 4,000 is? What do they stand for?

If you do not know, then Jesus is talking to you. He is saying look, these numbers are important. He is saying, if you want to understand the greater meaning of these two feeding miracles, which obviously relate to spiritual feeding miracles of true religions, then think first about the numbers of the provision baskets. Think about how many there were. This is the key.

To interpret this we apply the Numerical Principle to the baskets. Jesus is basically asking the reader if he has grasped the Numerical Principle! The meaning of numbers of things in the bible! So the 12 baskets are 12 days or 12 months or 12 years or administrations of food which does not come directly from Jesus, but comes as leftovers. Likewise the 7 baskets are 7 days or 7 months or 7 years or administrations of food not directly from Jesus but from leftovers - see [67].

And they began saying: Is this not Jesus the son of Joseph, whose father and mother we know? How is it that now he says: I have come down from heaven ? (John 6:42).

Well, how is it?? The Holy Spirit wishes you to think about this, and to ask yourself the very same question. Consider please the scripture below:

From the offspring of this [man] according to his promise God has brought to Israel a savior, Jesus, after John, <u>in advance of the entry of that one</u>, had preached publicly to all the people of Israel baptism of repentance (Acts 13:23,24).

This means that John the baptist preached publicly in advance of the entry, the coming down from heaven of an angel, God's firstborn and only begotten son, the angel Michael, into the human Jesus. Angelically possessing him at his baptism.

And the holy spirit in bodily shape like a dove came down upon him, and a voice came out of heaven: You are my Son, the beloved; I have approved you (Luke 3:22).

Q: What vehicle for a son of God has a bodily shape like a dove?
A: An angel.

John also bore witness, saying: I viewed the spirit coming down as a dove out of heaven, and it remained upon him (John 1:32).

Jesus was not called 'God's son the beloved' until after the dove had descended from heaven. This dove symbolised the entrance of the angel Michael into Jesus.

But the righteousness resulting from faith speaks in this manner: Do not say in your heart: Who will ascend into heaven? that is, to bring Christ down. Or: Who will descend into the abyss? that is, to bring Christ up from the dead (Romans 10:6,7)

The answer to both is Gabriel who angelically possessed John the Baptist for the purpose of presiding over the entrance of Michael into Jesus at his baptism. We are getting a bit deep here. For the full story see - Jesus was Michael, and John was Gabriel.

A Rather More Simple Reader Question from the Holy Spirit

For what benefit will it be to a man if he gains the whole world but forfeits his soul? or what will a man give in exchange for his soul?
(Matthew 16:26)
Jesus asked this question of his disciples, but quite obviously he is asking it of every man and woman who can read.

[C19] Helpful Tips

a. Get an electronic bible, preferably the New World Translation on disk available from the Watchtower - You'll have fun trying to get it without being cornered! Alternatively we are going to put our own electronic bible on the site for downloading soon. With this you can type in say: 'Holy spirit' and find every scripture mentioning it. This sort of capability is invaluable in bible research. You can download other electronic bibles from the web, but the translations may not be accurate enough. If you do not like computers, then you will need a comprehensive concordance and a New World Translation Bible, and a Greek Interlinear bible and a Hebrew Interlinear bible - see [books] We hope to have our paper bible available soon.
b. Do not try to squeeze a symbolic meaning into a fulfillment which you already understand. Even if you succeed you will have learned nothing new. We have made this mistake hundreds of times. Many religions know of no other way. To the Watchtower almost every time period in the second presence starts or ends in 1914, and whenever there are two groups in the bible, then one is the anointed remnant and the other is the great crowd. Do not be like this. Let the account lead you, this is letting the holy spirit lead you! Set your mind free. Accept any crazy interpretation in the creative phase and criticise it later - this is classic brainstorming technique.
c. 'Look!' This is a word that occurs 958 times in the NWT of the bible. When it occurs, treat it as a exhortation from the holy spirit itself to you. For that is what it is!
d. 'A man, a householder'. 'An enemy, a man'. This is wonderful and cryptic and disguised. It is a double designation and one of the two greater meanings refers to an angel. It is saying look there are two guys and one is a man. Which is really saying, the other is an angel.
e. 'Gather together'. 'Assemble'. These words when they occur are often a cryptic request from the spirit to add up all of those who are gathered together or assembled. The spirit is saying that their sum stands for something.
f. Distinguish between event symbolism and account symbolism. Event symbolism is the symbolism that Charles Russell and the second Adventists used on Daniel 4. They use the elements of the events

themselves as symbolising elements in the greater meaning. But account symbolism, uses the elements of the account of the events to symbolise elements in the greater meaning. So a king who is referred to as Nebuchadnezzar, as King Nebuchadnezzar, and as the King, can stand for two different people seperately and togehter, i.e. three different people/groups of people in the account symbolism but only for one person in the event symbolism.
g. If something happens at a certain hour, then it, or events related to it, happen 12 times in all, the number of hours in a Hebrew day:

Jesus answered: There are twelve hours of daylight, are there not? If anyone walks in daylight he does not bump against anything, because he sees the light of this world (John 11:9).

[C20] Elementary Counting and Cryptic Scriptures

We have so far discovered two dimensions of the holy book. The literal dimension and the symbolic dimension. But there is a third and a fourth.

There is a numerical count defined on every word of the bible. This count only works in the Hebrew and the Greek. It is not the count of Eli Rips or Michael Drosnin or other equidistant Hebrew letter sequence researchers, which can be found at www.biblecodes.com. We call this count the third dimension of the bible.

The 4th dimension, is a cryptic dimension, it is not a second symbolic dimension. There is no need for a 2nd symbolic dimension because the first symbolic dimension can have several meanings for the various different designations for the same person or thing in the account. The scriptures do have a cryptic side however, a newspaper crossword type side. This dimension appears to take the form of a series of discrete cryptic insights rather than a meaning for every word in every account as the other three dimensions give.

Now if you can see all four of these dimensions of the holy book then you are seeing the bible in colour rather than in black and white. For in our physical eyes, which God himself designed as a prophetic declaration of our spiritual vision (for everything the Jehovah does or declares is a prophetic declaration since as he is living all of his words and works are likewise living) we have cones, which see sharply in black and white, and we have rods, three types, which see slightly less sharply in colour. Is it red, green and blue? All of this structure is prefiguring the structure of the way in which we will see the bible, for the bible is a 4 dimensional book. The first dimension is the literal dimension and this corresponds to our cones, the ones that see in black and white, very sharply, unambiguously. The next three dimensions are the symbolic, the cryptic and the coded numeric dimensions, the red, the green and the blue rods. It is a beautiful book in glorious Technicolour. It is like Paul said:

In order that you may be thoroughly able to grasp mentally with all the holy ones what is the <u>breadth</u> and <u>length</u> and <u>height</u> and <u>depth</u>, and to know the love of Christ which surpasses knowledge (Ephesians 3:18,19).

4 dimensions. For Einstein discovered that the 3 dimensions of space are related to the 4th dimension of time via the Lorenz transformation. This results from the fact that the speed of light is a constant to all observers whether the light source is driving forwards in his Ford Escort with his halogens relative to the observer or orbiting backwards in his space shuttle with his laser beam. But the constancy of the spiritual source of light, the bible, which rather than emitting light at a constant speed independent of its relative motion, is a constant source, independent of time, emitting light at different speeds, is also manifested in 4 dimensions and these are:

- Literal
- Symbolic
- Cryptic
- Coded Numeric

For the same God made both types of light. The bible is a very fractal book, since it is pattern upon pattern, and yet man only discovered fractals in the last 20 years. Now Crick and Watson discovered slightly before the discovery of fractals, the molecular structure of the code of life, our genetic code, a 4 base code, written in terms of:

- Adenine
- Guamine
- Cytosine
- Thiamine

So we have 4 dimensions of space-time, 4 dimensions of human vision, and 4 bases of our genetic code & the 4 walls of the super temple of all Christianity with the 4 cornerstones but only one foundation stone, and we have the 4 living creatures in heaven: Courage, Power, Love and Wisdom (Ezekiel 1, Revelation 4). Now perhaps the reader will see what is the breadth, the length, the height and the depth, the 4 dimensions of the bible code. Perhaps he will realise that the works of Einstein and Crick and Watson, prophetically establish that there will be a further spiritual equivalent among God's covenanted people. For if Crick and Watson have been allowed to see the physical code of life, then we have been allowed to see the spiritual code of life. And it is the same God, Jehovah, who has made both of these codes, through his son. And his prophet, the now angelic apostle Paul, the one who has declared the 4 bases of the bible, has also declared this order of revealing, by saying:

The first is, not that which is spiritual, but that which is physical, afterward that which is spiritual (1 Corinthians 15:46).

Why is the sun 400 times bigger than the moon when it is 400 times further away from the earth than the moon. What a coincidence! How come these two completely unrelated bodies exactly fit over each other in a solar eclipse?

You will not find the answer in the department of astrophysics. You will find it in the book of Isaiah.

Do you people not know? Do you not hear? Has it not been told to you from the outset? Have you not applied understanding from the foundations of the earth?

There is one who is dwelling above the circle of the earth, the dwellers in which are as grasshoppers, the one who is stretching out the heavens just as a fine gauze, who spreads them out like a tent in which to dwell (Isaiah 40:21, 22).

Raise your eyes high up and see. Who has created these things? It is the one who is bringing forth the army of them even by number, all of whom he calls even by name. Due to the abundance of dynamic energy, he also being vigorous in power, not one [of them] is missing (Isaiah 40:26).

But do not think that we wish to condemn astrophysics, on the contrary we wish to save it. In order to understand the universe one needs first to understand that it was God who set the speed of light at 3×10^8 metres/sec. He set it at this value before Adam was born, 4027Tishri10 BC, to stop us screwing up the universe until we had learned how to behave.

At some time before Adam was born, light travelled a lot faster as we have mentioned above. The universe has not been around for billions of years at all. The speed of light was reset by God as a cage for men. In fact it was reset by the command: Let there be light! Because light must have existed before God made this statement.

On the first creative day of Genesis God said: **Let there be light**. And he said this after observing that there was darkness on the surface of the watery deep. In other words after he had created the planet earth in the literal meaning of the chapter:

**In [the] beginning God created the heavens and the earth.
Now the earth proved to be formless and waste and there was darkness upon the surface of [the] watery deep; and God's spirit was moving to and fro over the surface of the waters.
And God proceeded to say: "Let there be light." Then there came to be light** (Genesis 1:1-3).

But we know that light existed from the start of the Big Bang. Therefore light already existed when he said: Let there be light. This is the key realisation in understanding the meaning of Genesis 1. So God reset some feature of light or recreated it on day 1 in the literal meaning.

So just because it takes one constant value today does not mean that it has always taken this constant value, once you admit that there may be a God. But physics does not admit this. Until it does, it will never discover the truth about the universe. However if you can find it in your heart to believe that it was God who set the speed of light, rather than random chance, then please go to section [234], the Munrose Hypothesis, where we deduce the date of the Big Bang as being 11,513,689,593 BC, and find out what the initial value of the speed of light was during the Big Bang itself (it was not 300,000 km/s !) from Genesis 1.

And another thing! What do you think God could be symbolising by having the whole universe held together by gravity, a universal unquestioning attractive force? Where would the universe be without gravity? The same place the world would be without love. And that is where we are going right now!

And another thing, seeing as our scientific and technological advancement has been so rapid in the last few thousand years, how come our art is now worse than that of the cave man??

So returning to the count on the bible:

And they will be given into his hand for a time, times and half a time (Daniel 7:25).

It will be for an appointed time, appointed times and a half (Daniel 12:7).

There is where she is fed for a time, times and half a time (Revelation 12:14).

We can do no better here than to quote Gordon's first letter to the Watchtower Society, that they actually received, to describe the meaning of this strange way of saying: 3½. If the man on the Clapham omnibus is asked: What is half of seven? he replies: It is three and a half. He does not reply: It is one plus ones plus a half of one. It is therefore manifestly apparent that the true God, who is most certainly able to do anything that the man on the Clapham omnibus is able to do, having created that man, is saying a lot more than 'Three and a half times', when he says: A time, times and half a time. Hopefully the man on the Clapham omnibus will one day know what this greater meaning of this central expression in the bible really is.

We read in Revelation 12:

But the two wings of the great eagle were given the woman, that she might fly into the wilderness to her place; there is where she is fed for a time and times and half a time away from the face of the serpent (Revelation 12:14).

'Times' is obviously in the plural (since Greek has no dual number as Hebrew does). But earlier in the same chapter we read:

And the woman fled into the wilderness, where she has a place prepared by God, that they should feed her there a thousand two hundred and sixty days (Revelation 12:6).

In the actual vision, (but not in it's symbolic meaning) the two periods are the same period and so we are being told by holy spirit that the phrase 'a time, times and half a time' is 1260 days of the BLC (Biblical Lunar Calendar), which is 3.5 lunar years of 360 days. But a year is a time, a cycle, of the earth around the sun. So 3.5 years is 3.5 times

So 1 time + times + .5 time = 3.5 times

So times = 2 times

So this particular plural counts as a double, in this equation. Therefore, one of the things that is certainly being said is that plurals count as two times, since the word 'times' is interpreted as 720 days in the above scriptures. In this context singulars count as one time and halves count as half a time. If we now apply the Consistency Principle to this, then what this crazy phraseology is saying is not that 3.5 times is being expressed as a singular time, a plural time and a half time, but that everything in the bible can be expressed as a singular time a plural time or a half time.

For Solomon has said:

For everything there is an appointed time, even a time for every affair under the heavens (Ecclesiastes 3:1).

This is a repetition. So yes there is an appointed time for everything, but applying the Repetition Principle there is also another meaning to this scripture, a further fulfillment. This is that there is a time count on every sentence in the bible. David also spoke of this count under inspiration saying:

Show us just how to count our days in such a way as to bring a heart of wisdom in (Psalm 90:12).

Because days or years or months are all times, see - The Times Principle of the code. So the request is equivalent to: Show us how to count 'times'. So let's be like the tribe of Issachar, and the wise men of Persia:

And of the sons of Issachar having a knowledge of how to discern the times to know what Israel ought to do, there were two hundred head ones of theirs, and all their brothers were at their orders (1 Chronicles 12:32)

And the king proceeded to say to the wise men having knowledge of the times, for in this way the king's matter [came] before all those versed in law and legal cases (Esther 1:13)

Jesus said to his disciples:

It does not belong to you to get knowledge of the times or seasons which the Father has placed in his own jurisdiction (Acts 1:7).

But to us, this knowledge does belong. So we can apply a count to every word in the bible, assigning it one time if it is singular, two times if it is plural and half a time, if it is a half of something.

The philosophy of the count on each sentence is that the count is: The number of times represented by the sentence, which is the number of situations or actions in the sentence. The count works like this:

Singular words count as	one time
Plural words count as	two times
Fractions or parts of anything count as	half a time
Verbs	multiply
and, or, but, upon, with, after, before	add
into, out of, of, from, until, under	multiply
all, every	doubles

The count works on the Hebrew and Greek original text, not on any translation unless it is a count transparent translation, and no-one has yet made such a translation. The General basis of the count is that any sentence represents a number of times. For example the sentence:

'The kings ate the potatoes'

counts as 4 times, because this action effectively occurs 4 times because two kings are eating two potatoes and so a king is eating a potato 4 times. We say two kings because plurals count as 2 'times'. This is actually an integral part of Hebrew Grammar, which is the code of the language of the bible, from a linguistic point of view. Hebrew has singular, plural and dual (or double) mode. We take all plurals as duals from a counting point of view. The import of this is that in the greater meaning of the kings eating the potatoes, this meal could have lasted 4 days, 4 months or 4 years, or there might have been 4 greater meals.

We use the abbreviation 3x for 3 times and 2x for 2 times etc. 'All' or 'Every' counts as 2x and multiplies, it is understood as 'some plus the rest'. So that 'all of the horses' counts as 4x, or 4 times.

'In' is right distributive and adds like this: x in $2x = x$ in $x + x$ in $x = 2x+2x=4x$

x in $x = 2x$
$2x$ in $x = 3x$
$2x$ in $2x = 6x$
x in $2x = 4x$

Here are some examples:

all his belongings 4x
men in the house 3x
men in the houses 6x

You need a Greek Interlinear Bible and a Hebrew Interlinear Bible to work with this dimension of the Code. We quote count preserving translations here (interlinear ones normally are).

Some Simple Examples of the Count

This count takes some getting used to and it is most easily applied to single phrases such as:

Truly I say to you, He will appoint him over all his belongings (Matthew 24:47).

I tell you truthfully, He will appoint him over all his belongings (Luke 12:44).

All his belongings (πασιν τοις υπαρχουσιν) counts as 4x

So there are 4 appointments of slaves and stewards that Jesus makes. These are the 4 true Christian religions.

Look! I am sending to you people Elijah the prophet before the coming of the great and fear-inspiring day of Jehovah. And he must turn the heart of fathers back toward sons, and the heart of sons back toward fathers; in order that I may not come and actually strike the earth with a devoting [of it] to destruction (Malachi 4:5,6).

He must turn the heart of fathers back towards sons counts as 4x

So Elijah makes 4 reconciliations between actually previous and succeeding true religions. In fact there are 4 Elijah's, who were John, Paul, Russell and Gordon see - The 4 Elijah's.

Because Jesus said:

Indeed, which father is there among you who, if his son asks for a fish, will perhaps hand him a serpent instead of a fish? (Luke 11:11). And yes the third true religion has been in a position to offer its sons, the Great Crowd, who will form the basis of the 4th true religion 'a fish', i.e. entrance into the feeding of the two fishes - see [67]. But they haven't done that, they have offered them a serpent, Satan's internal corruption mouthpiece, corrupting the congregation (Eve) to get at the head one (Adam) - His Modus Operandi has not changed you blind ones!! One should be your head on earth just as one is your head in the heavens. Why therefore do you vote you hypocrites !!

For the serpent was found in the Tree of Knowledge of good and bad, representing God's Rulership over his people. It stands for the corruption from within the true religion. But Jesus also said:

In reply he said: Elijah, indeed, is coming and will restore all things (Matthew 17:11).

All things counts as 4x

So Elijah comes 4 times, to restore true worship and start 4 new religions.

The 'Great Crowd' of Revelation 7:9 is described as being:

Εκ παντος εθνους και φυλων και λαων και γλωσσων (Revelation 7:9 KI)
Out of every of nation and of tribes and of peoples and of tongues

2x.1x+2x+2x+2x=8x, i.e. 8 times, we take as 8 years from 2000Elul to 2008Elul

We know that it extends to the last day of Armageddon, since they are the ones who survive Armageddon. So it must start 8 years earlier i.e. in 2000Elul. So the first person is baptised into the New earthly covenant, the covenant for half a kingdom, in 2000Elul. Actually it was in 2000Tishri ! So evidently they come out of this period of 8 years.

Some More Complicated Examples of the Count

<u>Nebuchadnezzar's recital of his dream (Daniel 4:10-12, NIVHEOT, New International Version Hebrew English Old Testament)</u>

And visions of my head upon my bed, I was beholding	3x.
and look!	
a tree in the middle of the land	1½x
and height of him enormous	1x
he grew large the tree	1x
and he grew strong	1x
and height of him touched <u>to</u> the skies	2x
and visibility of him [touched] <u>to</u> end of all the earth	2x
leaf of him beautiful	1x
and fruit of him abundant	1x
and food of all in him	3x
under him she found shelter, beast of field	1x
and in branches of him they lived, birds of the airs	10x
and from him, he was fed, every creature	2x

Total of 26½x = 26½ times. But these are multiplied by the 3x of visions upon the bed:

3x.26½x=79½x, 79½ times, we take as 79½ years.

These run from 1914Tishri at the appointment of FDS3 to feed, until 1994Nisan at the appointment of FDS4 to feed. 'Birds of the airs' are the remnant of the circumcision of the spirit, spiritual Samaria. They took centre position in the earth when they were appointed over all belongings in Nisan 1918. Every creature is being fed 'at the proper time'. The branches of this tree of Moses are the 5 watches of the Watchtower.

The antetypical Pentecost (Joel 2:28 NIVHEOT)

And he will be, after this I will pour out spirit of me upon all flesh [I will pour out my spirit upon all flesh, after this]	4x
and they will prophesy, your sons and your daughters	4x
your old men, dreams they will dream	4x
your young men visions they will see	4x

16x, covenant of gifts, covenant of Keturah, new earthly covenant, covenant of Rachael, covenant for half a kingdom. Made in 1992Elul and lasting until 2008Elul.

The Fear Inspiring day of Jehovah (Joel 2:30 NIVHEOT)

And I will show wonders in the heavens	6x	1993Elul - 1999Elul
and in the earth, blood, fire and billows of smoke	5x	1999Elul - 2004Elul
the sun, he will be turned to darkness	1x	2004Elul - 2005Elul
and the moon to blood	1x	2005Elul - 2006Elul
before/to presence to come day of Jehovah the great and the one being dreadful	2x	2006Elul - 2008Elul

The day of Jehovah (Zephaniah 1:15,16 NIVHEOT)

The great day of Jehovah is near. It is near and there is a hurrying of it very much. The sound of the day of Jehovah is bitter. There is a mighty man letting out a cry.

Day of wrath, the day the that	1x	2008Elul - 2007Elul
Day of distress and anguish	2x	2007Elul - 2005Elul
Day of trouble and ruin	2x	2005Elul - 2003Elul
Day of darkness and gloom	2x	2003Elul - 2001Elul
Day of cloud and blackness	2x	2001Elul - 1999Elul
Day of trumpet and battlecry upon the cities, the ones being fortified and upon the corners, the towers	2x+2x+2x	1999Elul - 1993Elul

'Day of Jehovah' is the last 15x, of illumination spiritually, matched by bedarkening physically. The Lord's Witness trumpetted exclusively to the Jehovah's witnesses from 1993Elul (actually from 1992Elul) to 1999Elul. In 1999Elul we decided to go public. We are currently in the gloomy, cloudy dark period.

Finally here is a list that obviously was intended to be counted:

Revelation 18:11-13 (Greek Interlinear)

Also, the traveling merchants of the earth are weeping and mourning over her, because there is no one to buy their <u>full stock</u> anymore, a <u>full stock</u> of:

gold	1x
and silver	1x
and precious stone	1x
and pearls	2x
and fine linen	1x
and purple	1x
and silk	1x
and scarlet	1x
and every scented wood	2x
and every sort of ivory object	2x
and every sort of object out of most precious wood and of copper and of iron and of marble	2x+2x+2x+2x
also cinnamon	1x
and Indian spice	1x
and incenses	2x
and perfumed oil	1x
and frankincense	1x
and wine	1x
and olive oil	1x
and fine flour	1x
and wheat	1x
and cattle	2x
and sheep	2x
and horses	2x
and coaches	2x
and slaves	2x
and **human souls** (Revelation 18:11-13 NWT adapted from Greek).	2x
Total:	43x

43 months is 1290 days, the 1290 days of Daniel 9. Starting on 2004Elul16 when the last New Covenant Saint dies, and ending on 2008Nisan16 the first

day of Armageddon. Babylon is: the Harlot which is betrothed to Jesus in the symbolism of Revelation 18. This harlot is the Watchtower. Jesus has his full stock of all of the saints at the start of this period. Applying the Repetition Principle, we know that 'full stock' is the key symbolism of the account.

The Cryptic Dimension of the Code

We finish this section with two cryptic gems, which we have used to deduce the method of baptism for 'the life' - see [204]:

And as he was going out on his way, a certain man ran up and fell upon his knees before him and put the question to him: Good Teacher, what must I do to inherit everlasting life? (Mark 10:17).

Fine so one must fall upon one's knees for a start to get baptised.

A great number that became believers, turned upon the Lord (Acts 11:21 NWT/KI).

This means that there is a turning round in one's baptism.

[C21] The 'Bible Code' of Eli Rips and Michael Drosnin

Our initial problem with this work was the thought that Eli Rips (who founded ELS or Equidistant Hebrew Letter Sequence research) was still a Jew by Religious Persuasion. We thought that he cannot have this right because being a Jew by religion, he has not accepted the Jesus was God's son, the messiah, and so he has failed to understand the basic literal dimension of the holy book. It is therefore not reasonable to suppose that he can shed any light on any coded meanings correctly. It's rather like a man with no legs representing that he is a star football player! Gordon's other problem was that Satan always produces fakes to mask the original. There were many false Christs at the time of the true Christ, Jesus, in his first and his second presence:

Many will come on the basis of my name saying: I am the Christ, and mislead many (Matthew 24:5).

Our work showing that the bible is written in a symbolic code was published exclusively to the Governing Body of the Jehovah's Witnesses in 1992. But the first that the world really heard of any bible code was in 1994 (Newton's decoding activities were supressed when he was alive and only published very narrowly after he died), when the paper on ELS was submitted and published by the Statistical Science Journal in the US, Volume 9, Number 3,

August 1994. URL: www.torahcodes.co.il/wrr1/wrr1.htm. Gordon was prohibited by his understanding of the scriptures from going public until 1999Elul, 7 years after the first book was delivered to the HQ of the JWs by Massoud.

This ELS research appears now to have become a very large commercial empire for Amazon and Michael Drosnin and various publishers, more than it being a religious research program. There have to our knowledge been no further scientific papers in support of it since the first one in 1994, and one against it. Jesus said that you should judge a tree by its fruit. We can see no Christian fruit from this supposed decoding. We can see no academic fruit from this supposed decoding. We can see a whole load of commercial fruit. Recently there has been some good work which shows that ELS may well be just the result of random chance: www.prophezine.com/tcode/disclaim.html & www.direct.ca/trinity/codebreaker.html & www.direct.ca/trinity/closing.html .

Apparently if you translate the book of Revelation into English, and if you perform ELS on the English, ignoring all the vowels as Hebrew does, then you can find out something about William Gates Junior (Bill Gates) and Windows. If this is true then ELS is garbage, because the translation into English is a representation of inspired words but is not itself inspired at all, because there are many ways of translating Greek into English which use different words and yet have the same meaning. It is the Greek and the Hebrew texts that are the literal inspired words of God. So if an uninspired translation can tell you all about Bill Gates (or perhaps Steve Jobs), then so can War and Peace or any other book. But what the book of Revelation does say unequivocally is:

The bearing witness to Jesus is what inspires prophesying (Revelation 19:10).

Whereas there is no witness to Jesus in any of the ELS prophecies that we have seen and none in the best selling ELS book 'The Bible Code'. Although there are references to the Messiah (who is yet to put in an appearance!) So this work cannot be a true decoding in our opinion. We do not believe that the true God requires Christians to be able to speak Hebrew in order that they can understand his purposes. We will say this though, the originator of ELS, Eli Rips was a professor of Group theory, and Gordon started his PhD at Oxford in group theory, and group theory is beautiful and exact, it doesn't involve any statistics as does ELS. We cannot help thinking of the quote:

There are lies, damn lies and statistics.

What use is it telling Yitsac Rabin that he will be assasinated? As the ELS 'code' predicted. This is the sort of thing that fortune tellers do, and if they are wrong they are phoneys and if they are genuine they are getting their knowledge from Satan and are condemned in the literal meaning of the bible, being spirit mediums. 'Beware the Ides of March' was not from God. And it didn't help Julius Caesar. You know it's the same old wolf but in more modern sheep's clothing.

[C22] The Symbolic meaning of 7

If there are ' 7 things' in a bible account, then these things are successive in time.

Counting time in sevens was God's idea, he invented the week, the 7 creative days of the creative week are the first thing in the bible. It is not a natural thing for man, who counts in base ten, or in dozens, to count time in sevens. God instigated this 'base' for counting time.

<u>Time</u> is what he counts in sevens, with release after 7 times, counting to 7 exclusively or after 6 times counting 7 inclusively this being the Sabbath. The Sabbath is a concept which relates always to time. In the Hebrew language, the word for 'seven' and the word for 'Sabbath' are from the same root. Therefore the very language of God's people was and is declaring that 7 has to do with time. The concept that 7 relates to 7 things occurring one after the other with a release after or during the 7th one (depending on whether we count inclusively or exclusively), is enshrined in the language of the Old Testament.

But we fear that we have not laboured this seemingly trivial point enough. The Watchtower Society has 7 standing for 'divine completeness', but they miss the sense in which this completeness occurs, which is the temporal sense. It is a completeness in time, with the 7 repetitions occurring one after the other, consecutively, successively. For example, Daniel 9 literally says:

Seventy sevens, he is decreed for people of you and for city of holiness of you (Daniel 9:24 NIVHEOT).

From issuing of decree to restore and to rebuild Jerusalem until anointed one, ruler, sevens seven, and sevens sixty-two (Daniel 9:25 NIVHEOT).

It is implicit, it is understood that these sevens refer to time, and are therefore consecutive. It does not have to be spelt out. Similarly in the definition of the Jubilee, we see:

And you must count for yourself seven Sabbaths of years, seven times seven years, and the days of the seven Sabbaths of years must amount to forty-nine years for you (Leviticus 25:8).

A 'Sabbath' of years is here defined as 7 years. The holy spirit is actually equating, identifying 7 with the Sabbath. The Sabbath is a function of time, therefore the holy spirit is declaring 7 to be also a function of time, as regards its scriptural symbolism or significance.

So since Tuesday happens entirely after Monday, and since these two days have never coincided or even overlapped a little, and likewise for the whole week, the whole 7, the whole sabbath of days, we can deduce that 7 things means 7 successive things in scripture.

Example of the symbolism of 7: see [37]

[C23] The History of Event and Word Symbolism

Now here is the thing. Does a literal account have a straight symbolic meaning as well as a coded symbolic meaning? Does a symbolic account such as a dream or a parable or a vision have a straight symbolic meaning as well as a coded symbolic meaning?

These two questions troubled Gordon for 9 years until the end of 2001. But as usual once the question is asked in the correct way, the answer is not far off. As regards Gordon, who is the antetypical Daniel, who was named Belteshazzar by Nebuchadnezzar (he went in for slightly longer names than the Hebrews did), it is true in his experience, when he makes the effort that he should, then as the King himself said:

9 Oh Belteshazzar the chief of the magic-practicing priests, because I myself well know that the spirit of the holy gods is in you and that there is no secret at all that is troubling you, tell [me] the visions of my dream that I have beheld and its
interpretation (Daniel 4:9).

But this one thing about symbolic symbolism, straight symbolism and coded symbolism had eluded him for 9 years. During this time, Gordon had prayed many a time and had asked the true God and said to him: Oh Jehovah, who has chosen me out of all of the wise men on this earth to reveal his secrets to. If it pleases you, will you show this great bible code to others of your sons who can help me in the great work that I am commissioned to do. For I am but one man and your book was written by the Father of all minds for every human mind which can read or which can listen to another one who is reading. And the true God himself had for many years effectively been answering and saying: Oh Gordon, my son, it is you whom I have chosen to talk to face to face, and you can carry this burden, and I will help you to do so. For he has said in many places in the bible:

4 Jehovah has sworn (and he will feel no regret): You are a priest to time indefinite, according to the manner of Melchizedek! (Psalm 110:4).

And Gordon has known for a long time that these words apply to Jesus and himself and others. But he is made very happy by the true God when one of his brothers sorts out a biblical problem for him. Because then he knows that God has blessed his brother as he has blessed Gordon, and so Gordon is not alone in God's love in this respect. Of course it is wonderful to be a son, but it is better when you have some brothers and sisters.

If the reader is a boss, he will know how easy it is to get employees to park their backsides in his office, and yet how hard it is to get them to take their brains out of their parking spaces and use them to solve business problems. How happy a boss is when a member of staff expends brain power not on his own salary calculations or on his social advancement, or on making sure that come what may he is out of the office by 5:25 pm, but on the business which employs him. How wonderful it is when the business falters and someone else runs to pick it up before the boss gets there.

So this is what happened in the case of the number of types symbolic meanings that an account might have. Gordon asked the question at a study group:

Does the book of Revelation have a literal meaning of the type that, yes, John did actually see a harlot on a beast, and a straight symbolic meaning, the event symbolism, a simple symbolism (of the type that Jesus explained in the case of the parable of the Sower of Mark 4 - see [63]) and a coded symbolic meaning, the account symbolism, the word symbolism (of the type that Jesus explained in the case of the parable of the wheat and the weeds of Matthew 13). Or does it only have a literal meaning and a coded symbolic meaning?

It was Lee, who straight away came up with the answer, in the form of the first two verses of Revelation:

1 A revelation by Jesus Christ, which God gave him, to show his slaves the things that must shortly take place. And he sent forth his angel and presented [it] in signs through him to his slave John,
2 who bore witness to:

the word God gave
and to the witness Jesus Christ gave,
even to all the things he saw (Revelation 1).

Obviously 'all the things he saw' is the literal account, 'the word God gave' is another meaning and 'the witness Jesus Christ gave' is yet another meaning. So there must be both an Event symbolism and a Word symbolism.

As mentioned above John is bearing witness to 'The word God gave'. This therefore is a witness to God's words themselves which is the word symbolic meaning. John is also bearing witness to the (symbolically expressed) witness that Jesus gave him in the form of the vision, this then is the event symbolic account, the symbolic meaning of the events of the vision.

All the things he saw	Literal account of the vision
The Word God gave	Coded word symbolic meaning of the vision
The Witness Jesus Christ gave	Straight event symbolic meaning of the vision

By the Consistency Principle, this structure must apply to all symbolic accounts in the bible, such as parables, visions, dreams etc. Then Gordon was able to put the jigsaw together. Now in Daniel 4, the straight event symbolism cannot apply to the whole chapter as the Reverend John Aquila Brown, the second adventists and Charles Russell thought or you end up with Jesus being counselled as follows:

27 Therefore, Oh king, may my counsel seem good to you, and remove your own sins by righteousness, and your iniquity by showing mercy to the poor ones. Maybe there will occur a lengthening of your prosperity (Daniel 4:27).

which counsel plainly does not apply to Jesus. From this we deduce that literal accounts do not have straight symbolic meanings. So putting these together we get:

[1] Literal bible accounts only have a coded account symbolic meaning

[2] Symbolic bible accounts have a straight event symbolic meaning and a coded account symbolic meaning.

[3] Accounts which contain both literal and symbolic portions, such as dreams explanations and fulfilments, obey the two rules above for their respective portions.

So in the case of Daniel 4, since the chapter is not an entirely symbolic account, but contains various literal portions, it can not have one straight symbolic meaning that applies throughout the account. Such a meaning could not apply to the literal parts of the account, such as Daniel's explanation of the dream and the fulfilment of the dream. However the dream itself has both a straight symbolic explanation, which is the one that Daniel interpreted, and resulted in Nebuchadnezzar spending 7 years living like a wild animal. The coded symbolic interpretation of the dream gives the

Gentile Times and actually the chronology and activities of FDS3 and FDS4 - see [123].

This then is the true generalisation (as far as we can see it today) of the Reverend John Aquila Brown's astonishing interpretation of Daniel Chapter 4, as having a greater symbolic meaning relating to the Gentile Times. This generalisation extends his revelation to cover every literal and every symbolic portion of every chapter in the bible:

All symbolic portions of bible accounts have a straight symbolic meaning, the Event symbolism and a coded symbolic meaning, the Word Symbolism

All literal portions of bible accounts have only a coded symbolic meaning, the Word Symbolism

In fact a literal meaning is an event symbolic meaning with the identity (unity) symbolism. For non mathematicians, the identity symbolism is where an orange stands for an orange and a lemon stands for a lemon. It is the symbolism where the symbolic meaning is the literal meaning.

It was of course God, who through Jesus, opened Lee's eyes to help Gordon out here. We do not like to say this sort of thing very much, because these types of statements have been abused to the point of total numbness by so many false religions in the past. But when Gordon is too weak to carry on, or to tired to jump a particularly high fence, then the holy spirit just lifts him right up and it carries him right over. When the spirit helps, the answer is absolutely effortless! Most times one doesn't even realise that God has helped. Because notwithstanding all of the praise scattered throughout the bible, God is not interested in praise, he wants love and gratitude. The preponderance of praise exists to prevent his enemies from reading the bible. He doesn't go in for fanfare, trumpet blasts, drum rolls, medal pinning ceremonies, Oscar nominations, or long acceptance speeches. When Jesus died for all mankind, where was the applause? And who has done any better than him? When he cried out in his agony with his dying breath to the creator of every atom in the universe saying: Father receive my spirit, did God even make a response that he was aware of?

One day we, the grateful ones, will know how much God has done for us, and we will be flabbergasted. Until then, on the odd occasion when one realises that he has helped, one can feel his love in real time and that is something.

Yes, the true heroes of this system of things are unsung. They give without recompense from the world, they succeed without recognition from the world, they teach without qualifications from the world and they die with hardly a friend in the World. They save whilst being condemned by the world, they spread the truth whilst being lied to by the world, and lied about by the world, they keep their reason in a world with so little of it and they keep their love, a silent victory, whilst being drowned out by the deafening roar of self motivated self defeating hatred.

Glossary of Abbreviations

1AC   First Abrahamic Covenant (For citizenship of the Kingdom of God 2008 - 3008)
2AC   Second Abrahamic Covenant (For the physical promised land and exclusivity on God - terminated in 36Tishri)
3AC   Third Abrahamic Covenant (The legal basis for being born again as a spirit son of God).
1NC   First New Covenant (Leah)
1NCH First New Covenant helpers (Sons of Zilpah the maidservant of Leah)
2NC   Second New Covnenant (Rachel)
2NCH Second New Covenant helpers (Sons of Bilhah, the maidservant of Rachel)

FDS   Faithful and Discrete Slave of Matthew 24
FDS1 The administration of the first true Christian religion (33Nisan16 - 67Tishri) started by Jesus. The way.
FDS2 The administration of the second true Christian religion (67Tishri - 455Tishri) started by Paul, its first president
FDS3 The administration of the third true Christian religion (1884Tishri - 1994Tammuz30) The Watchtower, the truth.
FDS4 The administration of the fourth true Christian religion (1994Ab2 - 2007). The Lord's Witnesses, the life.

GNS   The Good For Nothing Slave of Matthew 25. The administration of the tail end of FDS1
WSS   The Wicked and Sluggish Slave of Matthew 25. The dual administration of the fallen FDS3
SS   The Sluggish Slave, the independent administration of the bible decoders in the Watchtower

BLC   Biblical Lunar Calendar
UN   United Nations
NGO   Non Governmental Organisation
NWT   New World Translation
NIVHEOT New International Version Hebrew English Old Testament
LITV   Green's Literal Version

Notes

Notes

Notes

Notes

Notes

Notes

Notes

Notes